CISA®
Certified Information Systems Auditor Practice Tests

Covers 2024–2029 Exam Objectives

CISA®
Certified Information Systems Auditor Practice Tests

Covers 2024–2029 Exam Objectives

Peter H. Gregory, CISA, CISSP

Mike Chapple, Ph.D., CISA, CISSP

SYBEX®
A Wiley Brand

Library of Congress Control Number: 2025908051

Print ISBN: 9781394290109
ePdf ISBN: 9781394290123
ePub ISBN: 9781394290116
oBook ISBN: 9781394324460

Cover Design: Wiley
Cover Image: © Jeremy Woodhouse/Getty Images
SKY10104395_042825

To my grandchildren – may they grow up in a safer world.
—Peter

To my wife, Renee. We are a quarter century into this adventure together and yet we still find ourselves standing on the precipice of change. Here's to what's next!
—Mike

Acknowledgments

Books like this involve work by many people, and as authors, we truly appreciate the hard work and dedication that the team at Wiley shows. We would especially like to thank our acquisitions editor, Jim Minatel, who jumped through some incredible hoops to make this project possible.

We also greatly appreciated the editing and production team for the book, including Christine O'Connor, the managing editor, who brought years of experience and great talent to the project; Archana Pragash, the project manager, who kept the train on the tracks; Bobby Rogers and Jessica Chang, the technical editors, who provided insightful advice and gave wonderful feedback throughout the book; and Liz Britten, the production editor, who guided us through layouts, formatting, and final cleanup to produce a great book. We would also like to thank the many behind-the-scenes contributors, including the graphics, production, and technical teams who made the book and companion materials into a finished product.

Shahla Pirnia, Elastos Chimwanda, Craig Sheffield, and Laurence Urbano, members of Mike's team at CertMike.com, were instrumental in helping us get all the details straightened out as we prepared the manuscript.

Our agent, Carole Jelen of Waterside Productions, continues to provide us with wonderful opportunities, advice, and assistance throughout our writing careers.

Finally, we would like to thank our families, who supported us through the late evenings, busy weekends, and long hours that a book like this requires to write, edit, and get to press.

About the Authors

Peter H. Gregory, CISSP, CISM, CISA, CRISC, CIPM, CDPSE, CCSK, A/CCRF, A/CCRP, A/CRMP, is the author of more than 60 books on security and technology, including *Solaris Security* (Prentice Hall, 2000), *The Art of Writing Technical Books* (Waterside, 2022), *CISA Certified Information Systems Auditor Study Guide* (John Wiley, 2025), *Chromebook For Dummies* (Wiley, 2023), and *Elementary Information Security* (Jones & Bartlett Learning, 2024).

Peter is a career semi-retired technologist and security executive. Earlier, he held security leadership positions at GCI (www.gci.com), Optiv Security (www.optiv.com), and Concur Technologies (www.concur.com). Peter is an advisory board member for the University of Washington and Seattle University for education programs in cybersecurity. He is a 2008 graduate of the FBI Citizens' Academy.

Peter resides in Central Washington State and can be found at www.peterhgregory.com.

Mike Chapple, PhD, CISA, CISSP, CISM, CIPP/US, CIPM, CCSP, CySA+, is the author of more than 50 books, including the best-selling *CISSP ISC2 Certified Information Systems Security Professional Official Study Guide* (Sybex, 2024), the *CISA Certified Information Systems Auditor Study Guide* (John Wiley, 2025), and the *CISSP ISC2 Official Practice Tests* (Sybex 2024). He is a cybersecurity professional with 25 years of experience in higher education, the private sector, and government.

Mike currently serves as teaching professor in the IT, Analytics, and Operations department at the University of Notre Dame's Mendoza College of Business, where he teaches undergraduate and graduate courses on cybersecurity, data management, and business analytics.

Mike previously served as executive vice president and chief information officer of the Brand Institute, a Miami-based marketing consultancy. He also spent four years in the information security research group at the National Security Agency and served as an active-duty intelligence officer in the US Air Force.

Mike earned both his BS and PhD degrees in computer science and engineering from Notre Dame. He also holds an MS in computer science from the University of Idaho and an MBA from Auburn University.

Learn more about Mike and his other security certification materials at his website, https://CertMike.com.

About the Technical Editors

Bobby Rogers is a senior cybersecurity professional with more than 30 years in the field. He serves as a cybersecurity auditor and virtual chief information security officer (vCISO) for a variety of clients. He works with a major engineering company in Huntsville, Alabama, helping to secure networks and manage cyber risk for its customers. In addition to numerous educational institutions, Bobby's customers have included the US Army, NASA, the State of Tennessee, and private/commercial companies and organizations. Bobby's specialties are cybersecurity engineering, security compliance, and cyber risk management, but he has worked in almost every area of cybersecurity, including network defense, computer forensics and incident response, and penetration testing.

He has narrated and produced more than 30 computer training videos for several training companies. He is the author of McGraw-Hill Education's *CompTIA CySA+ Cybersecurity Analyst Certification Passport (Exam CS0-002)*, 1st Edition and *CISSP Certification Passport*, 1st Edition; coauthor of *Certified in Risk and Information Systems Control (CRISC) All-in-One Certification Guide*, 1st and 2nd editions; and contributing author/ technical editor for the popular *CISSP All-in-One Exam Guide* (7th, 8th, and 9th editions).

Jessica Chang is a licensed CPA in the state of Colorado with more than 15 years of public accounting and general accounting experience in multiple leadership roles. She has worked in various industries, including telecommunications, hospitality, real estate, and e-commerce, and has served as the chief audit executive for multiple companies.

Contents at a Glance

Introduction

Congratulations on choosing to become a Certified Information Systems Auditor (CISA). Whether you have worked for several years in information systems auditing or have just recently been introduced to the world of controls, assurance, and security, don't underestimate the hard work and dedication required to obtain and maintain CISA certification. Although ambition and motivation are essential, the rewards of being CISA certified can far exceed the effort.

You probably never imagined yourself working in auditing or looking to obtain a professional auditing certification. Perhaps the increase in legislative or regulatory requirements for information system security led to your introduction to this field. Or, possibly, you noticed that CISA-related career options are increasing exponentially, and you have decided to get ahead of the curve. You aren't alone; since the inception of the CISA certification in 1978, more than 200,000 professionals worldwide reached the same conclusion and have earned this well-respected certification. Welcome to the journey and the amazing opportunities that await you.

How to Use This Book

This book is a companion to the *CISA Certified Information Systems Auditor Study Guide: Covers 2024 Exam Objectives (Sybex, 2025, Gregory/Chapple)*. If you're looking to test your knowledge before you take the CISA exam, this book will help you by providing a combination of 700 questions that cover the CISA domains with easily understood explanations for correct answers.

Since this is a companion to the *CISA Certified Information Systems Auditor Study Guide*, this book is designed to be similar to taking the CISA exam. It contains standard multiple-choice questions similar to those you may encounter in the certification exam itself. The book is divided into five chapters, each corresponding to the five domains in the CISA Job Practice.

We have compiled this information in both books to help you understand the commitment needed, prepare for the exam, and maintain your certification. Not only do we wish you to prepare for and pass the exam with flying colors, but we also provide you with the information and resources to maintain your certification and represent yourself and the professional world of information system (IS) auditing proudly with your new credentials.

If you're preparing for the CISA exam, you'll undoubtedly want to find as much information as possible about information systems and auditing. The more information you have, the better off you'll be when attempting the exam. The companion study guide was written with that in mind. The goal was to provide enough information to prepare you for the test, but not so much that you'll be overloaded with information outside the exam's scope.

Together, these books present the material at an intermediate technical level. Experience with and knowledge of security and auditing concepts will help you fully understand the challenges you'll face as an information systems auditor.

If you can answer 80% or more of the review questions correctly for a given domain, you can feel safe moving on to the next domain. If you're unable to answer that many correctly, reread the companion book chapter and try the questions again. Your score should improve.

 Don't just study the questions and answers! The questions on the actual exam will be different from the practice questions included in this book. The exam is designed to test your knowledge of a concept or objective, so use this book to learn the objectives behind the questions.

About ISACA

ISACA (formerly known as the Information Systems Audit and Control Association) is a recognized leader in control, assurance, and IT governance. Formed in 1967, this nonprofit organization represents more than 180,000 professionals in more than 188 countries. ISACA administers several exam certifications, including:

- Certified Information Systems Auditor (CISA)

- Certified Information Security Manager (CISM)

- Certified in Risk and Information Systems Control (CRISC)

- Certified Data Privacy Solutions Engineer (CDPSE)

- Certified in Governance of Enterprise IT (CGEIT)

- Certified Cybersecurity Operations Analyst (CCOA)

The certification program has been accredited under ISO/IEC 17024:2012, which means that ISACA's procedures for accreditation meet international requirements for quality, continuous improvement, and accountability.

If you're new to ISACA, we recommend you tour the organization's website (www.isaca. org) and familiarize yourself with the available guides and resources. In addition, if you're near one of the 225 local ISACA chapters in 99 countries worldwide, consider contacting the chapter board for information on local meetings, training days, conferences, or study sessions. You may be able to meet other IS auditors who can give you additional insight into the CISA certification and the audit profession.

Established in 1978, the CISA certification primarily focuses on audit, controls, assurance, and security. It certifies the individual's knowledge of testing and documenting IS controls and their ability to conduct formal IS audits. Organizations seek qualified personnel for assistance with developing and maintaining robust control environments. A CISA-certified individual is a great candidate for these positions.

The CISA Exam

The CISA exam is designed to be a vendor-neutral certification for information systems auditors. ISACA recommends this certification for those who already have experience in auditing and want to demonstrate that experience to current and future employers.

The exam covers five major domains:

1. Information Systems Auditing Process

2. Governance and Management of IT

3. Information Systems Acquisition, Development, and Implementation

4. Information Systems Operations and Business Resilience

5. Protection of Information Assets

These five areas include a range of topics, from enterprise risk management to evaluating cybersecurity controls. They focus heavily on scenario-based learning and the role of the information systems auditor in various scenarios. You'll need to learn a lot of information, but you'll be well rewarded for possessing this credential. ISACA reports that the average salary of CISA credential holders is more than $145,000. And according to *Certification Magazine*'s 2023 salary survey, ISACA credentials, including CISA, are among the top 10 highest paying in IT.

The CISA exam includes only standard multiple-choice questions. Each question has four possible answer choices, and only one of those answers is correct. When taking the test, you'll likely find some questions where you think multiple answers might be correct. In those cases, remember that you're looking for the *best* possible answer to the question!

The exam costs $575 for ISACA members and $760 for non-members. More details about the CISA exam and how to take it can be found at www.isaca.org/credentialing/cisa

You'll have four hours to take the exam and be asked to answer 150 questions during that time. Your exam will be scored on a scale ranging from 200 to 800, with a passing score of 450.

ISACA frequently does what is called *item seeding*, which is the practice of including unscored questions on exams. It does so to gather psychometric data, which is then used when developing new versions of the exam. Before you take the exam, you will be told that your exam may include these unscored questions. So, if you come across a question that does not appear to map to any of the exam objectives—or, for that matter, does not appear to belong in the exam—it is likely a seeded question. However, you never really know whether a question is seeded, so always try to answer every question.

Taking the Exam

Once fully prepared to take the exam, you can visit the ISACA website to register. Currently, ISACA offers two options for taking the exam: an in-person exam at a testing center and an at-home exam on your own computer through a remote proctoring service.

In-Person Exams

ISACA partners with PSI Exams testing centers, so your next step will be to locate a testing center near you. In the US, you can do this based on your address or your ZIP code, whereas non-US test takers may find it easier to enter their city and country. You can search for a test center near you on the PSI Exams website: https://www.psiexams.com

Now that you know where you'd like to take the exam, simply set up a PSI testing account and schedule an exam on the site.

On the day of the test, bring a government-issued identification card or passport that contains your full name (exactly matching the name on your exam registration), your signature, and your photograph. Be sure to show up with plenty of time before the exam starts. Remember that you cannot take your notes, electronic devices (including smartphones and watches), or other materials into the testing center with you.

At-Home Exams

ISACA also offers online exam proctoring. Candidates using this approach will take the exam at their home or office and be proctored over a webcam by a remote proctor.

Due to the rapidly changing nature of the at-home testing experience, candidates wishing to pursue this option should check the ISACA website for the latest details.

One critical fact worth noting is that you must have a computer with a webcam and full administrative control over the computer. You'll likely have some difficulty using an employer-based computer that restricts your control. We recommend that you use a personally owned computer instead.

After the CISA Exam

Once you have taken the exam, you will be notified of your score immediately, so you'll know if you passed the test right away. You should keep track of your score report with your exam registration records and the email address you used to register for the exam. You're now ready to begin the certification application process, described here.

Meeting the Experience Requirement

The CISA program is designed to demonstrate that an individual is a qualified information systems auditor. That requires more than just passing a test – it also requires real hands-on work experience.

The basic CISA work experience requirement is that you must have five years of work experience in information systems audit, controls, assurance, or security. If your work aligns with any job practice statements found later in this introduction, that experience likely qualifies.

You will be required to get your work experience verified by your supervisor or manager for each organization where you claim experience.

If you're a current information systems auditor or cybersecurity professional, you may find it easy to meet these requirements. If you don't yet meet the experience requirement, you may still take the exam, and then you'll have five years to gain the experience and become fully certified after passing the test.

Some waivers are available that can knock one, two, or three years off your experience requirement:

- If you hold an associate's degree in any field, you qualify for a one-year waiver.
- If you hold a bachelor's, master's, or doctoral degree in any field, you qualify for a two-year waiver.
- If you hold a master's degree in information systems or a related field, you qualify for a three-year waiver.
- If you hold full certification from the Chartered Institute of Management Accountants (CIMA), you qualify for a two-year waiver.
- If you are a member of the Association of Chartered Certified Accountants (ACCA), you qualify for a two-year waiver.

These waivers may not be combined. You may only use *one* of these waiver options against your certification requirements.

You must have earned all of the experience used toward your requirement within the 10 years preceding your application or within five years of the date you pass the exam.

Once you complete your application, you must acknowledge the ISACA Terms and Conditions Agreement and pay a US $50 application processing fee. When you have received final approval from ISACA, you can include the CISA moniker in your professional matters, including your email signature, resume, social media, and other materials.

Maintaining Your Certification

Information systems auditing is constantly evolving, with new threats and controls arising regularly. All CISA holders must complete continuing professional education annually to keep their knowledge current and their skills sharp. The guidelines around continuing professional education are somewhat complicated, but they boil down to two main requirements:

- You must complete 120 hours of credit every three years to remain certified.
- You must have at least 20 credit hours every year during that cycle.

You must meet both of these requirements. For example, if you earn 120 credit hours during the first year of your certification cycle, you still must earn 20 additional credits in each of the next two years.

Continuing education requirements follow calendar years, and your clock will begin ticking on January 1 of the year after you earn your certification. You are allowed to start earning credits immediately after you're certified. They'll just count for the following year.

There are many acceptable ways to earn CPE credits, many of which do not require travel or attending a training seminar. The important requirement is that you generally do not earn CPEs for work that you perform as part of your regular job. CPEs are intended to cover professional development opportunities outside of your day-to-day work. You can earn CPEs in several ways:

- Attending conferences
- Attending training programs
- Attending professional meetings and activities
- Taking self-study courses
- Participating in vendor marketing presentations
- Teaching, lecturing, or presenting
- Publishing articles, monographs, or books
- Participating in the exam development process
- Volunteering with ISACA
- Earning other professional credentials
- Contributing to the profession
- Mentoring

For more information on the activities that qualify for CPE credits, visit this site: www.isaca.org/credentialing/how-to-earn-cpe.

Additional Study Tools

This book has additional study tools to help you prepare for the exam. They include the following.

Go to www.wiley.com/go/Sybextestprep to register and gain access to this interactive online learning environment and test bank with study tools.

Sybex Test Preparation Software

Sybex's test preparation software lets you prepare with electronic test versions of the review questions from each chapter, the practice exam, and the bonus exam included in this book. You can build and take tests on specific domains or by chapter, or cover the entire set of CISA exam objectives using randomized tests.

Bonus Practice Exams

In addition to the practice questions for each chapter, this book includes two full 150-question practice exams. We recommend using them both to test your preparedness for the certification exam.

CISA Exam Objectives

ISACA publishes relative weightings for each of the exam's objectives. The following table lists the five CISA domains and the extent to which they are represented on the exam.

Domain	% of Exam
1. Information Systems Auditing Process	18%
2. Governance and Management of IT	18%
3. Information Systems Acquisition, Development, and Implementation	12%
4. Information Systems Operations and Business Resilience	26%
5. Protection of Information Assets	26%

Chapter

1

The Audit Process

THIS CHAPTER COVERS CISA DOMAIN 1, "INFORMATION SYSTEMS AUDITING PROCESS," AND INCLUDES QUESTIONS FROM THE FOLLOWING TOPICS:

- Audit management
- ISACA auditing standards and guidelines
- Audit and risk analysis
- Internal controls
- Performing an audit
- Control self-assessments
- Audit recommendations

The topics in this chapter represent 18% of the CISA examination.

This topic is fully covered in the companion guide, "CISA Certified Information Systems Auditor Study Guide," in Chapter 2.

Questions

You can find the answers to the questions in Appendix A.

1. The IT Assurance Framework consists of all of the following except:
   A. ISACA Code of Professional Ethics
   B. IS audit and assurance standards
   C. ISACA Audit Job Practice
   D. IS audit and assurance guidelines

2. An auditor is examining an IT organization's change control process. The auditor has determined that Change Advisory Board (CAB) meetings take place on Tuesdays and Fridays, where planned changes are discussed and approved. The CAB does not discuss emergency changes that are not approved in advance. What opinion should the auditor reach concerning emergency changes?
   A. The CAB should not be discussing changes made in the past.
   B. The CAB should be discussing recent emergency changes.
   C. Personnel should not be making emergency changes without CAB permission.
   D. Change control is concerned only with planned changes, not emergency changes.

3. A conspicuous video surveillance system would be characterized as what type(s) of control?
   A. Detective and deterrent
   B. Detective only
   C. Deterrent only
   D. Preventive and deterrent

4. Michael is developing an audit plan for an organization's data center operations. Which of the following will help Michael determine which controls require potentially more scrutiny than others?
   A. Security incident log
   B. Last year's data center audit results
   C. Risk assessment of the data center
   D. Data center performance metrics

5. An organization processes payroll and expense reports for thousands of corporate customers in an SAAS-based environment. Those customers want assurance that the organization's processes are effective. What kind of audit should the organization undertake?
   A. Compliance audit
   B. Operational audit
   C. Service provider audit
   D. IS audit

6. An audit project has been taking far too long, and management is beginning to ask questions about its schedule and completion. This audit may be lacking:

   A. Effective project management

   B. Cooperation from individual auditees

   C. Enough skilled auditors

   D. Clearly stated scope and objectives

7. An auditor is auditing the user account request and fulfillment process. The event population consists of hundreds of transactions, so the auditor cannot view them all. The auditor wants to view a random selection of transactions. This type of sampling is known as:

   A. Judgmental sampling

   B. Random sampling

   C. Stratified sampling

   D. Statistical sampling

8. An auditor is auditing an organization's user account request and fulfillment process. What is the first type of evidence collection the auditor will likely want to examine?

   A. Observation

   B. Document review

   C. Walkthrough

   D. Corroborative inquiry

9. A lead auditor is building an audit plan for a client's financial accounting system. The plan calls for periodic testing of a large number of transactions throughout the audit project. What is the best approach for accomplishing this?

   A. Reperform randomly selected transactions.

   B. Periodically submit test transactions to the audit client.

   C. Develop one or more CAATs.

   D. Request a list of all transactions to analyze.

10. A lead auditor is building an audit plan for a client's financial transaction processing system. The audit will take approximately three months. Which of the following is the best approach for reporting audit exceptions to the audit client?

   A. Report the exceptions to the audit committee.

   B. List the exceptions in the final audit report.

   C. Include the exceptions in a weekly status report.

   D. Advise the client of exceptions as they are discovered and confirmed.

11. Which of the following is true about the ISACA Audit Standards and Audit Guidelines?

   A. ISACA Audit Standards are mandatory.

   B. ISACA Audit Standards are optional.

   C. ISACA Audit Guidelines are mandatory.

   D. ISACA Audit Standards are only mandatory for SOX audits.

12. An auditor is auditing an organization's identity and access management program. The auditor has found that automated workflows are used to receive and track access requests and approvals. However, the auditor has identified a number of exceptions where subjects were granted access without the necessary requests and approvals. What remedy should the auditor recommend?

   A. Monthly review of access approvers

   B. Annual review of access approvers

   C. Annual user access reviews

   D. Monthly user access reviews

13. Why are preventive controls preferred over detective controls?

   A. Preventive controls are easier to justify and implement than detective controls.

   B. Preventive controls are less expensive to implement than detective controls.

   C. Preventive controls stop unwanted events from occurring, whereas detective controls only record them.

   D. Detective controls stop unwanted events from occurring, whereas preventive controls only record them.

14. For the purposes of audit planning, can an auditor rely on the audit client's risk assessment?

   A. Yes, in all cases.

   B. Yes, if the risk assessment was performed by a qualified external entity.

   C. No. The auditor must perform a risk assessment themselves.

   D. No. The auditor does not require a risk assessment to develop an audit plan.

15. An organization processes payroll and expense reports in an SAAS-based environment for thousands of corporate customers. Those customers want assurance that the organization's processes are effective. What kind of an audit should the organization undertake?

   A. AUP

   B. PA DSS

   C. PCI DSS

   D. SSAE18

16. An auditor is auditing an organization's system-hardening policy within its vulnerability management process. The auditor has examined the organization's system-hardening standards and wants to examine the configuration of some of the production servers. What is the best method for the auditor to obtain evidence?

   A. Capture screenshots from servers selected by the systems engineer during a walkthrough.

   B. Request screenshots from servers selected by the systems engineer.

   C. Request screenshots of randomly selected servers from the systems engineer.

   D. Capture screenshots from randomly selected servers during a walkthrough with the systems engineer.

17. An auditor is auditing the user account request and fulfillment process. The event population consists of hundreds of transactions, so the auditor cannot view them all. The auditor wants to view a random selection of transactions, as well as some of the transactions for privileged access requests. This type of sampling is known as:

   A. Judgmental sampling

   B. Random sampling

   C. Stratified sampling

   D. Statistical sampling

18. An auditor is auditing an organization's user account request and fulfillment process. The auditor has requested that the control owner describe the process to the auditor. What type of auditing is taking place?

   A. Observation

   B. Document review

   C. Walkthrough

   D. Corroborative inquiry

19. An external audit firm is performing an audit of a customer's financial accounting processes and IT systems. While examining a data storage system's user access permissions, the staff auditor discovered the presence of illegal content. What should the staff auditor do next?

   A. Notify law enforcement.

   B. Inform their supervisor.

   C. Notify the auditee.

   D. Notify the auditee's audit committee.

20. A QSA auditor in an audit firm has completed a PCI DSS audit of a client and found the client noncompliant with one or more PCI DSS controls. Management in the audit firm has asked the QSA auditor to sign off the audit as compliant, arguing that the client's level of compliance has improved from prior years. What should the QSA auditor do?

   A. Refuse to sign the audit report as compliant.

   B. Sign the audit report as compliant, under duress.

   C. Sign the audit report as compliant.

   D. Notify the audit client of the matter.

21. An organization wants to drive accountability for the performance of security controls to their respective control owners. Which activity is the best to undertake to accomplish this objective?

   A. Direct control owners to sign a document of accountability.

   B. Have the internal audit department audit the controls.

   C. Have an external audit firm audit the controls.

   D. Undergo control self-assessments (CSAs).

22. An auditor is evaluating a control related to a key card mechanism protecting a data center from unauthorized visitors. The auditor has determined that the key card control is ineffective because visitors often "piggyback" their way into the data center. What detective control should be implemented to compensate for this control deficiency?

   A. A video surveillance system with 90-day content retention that records all entrances into and exits from the data center

   B. A visitor's log inside the data center that all visitors would be required to sign

   C. A man trap

   D. A policy requiring all visitors to be escorted

23. A US-based organization processes payroll and expense reports in an SAAS-based environment for thousands of corporate customers. Customers outside the US want assurance that the organization's processes are effective. What kind of an audit should the organization undertake?

   A. ISO/IEC 27001

   B. SOC2

   C. ISAE3402

   D. SSAE18

24. A large merchant organization has commissioned a QSA (PCI) audit firm to perform a PCI DSS Report on Compliance (ROC). The audit firm has noted that the merchant's compliance deadline is less than one month away. What should the audit firm do next?

   A. File a compliance extension with the PCI Standards Council on behalf of the merchant.

   B. Inform the merchant that the ROC can be completed on time.

   C. Inform the merchant that the ROC cannot be completed on time and that an extension should be requested.

   D. File a compliance extension with the merchant's acquiring bank.

25. An auditor is developing an audit plan for an accounts payable function. Rather than randomly selecting transactions to examine, the auditor wants to select transactions from low, medium, and large payment amounts. Which sample methodology is appropriate for this approach?

    A. Judgmental sampling

    B. Stratified sampling

    C. Nonrandom sampling

    D. Statistical sampling

26. A cybersecurity audit firm has completed a penetration test of an organization's web application. The final report contains two findings that indicate the presence of two critical vulnerabilities. The organization disputes the findings because of compensating controls outside the web application interface. How should the audit proceed?

    A. The audit firm should remove the findings from the final report.

    B. The organization should select another firm to conduct the penetration test.

    C. The organization's management should protest the findings and include a letter accompanying the pen test report.

    D. The audit firm should permit the customer to include some management comments in the final report.

27. What is the objective of the ISACA audit standard on organizational independence?

    A. The auditor's placement in the organization should ensure that the auditor can act independently.

    B. The auditor should not work in the same organization as the auditee.

    C. To ensure that the auditor has the appearance of independence.

    D. To ensure that the auditor has a separate operating budget.

28. An auditor is auditing an organization's risk management process. During the walkthrough, the auditor asked the auditee to list all of the information sources contributing to the process. The auditee cited penetration tests, vendor advisories, nonvendor advisories, and security incidents as inputs. What conclusion should the auditor draw from this?

    A. The process is effective because risks are obtained from several disparate sources.

    B. The process is ineffective as risk assessments do not occur or contribute to the process.

    C. The process is effective because both internal and external sources are used.

    D. The process is ineffective because an anonymous tip line was not among the sources.

29. The capability wherein a server is constituted from backup media is known as which type of control?

    A. Primary control

    B. Manual control

    C. Compensating control

    D. Recovery control

30. Prior to planning an audit, an auditor would need to conduct a risk assessment to identify high-risk areas in all of the following situations *except*:

   A. When a client's most recent risk assessment is two years old

   B. When a client's risk assessment does not appear to be adequately rigorous

   C. A PCI "Report on Compliance" audit

   D. A SOC2 audit

31. Which of the following audit types is appropriate for a financial services provider such as a payroll service?

   A. SOC 1

   B. SAS70

   C. AUP

   D. Sarbanes-Oxley

32. Which of the following is the best method for ensuring that an audit project can be completed on time?

   A. Distribute a "provided by client" evidence request list at the start of the audit.

   B. Prepopulate the issues list with findings likely to occur.

   C. Increase the number of auditors on the audit team.

   D. Reduce the frequency of status meetings from weekly to monthly.

33. An auditor is about to start an audit of a user account access request and fulfillment process. The audit covers six months, from January through June. The population contains 1,800 transactions. Which of the following sampling methodologies is best suited for this audit?

   A. Examine the results of the client's control self-assessment (CSA).

   B. Submit some user account access requests and observe how they are performed.

   C. Request the first 30 transactions from the auditee.

   D. Request the first five transactions from each month in the audit period.

34. An auditor is auditing an organization's personnel onboarding process and examining the background check process. The auditor is mainly interested in whether background checks are performed for all personnel and whether background checks result in no-hire decisions. Which of the following evidence-collection techniques will support this audit objective?

   A. Request the full contents of background checks along with hire/no-hire decisions.

   B. Request the background check ledger that includes the candidates' names, results of background checks, and hire/no-hire decisions.

   C. Request the hire/no-hire decisions from the auditee.

   D. Examine the background check process, and note which characteristics of each candidate are included.

35. An auditor wants to audit the changes made to the DBMS configuration of a financial accounting system. What should the auditor use as the transaction population?

A. All of the transactions in the database

B. All of the requested changes in the change management process

C. All of the changes made to the database

D. All of the approved changes in the change management business process

36. A credit card payment processor undergoes an annual PCI DSS Report on Compliance (ROC) audit. What evidence of a passing audit should the payment processor provide to merchant organizations and others?

A. The signed Report on Compliance (ROC)

B. The signed attestation of compliance (AOC)

C. The signed report of validation (ROV)

D. The signed self-assessment questionnaire (SAQ)

37. Which of the following statements about the ISACA Audit Guidelines is correct?

A. ISACA Audit Guidelines apply only to audit firms and not to internal audit departments.

B. ISACA Audit Guidelines are required. Violations may result in fines for violators.

C. ISACA Audit Guidelines are required. Violations may result in loss of certifications.

D. ISACA Audit Guidelines are not required.

38. An external auditor is auditing an organization's third-party risk management (TPRM) process. The auditor has observed that the organization has developed an ISO 27001-based questionnaire sent to all third-party service providers annually. What value-added remarks can the auditor provide?

A. The process can be more efficient if the organization develops risk-based tiers to save time auditing low-risk vendors.

B. The organization should not be sending questionnaires to vendors every year.

C. The organization should structure its questionnaires based on CSA Star.

D. The organization should outsource its third-party management process.

39. What is the difference between SSAE18 Type I and SSAE18 Type II audits?

A. A Type I audit is an audit of process effectiveness, whereas a Type II audit is an audit of process effectiveness and design.

B. A Type I audit is an audit of process design and effectiveness, whereas a Type II audit is an audit of process design.

C. A Type I audit is an audit of process design, whereas a Type II audit is an audit of process design and effectiveness.

D. A Type I audit is an audit of process design and effectiveness, whereas a Type II audit is an audit of process effectiveness.

40. An auditor is auditing the payment systems for a retail store chain that has 80 stores in the region. The auditor needs to observe and take samples from some of the stores' systems. The audit client has selected two stores in the same city as the store chain headquarters and two stores in a nearby town. How should the audit of the store locations proceed?

    A. The auditor should learn more about the stores' systems and practices before deciding what to do.

    B. The auditor should audit the selected stores and proceed accordingly.

    C. The auditor should accept the sampling but select additional stores.

    D. The auditor should select which stores to examine and proceed accordingly.

41. As part of an audit of a business process, the auditor has discussed the process with the control owner and the control operators and has collected procedure documents and records related to the process. The auditor is asking internal customers of the business process to describe in their own words how the business process is operated. What kind of evidence collection are these discussions with internal customers?

    A. Reconciliation

    B. Reperformance

    C. Walkthrough

    D. Corroborative inquiry

42. Three months after the completion of an audit, the auditor contacted the auditee to inquire about the auditee's activities since the audit and whether the auditee has made any progress related to audit findings. What sort of communication is this outreach from the auditor?

    A. The auditor is a good audit partner and wants to ensure that the auditee is successful.

    B. The auditor is acting improperly by contacting the auditee outside of an audit and should be censored for unethical behavior.

    C. The auditee should assume that the auditor's outreach is personal in nature because this kind of communication is forbidden.

    D. The auditor clearly ensures that the auditee is happy with the auditor's work so that the auditor gets next year's audit assignment.

43. According to ISACA Audit Standard 1202, which types of risks should be considered when planning an audit?

    A. Fraud risk

    B. Business risk

    C. Cybersecurity risk

    D. Financial risk

44. An IT service desk department that provisions user accounts performs a monthly activity whereby all user account changes in the prior month are checked against the list of corresponding requests in the ticketing system. This activity is known as:

A. An audit

B. A monthly provisioning review

C. A control threat assessment (CTA)

D. A risk assessment

45. An organization that uses video surveillance at a work center has placed visible notices on building entrances that inform people that video surveillance systems are in use. The notices are an example of:

A. Administrative controls

B. Preventive controls

C. Detective controls

D. Deterrent controls

46. An auditor is planning an audit of a financial planning application. Can the auditor rely on a recent application penetration test as a risk-based audit?

A. No, because a penetration test does not reveal risks.

B. No, because a penetration test is not a risk assessment.

C. No: the auditor can make use of the pen test, but a risk assessment is still needed.

D. Yes, because the penetration test serves as a risk assessment in this case.

47. Which of the following is the best example of a control self-assessment of a user account provisioning process?

A. An examination of Active Directory to ensure that only domain administrators can make user account permission changes

B. Checks to see that only authorized personnel made user account changes

C. Confirmation that all user account changes were approved by appropriate personnel

D. Reconciliation of all user account changes against approved requests in the ticketing system

48. The proper sequence of an audit of an accounts payable process is:

A. Identify control owners, make evidence requests, perform walkthroughs, and perform corroborative interviews.

B. Make evidence requests, identify control owners, and perform corroborative interviews.

C. Identify control owners, perform corroborative interviews, make evidence requests, and perform walkthroughs.

D. Perform corroborative interviews, identify control owners, make evidence requests, and perform walkthroughs.

49. An auditor is auditing an accounts payable process and has found no exceptions. The auditor has decided to select additional samples to see whether any exceptions may be found. Which type of sampling is the auditor performing?

  A. Stop-or-go sampling

  B. Discovery sampling

  C. Judgmental sampling

  D. Exception sampling

50. Which of the following methods is best suited for an auditee to deliver evidence to an auditor during the audit of a background check process?

  A. FTP server

  B. Secure file transfer portal

  C. Email with SMTP over TLS

  D. Courier

51. An auditor has completed an audit, and the deliverable is ready to give to the audit client. What is the best method for delivering the audit report to the client?

  A. Courier

  B. Secure file transfer portal

  C. Email with SMTP over TLS

  D. In person, in a close-out meeting

52. What are the potential consequences if an IS auditor is a member of ISACA and CISA certified and violates the ISACA Code of Professional Ethics?

  A. Fines

  B. Imprisonment

  C. Termination of employment

  D. Loss of ISACA certifications

53. An auditor is auditing an accounts payable process and has discovered that a single individual has requested and also approved several payments to vendors. What kind of an issue has the auditor found?

  A. A separation-of-duties issue

  B. A split-custody issue

  C. A dual-custodian issue

  D. No issue has been identified

54. An organization uses an automated workflow process for request, review, approval, and provisioning of user accounts. Anyone in the organization can request access. Specific individuals are assigned to the review and approval steps. Provisioning is automated. What kind of control is the separation of duties between the review and approval steps?

  A. Compensating control

  B. Manual control

  C. Preventive control

  D. Administrative control

55. An auditor is planning an audit of a monthly terminated-users review procedure. The auditor is planning to ask the auditee for a list of current user accounts in Active Directory, as well as a list of current employees and a list of terminated employees from Human Resources so that the auditor can compare the lists. What kind of an audit is the auditor planning to perform?

  A. Reperformance

  B. Observation

  C. Corroboration

  D. Walk-back

56. An IT service desk manager is the control owner for the IT department change control process. In an audit of the change control process, the auditor has asked the IT service desk manager to provide all change control tickets whose request numbers end with the digit 6. What sampling methodology has the auditor used?

  A. Judgmental sampling

  B. Statistical sampling

  C. Stratified sampling

  D. Stop-or-go sampling

57. An audit firm is planning an audit of an organization's asset management records. For what reason would the auditor request a copy of the entire asset database from the third-party DBA versus a report of assets from the owner of the asset process?

  A. Honesty of the evidence provider

  B. Objectivity of the evidence provider

  C. Independence of the evidence provider

  D. Qualification of the evidence provider

58. An auditor has delivered a Sarbanes–Oxley audit report containing 12 exceptions to the audit client, who disagrees with the findings. The audit client is upset and is asking the auditor to remove six findings from the report. A review of the audit findings confirmed that all 12 findings are valid. How should the auditor proceed?

  A. Remove the three lowest-risk findings from the report.

  B. Remove the six lowest-risk findings from the report.

  C. Report the auditee to the Securities and Exchange Commission.

  D. Explain to the auditee that the audit report cannot be changed.

59. An auditor has delivered a Sarbanes–Oxley audit report containing 12 exceptions to the audit client, who disagrees with the findings. The audit client is upset and is asking the auditor to remove six findings from the report in exchange for a payment of $25,000. A review of the audit findings confirmed that all 12 findings are valid. How should the auditor proceed?

  A. The auditor should report the matter to their manager.

  B. The auditor should reject the payment and meet the auditee halfway by removing three of the findings.

  C. The auditor should reject the payment and remove six of the findings.

  D. The auditor should report the incident to the audit client's audit committee.

60. An auditor is auditing a change control process. During a walkthrough, the control owner described the process as follows: "Engineers plan their changes and send an email about their changes to the IT manager before 5 P.M. on Wednesday. The engineers then proceed with their changes during the change window on Friday evening." What, if any, findings should the auditor identify?

  A. The change control process is fine as is but could be improved by creating a ledger of changes.

  B. The change control process is fine as is.

  C. The change control process lacks a review step.

  D. The change control process lacks review and approval steps.

61. An organization utilizes a video surveillance system on all ingress and egress points in its work facility; surveillance cameras are concealed from view, and there are no visible notices. What type of control is this?

  A. Administrative control

  B. Secret control

  C. Detective control

  D. Deterrent control

62. An auditor is selecting samples from records in the user access request process. Although privileged access requests account for approximately 5% of all access requests, the auditor wants 20% of the samples to be requests for administrative access. What sampling technique has the auditor selected?

    A. Judgmental sampling

    B. Stratified sampling

    C. Statistical sampling

    D. Variable sampling

63. An auditor is auditing a change control process by examining change logs in a database management system and requesting change control records to show that those changes were approved. The auditor plans to proceed until the first exception is found. What sampling technique is being used here?

    A. Discovery sampling

    B. Stop-or-go sampling

    C. Attribute sampling

    D. Exception sampling

64. Which of the following is the best description of stop-or-go sampling?

    A. The auditor wants to select samples based on arbitrary criteria.

    B. The auditor wants to know how many transactions contain a certain range of values.

    C. The auditor wants to know the total value of the transaction population.

    D. The auditor believes the risk is low and wants to sample as few records as possible.

65. While auditing a payroll process, an auditor intends to keep selecting samples until an error is found. What type of sampling is being performed?

    A. Discovery sampling

    B. Stop-or-go sampling

    C. Attribute sampling

    D. Exception sampling

66. A staff auditor is auditing a process, which involves examining the contents of some employee laptop computers. The auditor has detected the presence of child pornography on one laptop computer. What should the auditor do next?

    A. Confront the user of the laptop computer.

    B. Delete the content from the laptop computer.

    C. Notify their supervisor.

    D. Notify law enforcement.

67. An audit firm has completed an audit of several auditee business processes. The audit firm is in the process of archiving information for the audit. Which of the following information can be excluded from the archiving process?

 A. Field notes

 B. Draft audit report

 C. Sampled transactions

 D. None of these

68. In an external audit of a client organization, one of the staff auditors realizes that their business partner in a side business is one of the auditee managers in the client organization. What should the staff auditor do about this?

 A. Maintain professional and ethical behavior during the audit.

 B. Refrain from discussing the side business with their business partner during the audit.

 C. Notify their supervisor about a potential conflict of interest.

 D. Request reassignment to another audit project.

69. An auditor is auditing a release management process by examining policies, procedures, and records and interviewing personnel. The auditor has determined that the personnel who initiate individual software releases are also the approvers. What might the auditor conclude from this?

 A. The process appears to have a segregation-of-duties issue.

 B. The process appears to have a race condition.

 C. The design of the process is appropriate and sound.

 D. Nothing can be concluded from this information.

70. An auditor is auditing an organization's vendor risk practices. The information security manager described the process to the auditor, which consists of the security manager performing a security scan of a new vendor's website to measure the level of risk and reaching a conclusion about the vendor's suitability solely based on the scan results. What might the auditor conclude from this?

 A. The organization's vendor management risk process is adequate because security scanning is the primary means for identifying risk.

 B. The organization's vendor management risk process is inadequate because an objective party should perform the scan.

 C. The organization's vendor management risk process is inadequate because the organization should also issue a questionnaire to the vendor.

 D. The organization's vendor management risk process is inadequate because it should be performed by an outside party instead of internally.

71. An auditor has completed fieldwork on a customer's SOC 2 audit and has briefed the customer on findings that will appear in the report. What should the customer do next?

   A. Challenge the auditor and ask them to prove their findings.

   B. Agree with the auditor.

   C. Ask for a second opinion from a different partner in the audit firm.

   D. Produce management comments that will appear in the published report.

72. Why would an organization's Internal Audit department conduct its own risk assessment versus relying on the risk assessment performed by the Information Security department?

   A. The auditor may not believe that the Information Security department is capable of conducting a proper risk assessment.

   B. As an objective, independent party, the Internal Audit department should conduct its own risk assessment.

   C. The internal auditor is prohibited by law from relying on the Information Security department's risk assessment.

   D. The internal auditor would put themselves in a conflict of interest situation.

73. An organization recently hired an experienced cybersecurity leader to make strategic improvements in the organization's cybersecurity capabilities. One item of interest to the cybersecurity leader is the matter of control owner–operators and their commitment to control effectiveness. Which of the following would best serve to improve this commitment?

   A. Control self-assessments

   B. Security awareness training

   C. Penetration testing

   D. An external audit

74. To save time in an audit, one of the staff auditors has decided to upload audit findings to a public LLM AI service to direct the service in composing the audit executive summary. The audit manager discovered this practice. What should the audit manager do next?

   A. Discipline the staff auditor for compromising the auditee's confidential information.

   B. Recognize and reward the staff auditor for innovation and efficiency.

   C. Update audit procedures so that other staff auditors will do the same.

   D. Notify law enforcement.

75. The director of Internal Audit in a new US-based public company has decided to staff its internal audit with contractors from a public accounting firm. This is an example of:

   A. Insourced external audit

   B. Outsourced external audit

   C. Outsourced internal audit

   D. Insourced internal audit

76. When planning an audit, a lead auditor must determine all of the following *except*:

 A. Findings

 B. Scope

 C. Purpose

 D. Schedule

77. An organization is required to comply with Sarbanes-Oxley, PCI DSS, ISO 27001, and NIST SP 800-53. What is the best approach for determining how the organization can plan to comply with these?

 A. Create separate controls and procedures for each framework.

 B. Map all controls together, thus creating the organization's General Computing Controls.

 C. Create separate controls, procedures, and records for each framework.

 D. Identify the scope for each framework, and map common controls.

78. Two cybersecurity staff members are arguing about the classification of the organization's video surveillance system. One argues that video surveillance is a deterrent control, and the other argues that video surveillance is a detective control. Who is right, and why?

 A. Video surveillance is neither deterrent nor detective.

 B. Video surveillance is a detective control.

 C. Video surveillance is both deterrent and detective.

 D. Video surveillance is a deterrent control.

79. An online retail merchant organization with an online product catalog accepts credit card payments from customers but does not store credit card data. A third-party organization accepts payments through a gateway. The CFO argues that the organization is not required to comply with PCI DSS because the organization does not store credit card data. What, if any, are the organization's requirements for complying with PCI DSS?

 A. The organization is required to comply because its website directs payments to the third-party payment gateway.

 B. The organization is not required to comply because it does not store credit card data.

 C. The organization is required to comply because it advertises its acceptance of credit cards for payment.

 D. The organization is not required to comply because another organization accepts payments on its behalf.

80. The advantages of control self-assessments include all of the following *except*:

 A. Control risks can be identified earlier.

 B. Favorable self-assessments can result in audits being delayed.

 C. Relationships with control owners can improve through collaboration.

 D. More personnel will be aware of the need for effective controls.

Chapter

2

Governance and Management of IT

THIS CHAPTER COVERS CISA DOMAIN 2, "GOVERNANCE AND MANAGEMENT OF IT," AND INCLUDES QUESTIONS FROM THE FOLLOWING TOPICS:

- Business alignment
- Security strategy development
- Security governance
- Information security strategy development
- Resources needed to develop and execute a security strategy
- Information security metrics

The topics in this chapter represent 18% of the CISA examination.

This topic is fully covered in the companion guide, "CISA Certified Information Systems Auditor Study Guide," in Chapter 1.

Questions

You can find the answers to the questions in Appendix A.

1. Management's control of information technology processes is best described as:
   A. Information technology policies
   B. Information technology policies, along with audits of those policies
   C. Information technology governance
   D. Metrics as compared to similar organizations

2. What is the best method for ensuring that an organization's IT department achieves adequate business alignment?
   A. Find and read the organization's articles of incorporation.
   B. Understand the organization's vision, mission statement, and objectives.
   C. Determine who the CIO reports to in the organization.
   D. Study the organization's application portfolio.

3. Roberta has located her organization's mission statement and a list of strategic objectives. What steps should Roberta take to ensure that the IT department aligns with the business?
   A. Discuss strategic objectives with business leaders to better understand what they wish to accomplish and what steps are being taken to achieve the objectives.
   B. Develop a list of activities that will support the organization's strategic objectives, and determine the cost of each.
   C. Select those controls from the organization's control framework that align with each objective, and then ensure that those controls are effective.
   D. Select the policies from the organization's information security policy that are relevant to each objective, and ensure that those policies are current.

4. Michael wants to improve the risk management process in his organization by creating content that will help management understand when certain risks should be accepted and when certain risks should be mitigated. The policy that Michael needs to create is known as:
   A. A security policy
   B. A control framework
   C. A risk appetite statement
   D. A control testing procedure

5. In a typical risk management process, the best person to make a risk treatment decision is:
   A. The chief risk officer (CRO)
   B. The chief information officer (CIO)
   C. The department head associated with the risk
   D. The chief information security officer (CISO)

6. The ultimate responsibility for an organization's cybersecurity program lies with:

   A. The board of directors

   B. The chief executive officer (CEO)

   C. The chief information officer (CIO)

   D. The chief information security officer (CISO)

7. In a US public company, a CIO will generally report the state of the organization's IT function to:

   A. The Treadway Commission

   B. Independent auditors

   C. The US Securities and Exchange Commission

   D. The board of directors

8. A new CIO in an organization is building its formal IT department from the ground up. To ensure collaboration among business leaders and department heads in the organization, the CIO should form and manage:

   A. A technology committee of the board of directors

   B. An IT steering committee

   C. An audit committee of the board of directors

   D. A business-aligned IT policy

9. The best person or group to make risk treatment decisions is:

   A. The chief information security officer (CISO)

   B. The audit committee of the board of directors

   C. The cybersecurity steering committee

   D. External auditors

10. Which is the best party to conduct access reviews?

    A. Users' managers

    B. Information security manager

    C. IT service desk

    D. Department head

11. Which is the best party to make decisions about the configuration and function of business applications?

    A. Business department head

    B. IT business analyst

    C. Application developer

    D. End user

12. Which of the following is the best definition of custodial responsibility?

A. The custodian protects assets based on the customer's defined interests.

B. The custodian protects assets based on its own defined interests.

C. The custodian makes decisions based on its own defined interests.

D. The custodian makes decisions based on the customer's defined interests.

13. What is the primary risk of IT acting as custodian for a business owner?

A. IT may not have enough interest to provide quality care for business applications.

B. IT may not have sufficient staffing to properly care for business applications.

C. IT may have insufficient knowledge of business operations to make good decisions.

D. Business departments may not give IT sufficient access to properly manage applications.

14. An organization needs to hire an executive who will build a management program that considers threats and vulnerabilities. The best job title for this position is:

A. CSO

B. CRO

C. CISO

D. CIRO

15. An organization needs to hire an executive who will be responsible for ensuring that the organization's policies, business processes, and information systems are compliant with laws and regulations concerning the proper collection, use, and protection of personally identifiable information. What is the best job title for the organization to use for this position?

A. CSO

B. CIRO

C. CISO

D. CPO

16. The Big Data Company is adjusting several position titles in its IT department to reflect industry standards. Included in the consideration are two individuals. The first is responsible for the overall relationships and data flows among the company's internal and external information systems. The second is responsible for the overall health and management of systems containing information. Which two job titles are most appropriate for these two roles?

A. Systems architect and database administrator

B. Data architect and data scientist

C. Data scientist and database administrator

D. Data architect and database administrator

17. What is the primary distinction between a network engineer and a telecom engineer?

   A. A network engineer is primarily involved with networks and internal network media, whereas a telecom engineer is primarily involved with networks and external (carrier) network media.

   B. A network engineer is primarily involved with networks and external (carrier) network media, whereas a telecom engineer is primarily involved with networks and internal network media.

   C. A network engineer is primarily involved with Layer 3 protocols and above, whereas a telecom engineer is primarily involved with Layer 1 and Layer 2 protocols.

   D. There is no distinction, as both are involved in all aspects of an organization's networks.

18. An organization that is a US public company is redesigning its access management and access review controls. What is the best role for Internal Audit in this redesign effort?

   A. Develop procedures.

   B. Design controls.

   C. Provide feedback on control design.

   D. Develop controls and procedures.

19. A security operations manager proposes that engineers who design and manage information systems play a role in monitoring those systems. Is design and management compatible with monitoring? Why or why not?

   A. No. Personnel who design and manage systems should not perform a monitoring role, as this is a conflict of interest.

   B. Yes. Personnel who design and manage systems will be more familiar with the steps to take, as well as the reasons to take them when alerts are generated.

   C. No. Personnel who design and manage systems will not be familiar with response procedures when alerts are generated.

   D. No. Personnel who design and manage systems are not permitted access to production environments and should not perform monitoring.

20. The purpose of metrics in an IT department is to:

   A. Measure the performance and effectiveness of controls.

   B. Measure the likelihood of an attack on the organization.

   C. Predict the likelihood of an attack on an organization.

   D. Predict the next IT service outage.

21. Which security metric is best considered a leading indicator of an attack?

   A. Number of firewall rules triggered

   B. Number of security awareness training sessions completed

   C. Percentage of systems scanned

   D. Mean time to apply security patches

22. Steve, a CISO, has vulnerability management metrics and needs to build business-level metrics. Which of the following is the best business-level leading indicator metric suitable for his organization's board of directors?

    A. Average time to patch servers supporting manufacturing processes

    B. Frequency of security scans of servers supporting manufacturing processes

    C. Percentage of servers supporting manufacturing processes that are scanned by vulnerability scanning tools

    D. Number of vulnerabilities remediated on servers supporting manufacturing processes

23. The metric "percentage of systems with completed installation of advanced anti-malware" is best described as:

    A. A key operational indicator (KOI)

    B. A key performance indicator (KPI)

    C. A key goal indicator (KGI)

    D. A key risk indicator (KRI)

24. A member of the board of directors has asked Ravila, a CIRO, to produce a metric showing the reduction of risk as a result of the organization making key improvements to its security information and event management system. Which type of metric is most suitable for this purpose?

    A. KGI

    B. RACI

    C. KRI

    D. ROSI

25. A common way to determine the effectiveness of IT metrics is the SMART method. SMART stands for:

    A. Security Metrics Are Risk Treatment

    B. Specific, Measurable, Attainable, Relevant, Timely

    C. Specific, Measurable, Actionable, Relevant, Timely

    D. Specific, Manageable, Actionable, Relevant, Timely

26. The statement "Complete migration of flagship system to the latest version of vendor-supplied software" is an example of:

    A. A mission statement

    B. A vision statement

    C. A purpose statement

    D. An objective statement

27. Ernie, a CIO who manages a large IT team, wants to create a mission statement for the team. What is the best approach for creating this mission statement?

    A. Start with the organization's mission statement.

    B. Start with Ernie's most recent performance review.

    C. Start with the results of the most recent risk assessment.

    D. Start with the body of open items in the project portfolio.

28. Which of the following statements is the best description for the purpose of performing risk management?

    A. Identify and manage vulnerabilities that may permit security events to occur.

    B. Identify and manage threats that are relevant to the organization.

    C. Assess the risks associated with third-party service providers.

    D. Assess and manage risks associated with doing business online.

29. Key metrics showing the effectiveness of a risk management program would *not* include:

    A. Reduction in the number of security events

    B. Reduction in the impact of security events

    C. Reduction in the time to remediate vulnerabilities

    D. Reduction in the number of patches applied

30. Examples of security program performance metrics include all of the following *except*:

    A. Time to detect security incidents

    B. Time to remediate security incidents

    C. Time to perform security scans

    D. Time to discover vulnerabilities

31. Two similar-sized organizations are merging. Paul will be the CIO of the new combined organization. What is the greatest risk that may occur as a result of the merger?

    A. Differences in practices that may not be understood

    B. Duplication of effort

    C. Gaps in coverage of key processes

    D. Higher tooling costs

32. The purpose of value delivery metrics is:

    A. Long-term reduction in costs

    B. Reduction in ROSI

    C. Increase in ROSI

    D. Increase in net profit

33. Joseph, a CIO, is collecting statistics on several operational areas and needs to find a standard way of measuring and publishing information about the effectiveness of his program. Which of the following is the best approach to follow?

- **A.** Scaled score
- **B.** NIST Cybersecurity Framework (CSF)
- **C.** Business Model for Information Security (BMIS)
- **D.** Balanced scorecard (BSC)

34. Which of the following is the best description of the Business Model for Information Security (BMIS)?

- **A.** Describes the relationships (as dynamic interconnections) between policy, people, process, and technology
- **B.** Describes the relationships (as dynamic interconnections) between people, process, technology, and the organization
- **C.** Describes the primary elements (people, process, and technology) in an organization
- **D.** Describes the dynamic interconnections (people, process, and technology) in an organization

35. What is the correct name for the model shown here?

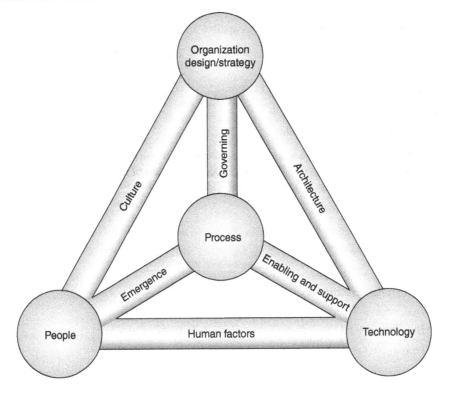

    A. COBIT Model for Information Technology

    B. COBIT Model for Information Security

    C. Business Model for Information Security

    D. Business Model for Information Technology

36. Jacqueline, an experienced CISO, is reading the findings in a recent risk assessment that describes deficiencies in the organization's vulnerability management process. How would Jacqueline use the Business Model for Information Security (BMIS) to analyze the deficiency?

    A. Identify the elements connected to the process dynamic interconnection (DI).

    B. Identify the DIs connected to the process element.

    C. Identify the dynamic elements connected to human factors.

    D. Identify the dynamic elements connected to technology.

37. Which of the following would constitute an appropriate use of the Zachman enterprise framework?

    A. An IT service management model, as an alternative to ITIL

    B. Identifying system components, followed by high-level design and business functions

    C. Development of business requirements, translated top-down into technical architecture

    D. IT systems described at a high level and then in increasing levels of detail

38. An IT architect needs to document the flow of data from one system to another, including external systems operated by third-party service providers. What kind of documentation does the IT architect need to develop?

    A. Data flow diagrams (DFDs)

    B. Entity relationship diagrams (ERDs)

    C. A Zachman architecture framework

    D. Visio diagrams showing information systems and data flows

39. Carole is a CISO in a new organization with a fledgling security program. Carole needs to identify and develop mechanisms to ensure desired outcomes in selected business processes. What is a common term used to define these mechanisms?

    A. Checkpoints

    B. Detective controls

    C. Controls

    D. Preventive controls

40. What is the best approach to developing security controls in a new organization?

    A. Start with a standard control framework and make risk-based adjustments as needed.

    B. Start from scratch and develop controls based on risk as needed.

    C. Start with NIST CSF and move up to ISO 27001 and then NIST 800-53 as the organization matures.

    D. Develop controls in response to an initial risk assessment.

41. Which of the following is the best description of the COBIT framework?

  A. A security process and controls framework that can be integrated with ITIL or ISO 20000

  B. An IT controls and process framework on which IT controls and processes can be added at an organization's discretion

  C. An IT process framework with optional security processes when Extended COBIT is implemented

  D. An IT process framework that includes security processes that are interspersed throughout the framework

42. One distinct disadvantage of the ISO 27001 standard is:

  A. The standard is costly (over US$100 per copy).

  B. The standard is available only for use outside the US.

  C. The standard is available only for use in the US.

  D. The standard is suitable only for large organizations.

43. Which of the following statements about ISO 27001 is correct?

  A. ISO 27001 consists primarily of a framework of security controls, followed by an appendix of security requirements for running a security management program.

  B. ISO 27001 consists primarily of a body of requirements for running a security management program, along with an appendix of security controls.

  C. ISO 27001 consists of a framework of information security controls.

  D. ISO 27001 consists of a framework of requirements for running a security management program.

44. The US law that regulates the protection of data related to medical care is:

  A. PIPEDA

  B. HIPAA

  C. GLBA

  D. GDPR

45. The regulation "Security and Privacy Controls for Federal Information Systems and Organizations" is better known as:

  A. ISO/IEC 27001

  B. ISO/IEC 27002

  C. NIST CSF

  D. NIST SP 800-53

46. What is the best explanation for the Implementation Tiers in the NIST Cybersecurity Framework?

   A. Implementation Tiers are levels of risk as determined by the organization.

   B. Implementation Tiers are stages of implementation of controls in the framework.

   C. Implementation Tiers are likened to maturity levels.

   D. Implementation Tiers are levels of risk as determined by an external auditor or regulator.

47. Jeffrey is a CIO in an organization that provides financial services for private organizations, government agencies, and federal agencies in the US. Which is the best information security controls framework for this organization?

   A. CIS

   B. ISO 27001

   C. NIST CSF

   D. NIST SP 800-53

48. The scope of requirements of PCI DSS is:

   A. All systems that store, process, and transmit credit card numbers, as well as all other systems that can communicate with these systems

   B. All systems that store, process, and transmit credit card numbers

   C. All systems that store, process, and transmit unencrypted credit card numbers

   D. All systems in an organization where credit card numbers are stored, processed, and transmitted

49. Which of the following statements is true about controls in the Payment Card Industry Data Security Standard?

   A. Many controls are required, whereas some are "addressable," or optional, based on risk.

   B. All applicable controls are required, regardless of actual risk.

   C. The required controls are determined for each organization by the acquiring bank.

   D. In addition to core controls, each credit card brand has its own unique controls.

50. The PCI DSS is an example of:

   A. An industry regulation that is enforced with fines

   B. A private industry standard that is enforced with contracts

   C. A voluntary standard that, if used, can reduce cyber insurance premiums

   D. An international law enforced through treaties with member nations

51. What are three factors that a risk manager might consider when developing an information security strategy?

   A. Threats, risks, and solutions

   B. Prevention, detection, and response

   C. Risk levels, staff qualifications, and security tooling

   D. Risk levels, operating costs, and compliance levels

52. The responsibility for facilitation of an organization's cybersecurity program lies with:

   A. The board of directors

   B. The chief executive officer (CEO)

   C. The chief information officer (CIO)

   D. The chief information security officer (CISO)

53. The Zachman framework is:

   A. An IT process framework

   B. An enterprise architecture framework

   C. A security governance framework

   D. An IT governance framework

54. An enterprise architect wants to create a visual artifact that illustrates information moving between systems. This artifact is a/an:

   A. Data flow diagram

   B. Entity-relationship diagram

   C. Gantt chart

   D. Zachman model

55. The philosophy whereby persons' and systems' identities are considered untrusted by default is known as:

   A. Least privilege

   B. Trust but verify

   C. Zero trust

   D. Transitive trust

56. In an organization with numerous business locations, including sales offices, corporate offices, warehouses, and data centers, IT and security leaders want to develop a more consistent approach to protective measures in these locations. The IT and security leaders should develop:

   A. A data classification policy

   B. A site classification policy

   C. An access control policy

   D. An access control guideline

57. Who in an organization should be authorized to represent the organization on social media sites?

  A. Data privacy officer

  B. Chief information officer

  C. Chief information security officer

  D. Public information officer

58. An IT worker is reading a document that contains helpful information for implementing an encryption algorithm within a software program. What kind of a document is the IT worker reading?

  A. A policy

  B. A guideline

  C. A standard

  D. A procedure

59. All of the following are options for risk treatment *except*:

  A. Transfer

  B. Avoid

  C. Accept

  D. Defer

60. In the context of risk management, what should be considered as assets in an organization?

  A. All systems, data, equipment, intellectual property, buildings and property, and personnel

  B. All systems, data, equipment, intellectual property, and buildings and property

  C. All systems, software, and devices

  D. All systems, software, data, and devices

61. A new cybersecurity manager is setting up a risk management program in an organization that lacks an asset management system. What sources should the manager utilize to get a reasonably complete list of assets?

  A. Financial system asset inventory, network discovery scans, and endpoint management system data

  B. Network discovery scans

  C. Network discovery scans and endpoint management system data

  D. Financial system asset inventory and network discovery scans

62. While conducting a risk assessment of a group of business processes and supporting systems, the risk manager identified a number of risks. What further analysis, if any, should the risk manager conduct on those identified risks?

    A. No further analysis is required; identified risks can be brought up for risk treatment decisions.

    B. One or more risk mitigation options should be developed for each identified risk.

    C. One or more risk treatment options should be developed for each identified risk.

    D. Quantified risk analysis should then be performed on identified risks.

63. A risk analyst is conducting a risk assessment on a group of systems. The risk analyst first conducted research into the potential threats against these systems. What should the risk analyst do next?

    A. Continue with quantitative or semi-quantitative risk analysis.

    B. Identify vulnerabilities in the systems.

    C. Calculate the probability of occurrence for those threat events.

    D. Develop a rank-ordered list of mitigation tasks.

64. In the context of cybersecurity risk management, which of the following statements about probability and impact is true?

    A. Both probability and impact are relatively easy to quantify.

    B. Both probability and impact are relatively difficult to quantify.

    C. Impact is relatively difficult to quantify, whereas probability is easy to quantify.

    D. Impact is relatively easy to quantify, whereas probability is not easy to quantify.

65. Missing security patches, non-expiring passwords, and incorrect configuration settings are examples of:

    A. Incidents

    B. Vulnerabilities

    C. Threats

    D. Risks

66. Which of the following is the best description of exposure factor (EF)?

    A. The financial loss that results from the realization of a threat, expressed as the asset's total value

    B. The financial loss that results from the realization of a threat, expressed as a percentage of the asset's total value

    C. The probability of occurrence of a single instance of a threat event

    D. The probability of occurrence of all instances of a threat event

67. An estimate of the number of times that a threat may occur within a single year is known as:

   A. Annualized rate of occurrence (ARO)

   B. Exposure factor (EF)

   C. Annualized loss expectancy (ALE)

   D. Annualized exposure factor (AEF)

68. How is annualized loss expectancy (ALE) calculated?

   A. Asset value (AV) divided by exposure factor (EF)

   B. Asset value (AV) times exposure factor (EF)

   C. Single loss expectancy (SLE) times annualized rate of occurrence (ARO)

   D. Single loss expectancy (SLE) divided by the annualized rate of occurrence (ARO)

69. The acquisition of a cyber insurance policy is an example of:

   A. Risk avoidance

   B. Risk transfer

   C. Risk mitigation

   D. Risk acceptance

70. A Europe-based organization has performed a risk assessment on a new online service. The risk assessment identified a high-rated risk related to the privacy of customers. In risk treatment, the organization's executives selected risk avoidance as its risk treatment decision. What does this decision mean?

   A. The organization will enact one or more controls to reduce risk.

   B. The organization will purchase cyber incident insurance to protect the new online service.

   C. The organization will mitigate risks associated with the new online service.

   D. The organization will discontinue the new online service.

71. An internal publication describing compensation, benefits, dress code, paid time off, and conduct is known as:

   A. An employee policy manual

   B. An intranet

   C. An employment agreement

   D. A notice of employment practices

72. In the financial services industry, what is the purpose of mandatory vacations?

   A. Gives other employees an opportunity to cross-train

   B. Reduces employers' financial obligations

   C. Provides extended time for rest and relaxation

   D. Provides adequate time for auditors to examine an employee's behavior while absent from work

73. Which of the following is the best description of the accumulation of privilege?

    A. Gaining access rights over an extended period of time

    B. Gaining new user accounts over an extended period of time

    C. Building up a long history of passwords that have been used

    D. Being given local administrator rights based on trust

74. Which of the following best explains how accumulation of privileges occurs?

    A. Long-time IT administrators are given more administrative rights over time.

    B. Long-time employees slowly accumulate privileges, particularly when transferring from department to department.

    C. A malware attack gives attackers access to more systems and devices over time.

    D. AI-generated phishing emails convince many more employees to click on links or open attachments.

75. IS auditors have detected several instances of lack of segregation of duties in a small organization's accounting department. How can risk best be reduced?

    A. Hire additional personnel.

    B. Perform additional activity reviews to detect any wrongdoing.

    C. Adopt a strict "need to know" access policy.

    D. Adopt a strict "least privilege" access policy.

76. A metric that is used to depict the probability and/or impact of cyber threat events is known as:

    A. A key risk indicator (KRI)

    B. A key performance indicator (KPI)

    C. A key compliance indicator (KCI)

    D. A trailing indicator

77. Which of the following supports the notion of source code vulnerabilities as a quality problem?

    A. Source code vulnerabilities reduce developer productivity.

    B. Source code vulnerabilities require more debugging time.

    C. Source code vulnerabilities are defects that may permit an attacker to more easily compromise a system.

    D. Source code vulnerabilities may lead to application malfunction.

78. The prospect of an organization running afoul of an applicable cyber regulation is known as:

    A. An unacceptable risk

    B. The cost of doing business

    C. Cyber risk

    D. Compliance risk

79. An auditor is reviewing an organization's risk management program policies, procedures, and records. The auditor has noted that, in the risk treatment process, risks that are accepted are accepted in perpetuity. What should the auditor conclude from this practice?

    A. The auditor should notify the organization's board of directors.

    B. There is insufficient information on what the auditor should do.

    C. The auditor should document a finding.

    D. The auditor should note that the organization is following best practices.

80. An auditor is reviewing an organization's risk management program and has determined that the risk manager (who reports to the CISO) performs risk assessments and makes the organization's risk treatment decisions. What should the auditor conclude from this practice?

    A. The auditor should document a finding because a business leader should be making risk treatment decisions.

    B. The auditor should document a finding because the CISO should be making risk treatment decisions.

    C. The auditor should note that the organization is following best practices.

    D. The auditor should suggest that business leaders be informed of risk treatment decisions.

Chapter
3

IT Life Cycle Management

THIS CHAPTER COVERS CISA DOMAIN 3, "INFORMATION SYSTEMS ACQUISITION, DEVELOPMENT, AND IMPLEMENTATION," AND INCLUDES QUESTIONS FROM THE FOLLOWING TOPICS:

- Program and project management
- The systems development life cycle (SDLC)
- Infrastructure development and implementation
- Maintaining information systems
- Business processes and business process reengineering
- Managing third-party risk
- Application controls

The topics in this chapter represent 12% of the CISA examination.

This topic is fully covered in the companion guide, "CISA Certified Information Systems Auditor Study Guide," in Chapter 3.

Questions

You can find the answers to the questions in Appendix A.

1. What is the best reason for considering a proof of concept?
   A. The system being considered is too expensive to implement all at once.
   B. The system being considered will be a fully customized solution.
   C. The system being considered is too complicated to evaluate fully.
   D. The system being considered is not yet available.

2. A formal process whereby the organization gathers all business and technical requirements and forwards them to several qualified vendors, who then respond to them, is called:
   A. Request for information (RFI)
   B. Request for proposals (RFP)
   C. Request for evaluation (RFE)
   D. Request for quote (RFQ)

3. An organization that wishes to acquire IT products or services that it fully understands should issue what kind of document?
   A. Request for proposals (RFP)
   B. Request for information (RFI)
   C. Statement of work (SOW)
   D. Bid schedule

4. Which SEI CMM maturity level states that there is some consistency in the ways that individuals perform tasks from one time to the next, as well as some management planning and direction to ensure that tasks and projects are performed consistently?
   A. Initial
   B. Defined
   C. Repeatable
   D. Managed

5. At what stage in the acquisition process should a project team develop requirements?
   A. After writing the test plan
   B. After operational process development
   C. Prior to writing the test plan
   D. Prior to operational process development

6. All of the following are activities a project manager must perform to ensure that a project is progressing in accordance with its plan *except*:

   A. Designing and testing the system

   B. Tracking project expenditures

   C. Recording task completion

   D. Managing the project schedule

7. During which phase of the infrastructure development life cycle are all changes to the environment performed under formal processes, including incident management, problem management, defect management, change management, and configuration management?

   A. Testing

   B. Design

   C. Implementation

   D. Maintenance

8. Which management processes cover the post-implementation phase of the SDLC?

   A. Maintenance management and change management

   B. Change management and configuration management

   C. Service management and configuration management

   D. Incident management and problem management

9. Change management and configuration management are key to which phase of the SDLC?

   A. Requirement definition

   B. Design

   C. Maintenance

   D. Testing

10. Which of the following is a formal verification of system specifications and technologies?

   A. Design review

   B. User acceptance testing (UAT)

   C. Implementation review

   D. Quality assurance testing (QAT)

11. All of the following are considerations when selecting and evaluating a software vendor *except*:

   A. Source code languages

   B. Financial stability

   C. References

   D. Vendor supportability

12. Which type of quality assurance method involves the users rather than IT or IS personnel?

    A. System testing

    B. Functional testing

    C. Quality assurance testing (QAT)

    D. User acceptance testing (UAT)

13. All of the following are considered risks to a software development project *except*:

    A. The delivered software did not adequately meet business needs.

    B. The delivered software is not meeting efficiency needs.

    C. Termination of the project manager.

    D. Project falling behind schedule or exceeding budget.

14. Analysis of regulations and market conditions normally takes place during which activity of the SDLC?

    A. Testing phase

    B. Feasibility study

    C. Design phase

    D. Requirements definition phase

15. Which term describes a scrum project and is a focused effort to produce some portion of the total project deliverable?

    A. Milestone

    B. Objective

    C. Daily Scrum

    D. Sprint

16. For what reason would an Internet-based financial application record the IP addresses of users who log in?

    A. This permits application performance testing.

    B. This provides localization information to the application.

    C. This provides authentication information to the application.

    D. This provides forensic information that can be used later.

17. In the context of logical access controls, the terms *subject* and *object* refer to:

    A. *Subject* refers to the person who is accessing the data, and *object* refers to the data being accessed.

    B. *Subject* refers to the data being accessed, and *object* refers to the file that contains the data.

    C. *Subject* refers to the security context, and *object* refers to the data.

    D. *Subject* refers to the data, and *object* refers to the person or entity accessing the data.

18. In the context of logical access control, what does the term *fail closed* mean?

   A. In the event of a power outage, all access points are closed.

   B. If access is denied, a database table will be closed or locked to changes.

   C. If an access control mechanism fails, all access will be denied.

   D. If an access control mechanism fails, all access will be allowed.

19. When would you design an access control to fail open?

   A. In the case of fire suppression controls, which would need to activate immediately if a fire is detected

   B. In the case of building access controls, which would need to permit the evacuation of personnel in an emergency

   C. In the event of an emergency, where data access controls would need to allow anyone access to data so it could be backed up successfully and removed from the site

   D. In the case of an incident where outside investigators would require immediate and complete access to restricted data

20. What are the three levels of the Constructive Cost Model (COCOMO) method for estimating software development projects?

   A. Basic, Intermediate, and Detailed

   B. Levels I, II, and III

   C. Initial, Managed, and Optimized

   D. Organic, Semi-detached, and Embedded

21. The best source for requirements for an RFP project is:

   A. Published industry standards

   B. The incumbent system's specifications

   C. Vendors and suppliers

   D. The organization's own business, technical, and security requirements

22. An organization wants to build a new application, but it has not yet defined precisely how end-user interaction will work. Which application development technique should be chosen to determine end-user interaction?

   A. Prototyping

   B. RAD

   C. Waterfall

   D. Scrum

23. A project manager regularly sends project status reports to executive management. Executives are requesting that status reports include visual diagrams showing the project schedule and project critical paths from week to week. Which type of chart should the project manager use?

    A. WBS

    B. PRINCE2

    C. PERT

    D. Gantt

24. During which phase of the SDLC are functionality and design characteristics verified?

    A. Maintenance

    B. Implementation

    C. Testing

    D. Design

25. Which kind of testing ensures that data is being formatted properly and inserted into the new application from the old application?

    A. Unit testing

    B. Migration testing

    C. Regression testing

    D. Functional testing

26. Which entity commissions feasibility studies to support a business case?

    A. Project team

    B. Project manager

    C. CISO

    D. IT steering committee

27. What is the purpose of a configuration management database?

    A. Storage of every change made to system components

    B. Storage of available configurations for system components

    C. Storage of approvals for configuration changes to a system

    D. Storage of the most recent change made to system components

28. When is the best time for an organization to measure the business benefits of a new system?

    A. During unit testing

    B. One year after implementation

    C. During requirements definition

    D. During user acceptance testing

29. Which of the following represents the components of the project in graphical or tabular form and is a visual or structural representation of the system, software, or application?

    A. Data flow diagram (DFD)

    B. Work breakdown structure (WBS)

    C. Zachman model

    D. Object breakdown structure (OBS)

30. Which type of tests will determine whether there are any failures or errors in input, processing, or output controls in an application?

    A. Referential integrity tests

    B. Data conversion tests

    C. Data integrity tests

    D. Static data storage tests

31. Which quantitative method of sizing software projects is repeatable for traditional programming languages but is not as effective with newer, nontextual languages?

    A. Source lines of code (SLOC)

    B. Work breakdown structure (WBS)

    C. Object breakdown structure (OBS)

    D. Constructive Cost Model (COCOMO)

32. Which type of testing, usually performed by developers during the coding phase of the software development project, is used to verify that the code in various parts of the application works properly?

    A. Unit testing

    B. Regression testing

    C. Functional testing

    D. User acceptance testing

33. An organization is considering acquiring a key business application from a small software company. What business provision should the organization require of the software company?

    A. Bonding

    B. Liability insurance

    C. Developer background checks

    D. Place source code in escrow

34. Which phase of the SDLC is continually referenced during the development, acquisition, and testing phases to ensure that the system is meeting the required specifications?

   A. Testing

   B. Requirements definition

   C. Design

   D. Implementation

35. What is the purpose of the review process after each phase of the SDLC?

   A. To establish additional requirements

   B. To change existing requirements

   C. To ensure that project deliverables meet the agreed-on requirements

   D. To provide end users with a progress check on system development

36. The result of strategic planning, process development, and systems development is:

   A. Benefits actualization

   B. Benefits realization

   C. Business viability

   D. Business realization

37. An organization of many large, complex activities that work together to fulfill one or more business objectives is known as:

   A. A program

   B. A repository

   C. A business unit

   D. A department

38. The document that defines and describes a program is known as a:

   A. WBS

   B. RACI

   C. Policy

   D. Charter

39. An organization's business leader wants to develop a new business idea and needs to do some work to determine whether the idea is favorable. The business leader should conduct a:

   A. Feasibility analysis

   B. Business case

   C. Project proposal

   D. Project plan

40. An organization recently launched a new service, only to realize that costs were higher than expected, and there was a lack of consensus on whether the launch was successful. What should the organization have done first that might have resulted in a better outcome?

A. Focus groups

B. Project plan

C. Business case

D. Quantitative analysis

41. An organization implemented a new business application that was two years in a feasibility study, business case, requirements, design, and development. A few weeks after implementation, the IT department conducted measurements to determine business benefits, and the benefits fell far short of expectations. What should the organization have done differently?

A. Forego business benefit measurements as they are often misleading.

B. Defined the business benefit measurements in the requirements phase of the project.

C. Outsourced the business benefit study to eliminate any potential biases.

D. Conducted business benefit measurements 6–12 months after implementation instead of right away.

42. A large organization with several departments has project managers in each department and subdepartment. An initiative to improve business efficiency is underway, and one idea proposed is to move all project managers into a centralized PMO. What is one distinct disadvantage of forming a centralized PMO?

A. Project managers will be more isolated from the departments they serve and be less familiar with their practices.

B. Project managers may be forced to adopt a single project management methodology.

C. Some organizations struggle with implementing matrix management.

D. Departments will have more difficulty controlling project managers.

43. A software development organization has large numbers of software developers organized by the type of languages and systems used. The organization then organizes teams of developers that are dedicated to specific long-term projects. In this arrangement, each software developer has two supervisors: a supervisor for the team of like developers and a supervisor in the project they are assigned to. This type of structural arrangement is known as:

A. Bifurcated teams

B. RACI management

C. Matrix management

D. Agile methodology

44. The following figure is an example of:

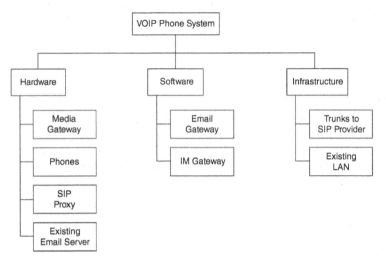

A. Gate process

B. Object breakdown structure

C. Work breakdown structure

D. Gantt chart

45. The following figure is an example of:

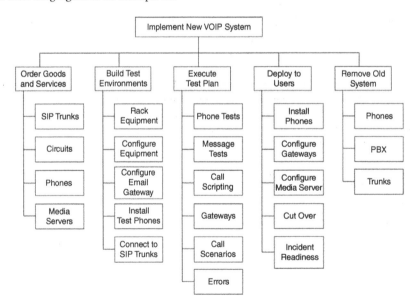

A. Gate process

B. Object breakdown structure

C. Work breakdown structure

D. Gantt chart

46. All of the following are typical responsibilities of a project manager *except*:

A. Approving project changes

B. Building the project schedule

C. Tracking project costs

D. Communicating project status

47. A large, multiyear project in an organization is over time and over budget. Which of the following people is responsible for getting the project back on track?

A. Program manager

B. Project manager

C. Department head

D. Scrum master

48. An organization has organized a group of individuals who are department head leaders or their delegates. The group meets monthly to discuss IT priorities and issues. This group is better known as:

A. IT Leadership Team

B. IT Standards Board

C. IT Steering Committee

D. IT Focus Group

49. While reviewing the status and schedule of a multiquarter project, the project manager realizes that the project is likely to be completed at least a month later than originally scheduled. Assuming there are no notification stipulations in place, the project manager should inform the project sponsor of this:

A. Never

B. At the next monthly project review

C. At the next weekly project meeting

D. Immediately

50. What party should be responsible for creating cybersecurity requirements in a software development project?

A. COO

B. IT department

C. Cybersecurity team

D. Software engineers

51. What party should be responsible for implementing cybersecurity requirements in a software development project?

   A. CISO

   B. End users

   C. Cybersecurity team

   D. Software engineers

52. In a software development project, what party should be responsible for performing unit testing?

   A. Software developers

   B. Project manager

   C. Cybersecurity team

   D. Project sponsor

53. Members of a project team have been exhibiting confusion over roles and responsibilities. To alleviate this situation, the project manager should develop a:

   A. ARCI model

   B. BMIS model

   C. Project plan

   D. Gantt chart

54. A large project team has been organized to carry out a significant systems development project. As a part of organizing the project, the project manager has developed a RACI chart. What purpose will the RACI chart serve?

   A. It defines requirements and standards.

   B. It defines requirements.

   C. It defines roles and responsibilities in detail.

   D. It defines the composition of the project team.

55. On a project team, which party is responsible for tracking the completion of individual tasks?

   A. The persons responsible for performing individual tasks

   B. The project manager

   C. The project sponsor

   D. None of these

56. The purpose of a SLOC tool is:

    A. Estimate the effort required to develop source code.

    B. Identify defects in source code.

    C. Contain use cases for source code testing.

    D. Measure the efficiency of code.

57. The following diagram is an example of:

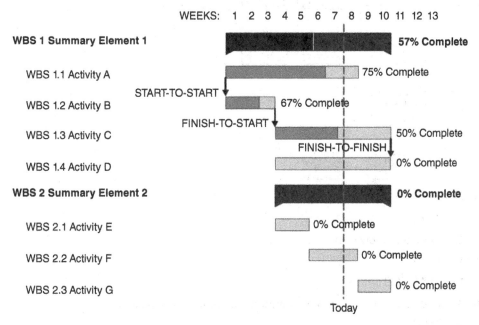

    A. Gantt chart

    B. PERT chart

    C. COCOMO grid

    D. Project plan

58. Which of the following tools is used to estimate the resources required for a software development project?

    A. RACI diagrams

    B. Gantt charts

    C. Function point analysis

    D. Intersectionality analysis

59. The following diagram is an example of:

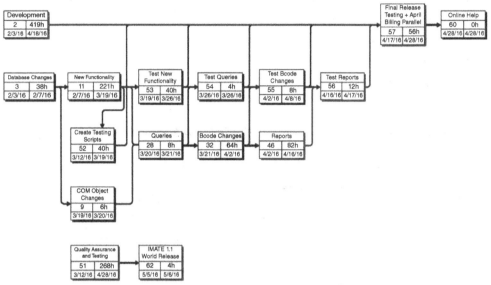

(Image courtesy of Digital Aardvark, Inc.)

   A. RACI chart
   B. Work breakdown structure
   C. Gantt chart
   D. PERT chart

60. A period in which a project or task must be completed is known as a:
   A. Timebox
   B. Taskbox
   C. Constraint
   D. Epoch

61. The name of the iterative and incremental process commonly used to manage agile software development projects is:
   A. Waterfall
   B. Scrum
   C. Agile
   D. PRINCE2

62. In a scrum-managed project, which party should be assigned to the role of ScrumMaster?

    A. End user

    B. Product owner

    C. Project manager

    D. Project sponsor

63. In a daily standup, the ScrumMaster describes the contents of the product backlog. What is the ScrumMaster doing?

    A. Describing the list of project deliverables that have not yet been approved

    B. Describing the list of required project deliverables that are late

    C. Describing the list of required project deliverables for the current sprint

    D. Describing the list of required project deliverables for the entire project

64. The following diagram is a depiction of:

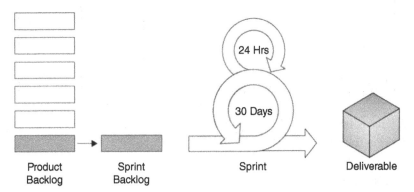

    A. The sprint process

    B. The scrum process

    C. The agile process

    D. The waterfall process

65. The greatest strength of Kanban is:

    A. Its visual display of planned tasks, work in progress, and completed tasks

    B. Its visual depiction of project task interdependencies

    C. Its visual depiction of a project's critical path(s)

    D. Its requirements traceability

66. The following diagram is:

Backlog	In Progress (3)	Peer Review (3)	In Test (1)	Done	Blocked
📄	📄	📄	📄	📄	
📄	📄	📄		📄	📄
📄	📄			📄	
📄				📄	
📄					
📄					
📄					
Fast Track/ Defect		📄			

- **A.** A Kanban board
- **B.** A sprint backlog
- **C.** A Gantt chart
- **D.** A PERT chart

67. After reviewing the history of large processes in the past, a program manager wants to institute a gate process for future projects. What additional step will be present in future projects as a result?

- **A.** Approvals are required for requirements not met.
- **B.** Approvals are required before a project is completed.
- **C.** Approvals are required before projects may proceed to the next step.
- **D.** Approvals are required before a project is started.

68. What is meant by requirements traceability?

- **A.** Each requirement can be matched with the developer who will implement it.
- **B.** Each requirement can be matched with the person or team who will test it.
- **C.** Each requirement can be traced back to the law or standard.
- **D.** Each requirement can be traced back to the person who requested it.

69. What is the proper interpretation of the following figure?

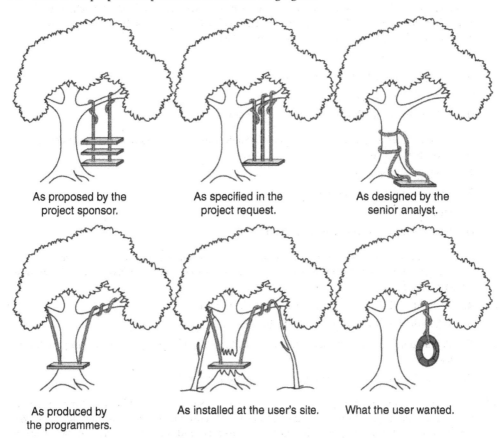

As proposed by the project sponsor.

As specified in the project request.

As designed by the senior analyst.

As produced by the programmers.

As installed at the user's site.

What the user wanted.

A. Project managers often lose control of projects.

B. User requirements are often not stated clearly and with sufficient detail.

C. Project teams often suffer from poor communication.

D. Project members often disagree with how to implement requirements.

70. The principal design characteristic of the waterfall process is:

A. Formal approvals are required before one step may progress to the next.

B. Each phase of the project must be fully complete before the next phase can begin.

C. Multiple phases of a project can be performed in parallel.

D. Projects move forward at great velocity and are difficult to control.

71. A project sponsor contracts with a small software development firm to develop a custom business application. The software development firm is two years old. What mechanism should be put in place to ensure that the customer will be able to support the business application if the software development firm goes out of business?

    A. Source code escrow

    B. An open-source license agreement

    C. A beneficiary clause

    D. Symbol tables in all compiled software modules

72. What is one of the greatest challenges facing SaaS companies related to the multitenant nature of their systems?

    A. Managing system performance

    B. Managing software releases

    C. Disaster recovery planning

    D. Effectively segregating customer data

73. An organization has issued an RFP to replace a large business application. The organization has evaluated and scored RFP responses, resulting in three finalists. How should the organization proceed?

    A. Proceed to the request for information (RFI) phase.

    B. Select the finalist, and purchase the business application.

    C. Begin contract negotiations with two or three of the finalists prior to making the final award.

    D. Select the finalist, and begin contract negotiation.

74. An organization plans to begin a project in which SaaS software will be used for a principal line-of-business application. The CISO argues that Secure SDLC processes should be utilized for this project, but IT is against it. For what reason should the organization utilize its Secure SDLC project in this instance?

    A. Other SDLC activities, including requirements, design, integration, testing, and implementation, still take place.

    B. Secure SDLC standards have always asserted that software development is not a requirement of SDLC.

    C. The organization should not utilize the SDLC process because no software development is being done for this project.

    D. Other SDLC activities, including requirements, design, integration, testing, and implementation, are not taking place.

75. Source code repositories should have all of the following safeguards implemented *except*:

   A. Compilation is required before check-in

   B. Multifactor authentication

   C. Code check-out only when associated with a bug-fix ticket

   D. Code check-in requires a completed static code scan

76. How do unit testing and system testing differ?

   A. System testing is a test of an entire system, whereas unit testing is a single step in system testing.

   B. Unit testing is a test of software modules, whereas system testing is a test of an application's supporting infrastructure.

   C. System testing is a test of an individual module, whereas unit testing is a test of an entire system.

   D. Unit testing is a test of an individual module, whereas system testing is a test of an entire system.

77. An organization's CIO insists that all phases and aspects of testing of a new primary software environment are complete and that all relevant issues have been remedied. The CIO asserts that the organization should perform an "all at once" cutover versus a "parallel" cutover. What argument best refutes this approach?

   A. Parallel testing is different from unit testing.

   B. The CIO is right in saying that a parallel cutover is unnecessary because UAT went so well.

   C. The possibility of differences in processing results in parallel testing could uncover defects not detected in earlier testing.

   D. It is the role of the IT Steering Committee to dictate the test regimen for new applications.

78. How do DevOps and DevSecOps differ?

   A. They are not different; DevOps and DevSecOps are essentially the same thing.

   B. DevSecOps is DevOps with security testing as a part of the automated development platform.

   C. DevSecOps is DevOps with security integrated into the IDE.

   D. DevOps is DevSecOps minus secure coding policy.

79. Which of the following best describes web-based application development?

   A. The result is a web-based application.

   B. Application development tools are web-based.

   C. Application development tools can be run within a browser.

   D. The application's detailed design resembles that of a web application.

80. The following figure is an example of:

CUSTOMER	CUSTOMER DATA		
	PLATFORM, APPLICATIONS, IDENTITY AND ACCESS MANAGEMENT		
	OPERATING SYSTEM, NETWORK AND FIREWALL CONFIGURATION		
	CLIENT-SIDE DATA ENCRYPTION AND DATA INTEGRITY AUTHENTICATION	SERVER-SIDE ENCRYPTION (FILE SYSTEM AND/OR DATA)	NETWORKING TRAFFIC PROTECTION (ENCRYPTION, INTEGRITY, IDENTITY)
AWS	SOFTWARE		
	COMPUTER	STORAGE	DATABASE	NETWORKING
	HARDWARE/AWS GLOBAL INFRASTRUCTURE		
	REGIONS	AVAILABILITY ZONES	EDGE LOCATIONS

- **A.** An SDLC
- **B.** A Zachman architecture
- **C.** A cloud responsibility model
- **D.** A cloud architecture model

Chapter 4

IT Service Management and Continuity

THIS CHAPTER COVERS CISA DOMAIN 4, "INFORMATION SYSTEMS OPERATIONS AND BUSINESS RESILIENCE," AND INCLUDES QUESTIONS FROM THE FOLLOWING TOPICS:

- Information systems operations
- Information systems hardware
- Information systems architecture and software
- Network infrastructure, technologies, models, and protocols
- Business continuity and disaster recovery planning
- Auditing infrastructure, operations, and business continuity and disaster recovery planning

The topics in this chapter represent 26% of the CISA examination.

This topic is fully covered in the companion guide, "CISA Certified Information Systems Auditor Study Guide," in Chapters 4, 5, and 6.

Questions

You can find the answers to the questions in Appendix A.

1. A device that forwards packets to their destination based on their destination IP address is known as a:
   A. Bridge
   B. Gateway
   C. Router
   D. Switch

2. A manager is planning to implement a first-time use of a vulnerability scanning tool in an organization. What method should the security manager use to confirm that all assets are scanned?
   A. Compare the scan results with the accounting department's asset inventory.
   B. Compare the scan results with the contents of the CMDB.
   C. Compare the scan results with a discovery scan performed by the vulnerability scanning tool.
   D. Compare the scan results with the latest network diagram.

3. Which of the following methods should be used to create a point-in-time copy of a large production database?
   A. Storage system snapshot
   B. Storage system replication
   C. E-vaulting
   D. Export to a flat file that is backed up to tape

4. All of the following protocols are used for federated authentication *except*:
   A. OAuth
   B. SAML
   C. WSDL
   D. HMAC

5. What is typically the most significant risk associated with end users being local administrators on their workstations?
   A. End users will have access to all confidential information.
   B. End users can install unauthorized software.
   C. Malware can run at the highest privilege level.
   D. End users can use tools to crack all domain passwords.

6. Which of the following people is best suited to approve users' access to sensitive data in a customer database?

    A. Customer service manager

    B. IT service desk personnel

    C. Information security manager

    D. IT manager

7. An organization is planning a new SaaS service offering and is uncertain about the resources required to support the service. How should the organization proceed?

    A. Calculate projected performance using CMMI tools.

    B. Calculate projected performance using Zachman tools.

    C. Measure actual performance metrics in production.

    D. Build a working prototype and perform load tests.

8. What is the best definition of a problem in ITIL-based service management?

    A. Chronic exceptions in audits of IT systems.

    B. The same incident occurs repeatedly.

    C. Repeated unscheduled downtime.

    D. Unscheduled downtime that exceeds SLAs.

9. Which of the following is the best relationship between system security and the use of vulnerability scanning tools?

    A. Vulnerability scanning is performed proactively, and it drives the security patching and hardening functions.

    B. Vulnerability scanning is performed proactively, and it drives the security patching function.

    C. Patching and hardening are performed proactively, and vulnerability scanning is used to verify their effectiveness.

    D. Patching is performed proactively, and vulnerability scanning is used to verify its effectiveness.

10. An SaaS provider and a customer are having a dispute about the availability of service, quality of service, and issue resolution provided by the SaaS provider. What type of legal agreement should the parties add to their contract to better define these problems and their resolution?

    A. Pricing table

    B. Exit clause

    C. Performance addendum

    D. Service-level agreement

11. What is the purpose of a business impact analysis?

    A. It defines the most critical business processes.

    B. It defines the most critical IT applications.

    C. It defines the most critical service providers.

    D. It defines the disaster recovery plan.

12. An IT architect needs to increase the resilience of a single application server. Which of the following choices will *least* benefit the server's resilience?

    A. Active–active cluster

    B. Active–passive cluster

    C. Geo-cluster

    D. Redundant power supply

13. Which of the following backup schemes best protects an organization from ransomware?

    A. Storage system replication

    B. Storage system mirroring

    C. Storage system snapshots

    D. RAID-5

14. A mail order organization wants to develop procedures to be followed in the event that the main office building cannot be occupied, so that customer orders can still be fulfilled. What kind of a plan does the organization need to develop?

    A. Business impact analysis

    B. Business continuity plan

    C. Disaster recovery plan

    D. Emergency evacuation plan

15. An IT department is planning on implementing disaster recovery capabilities in some of its business systems. What means should be used to determine which applications require DR capabilities and to what level of recoverability?

    A. Business continuity plan

    B. Disaster recovery plan

    C. Risk assessment

    D. Business impact analysis

16. Which of the following is the most compelling reason for an organization to *not* automate its data purging jobs in support of data retention policies?

    A. DR planning

    B. Referential integrity

    C. Privacy breaches

    D. Legal holds

17. Which of the following schemes is most likely to be successful for workstations used by a mobile workforce?

    A. Automated patching followed by a system restart that the end user can control.

    B. Automated patching and restarts.

    C. End-user-initiated patching and restarts.

    D. Only those patches that do not require a system restart are applied.

18. An IT department completed a data discovery assessment and found that numerous users were saving files containing sensitive information on organization-wide readable file shares. Which of the following is the best immediate remediation for this matter?

    A. Remove the offending files from the org-wide share.

    B. Announce to users that the org-wide readable share is not for sensitive data.

    C. Change the org-wide readable share to read-only for most users.

    D. Change the org-wide readable share to write-only for most users.

19. For which users or groups should the SQL listener on a database management system be accessible?

    A. For the application accounts only

    B. For the application and DBA accounts only

    C. For DBA accounts only

    D. For DBA accounts plus all users of the application

20. An organization's financial accounting system crashes every Friday night after backups have been completed. In ITIL terms, what process should be invoked?

    A. Problem management

    B. Incident management

    C. Capacity management

    D. Business continuity management

21. An IT organization is investigating a problem in its change management process whereby many changes must be backed out because they could not be completed or because verifications failed. Which is the best remedy for this situation?

    A. Increase the size of change windows.

    B. Require a separate person to verify changes.

    C. Require change requests to have better backout procedures.

    D. Require more rigorous testing in a test environment prior to scheduling changes in production.

22. Which language is used to change the schema in a database management system?

    A. DDL

    B. SQL

    C. Stored procedures

    D. JCL

23. A DBA has been asked to limit the tables, rows, or columns that are visible to some users with direct database access. Which solution would best fulfill this request?

    A. Create alternate user accounts.

    B. Move those users into different AD groups.

    C. Create one or more views.

    D. Change the schema for those users.

24. An organization's IT department developed DR capabilities for some business applications prior to a BIA ever being performed. Now that a BIA has been performed, it has been determined that some IT applications' DR capabilities exceed what is called for in the BIA and that other applications fall short. What should be done to remedy this?

    A. Redo the BIA using existing DR capabilities as inputs.

    B. Make no changes, as this is the expected result.

    C. Change IT application DR capabilities to align with the BIA.

    D. Change the BIA to align with IT application DR capabilities.

25. What is the purpose of hot-pluggable drives in a storage system?

    A. Ability to replace drives that have crashed or overheated

    B. Ability to replace drives while the storage system is still running

    C. Ability to replace drives without the risk of harm to personnel

    D. Ability to install additional drives without powering down the system

26. What is the primary purpose of data restoration testing?

    A. To meet regulatory requirements

    B. To prove that bare-metal restores can be performed

    C. To see how long it takes to restore data from backup

    D. To ensure that backups are actually being performed

27. Which of the following should approve RTO and RPO targets?

    A. Senior business executives

    B. Board of directors

    C. CISO

    D. CIO

28. An organization has developed its first-ever disaster recovery plan. What is the best choice for the first round of plan testing?

   A. Cutover test

   B. Walkthrough

   C. Simulation

   D. Parallel test

29. Which of the following best describes the purpose of a hypervisor?

   A. It creates and manages virtual desktops.

   B. It creates and manages containers.

   C. It installs software on virtual machines.

   D. It creates and manages virtual machines.

30. Which of the following best fits the definition of a set of structured tables with indexes, primary keys, and foreign keys?

   A. Hierarchical database

   B. Object database

   C. Relational database

   D. Network database

31. An organization uses its vulnerability scanning tool as its de facto asset management system. What is the biggest risk associated with this approach?

   A. Network engineers could build new IP networks not included in the scanning tool's configuration.

   B. System engineers could implement new servers that the scanning tool won't see.

   C. System engineers could implement new virtual machines that the scanning tool won't see.

   D. IP source routing could prevent the scanning tool from seeing all networks.

32. Which of the following systems should be used to populate the IT asset database in an elastic cloud environment?

   A. Hypervisor

   B. Vulnerability scanning tool

   C. Patch management tool

   D. CMDB

33. What is a typical frequency for running a job that checks Active Directory for unused user accounts?

A. Every hour

B. Every 24 hours

C. Every 7 days

D. Every 90 days

34. The system interface standard that includes process control, IPC, and shared memory is known as:

A. UNIX

B. POSIX

C. ActiveX

D. Ultrix

35. An environment consisting of centralized servers running end-user operating systems that display on users' computers is known as:

A. Hosted hypervisor

B. Bare-metal hypervisor

C. Virtual desktop infrastructure

D. Reverse Telnet

36. A data privacy officer recently commissioned a data discovery exercise to understand the extent to which sensitive data is present on the company's world-readable file share. The exercise revealed that dozens of files containing large volumes of highly sensitive data were present on the file share. What is the best first step the data privacy officer should take?

A. Remove all instances of files containing large volumes of highly sensitive data.

B. Investigate each instance to see whether any files are a part of business processes.

C. Sanction the users who placed the files there for violations of internal privacy policy.

D. Do nothing, as this is an acceptable practice for files of this type.

37. A new IT manager is making improvements in the organization's management of unplanned outages. The IT manager has built a new process where repeated cases of similar outages are analyzed to identify their cause. What process has the IT manager created?

A. Problem management

B. Incident management

C. Root cause analysis

D. Security event management

38. A new IT manager is making improvements in the organization's management of the detailed settings on servers and network devices. The process that the IT manager has made is a part of:

   A. Vulnerability management

   B. System hardening

   C. Configuration management

   D. Performance management

39. A new IT manager is making improvements in the organization's management of the detailed settings on servers and network devices. The process includes the creation of a repository for storing details about this information. This repository is known as:

   A. An asset management database

   B. A vulnerability management database

   C. A configuration management database

   D. A system hardening standard

40. A new IT manager is making improvements to the organization's need to make its systems and devices more resilient to attacks. The IT manager should update:

   A. The vulnerability management process

   B. The system and device hardening standard

   C. The configuration management database

   D. The security incident response plan

41. A customer of an SaaS provider is complaining about the SaaS provider's lack of responsiveness in resolving security issues. What portion of the contract should the customer refer to when lodging a formal complaint?

   A. Service description

   B. System availability

   C. Service-level agreement

   D. Security controls

42. Computer code that is found within the contents of a database is known as a:

   A. Blob

   B. Function

   C. Stored procedure

   D. Subroutine

43. An organization is starting its first-ever effort to develop a business continuity and disaster recovery plan. What is the best first step to perform in this effort?

    A. Criticality analysis

    B. Business impact analysis

    C. Setting recovery targets

    D. Selecting a DR site

44. What is the purpose of connecting two redundant power supplies to separate electrical circuits?

    A. System resilience in case one electrical circuit fails

    B. To balance the electrical load between the circuits

    C. To balance the phasing between the circuits

    D. To avoid overloading a single electrical circuit

45. An IT organization is modernizing its tape backup system by replacing its tape library system with a storage array while keeping its tape backup software system. What has the organization implemented?

    A. E-vaulting

    B. S-vaulting

    C. Virtual tape library

    D. Mirroring

46. An IT organization is modernizing its tape backup system by sending data to a cloud storage provider. What has the organization implemented?

    A. Replication

    B. Mirroring

    C. Virtual tape library

    D. E-vaulting

47. A city government department that accepts payments for water use has developed a procedure to be followed by end users when the IT application for processing payments is unavailable. What type of procedure has been developed?

    A. Business continuity plan

    B. Disaster recovery plan

    C. Business impact analysis

    D. Backout plan

48. A city government IT department has developed a procedure to be followed when the primary application for accepting water usage payments has been incapacitated. The procedure, to be carried out by IT personnel, calls for the initiation of a secondary application in a different data center. What type of procedure has been developed?

   A. Business continuity plan

   B. Backout plan

   C. Security incident response plan

   D. Disaster recovery plan

49. What is the most important factor to consider in the development of a disaster recovery plan?

   A. The safety of personnel

   B. The availability of critical data

   C. Notification of civil authorities

   D. The continuity of critical operations

50. An SSD is most used as:

   A. Backup storage

   B. Removable storage

   C. Main storage

   D. Secondary storage

51. The phrase "you can't protect what you don't know about" refers to which key IT process?

   A. Vulnerability management

   B. License management

   C. Patching

   D. Asset management

52. The SOAP protocol is related to:

   A. The patch management process

   B. The exchange of data through an API

   C. The vulnerability management process

   D. Memory garbage collection

53. Restricting USB-attached storage on end-user workstations addresses all of the following *except*:

   A. Leakage of intellectual property

   B. Malware infection

   C. System capacity management

   D. Personal use of a workstation

54. The primary purpose of a dynamic DLP system is:

    A. To detect unauthorized personal use of a workstation

    B. To detect unauthorized use of personal webmail

    C. To control unauthorized access to sensitive information

    D. To control unauthorized movement of sensitive information

55. What is the suitability for the use of a SIEM to alert personnel of system capacity and performance issues?

    A. If Syslog events are generated, use cases related to performance and capacity can be developed.

    B. A SIEM can only be used to alert personnel of security events.

    C. Use cases for non-security-related events do not function on a SIEM.

    D. Alerts for non-security-related events do not function on a SIEM.

56. After analyzing events and incidents from the past year, an analyst has declared the existence of a problem. To what is the analyst referring?

    A. One or more controls are in a state of failure.

    B. The analyst is unable to access all incident data for the entire year.

    C. One or more high-criticality incidents have occurred.

    D. A specific type of incident is recurring.

57. A DBA has determined that it is not feasible to directly back up a large database. What is the best remedy for this?

    A. Defragment the database to permit a linear backup.

    B. Change the database to read-only during a backup to preserve integrity.

    C. Compress the database to recover free space.

    D. Export the database to a flat file, and back up the flat file.

58. What is the feasibility of using the results of a BIA in the creation of a system classification plan?

    A. A BIA will indicate the sensitivity of specific data that is associated with critical business processes.

    B. A BIA will indicate the operational criticality of specific data that is associated with critical business processes.

    C. A BIA does not correlate to specific information systems.

    D. A BIA does not correlate to specific data sets.

59. A system engineer is reviewing critical systems in a data center and maps them to individual electrical circuits. The engineer identified a system with two power supplies that are connected to the same plug strip. What should the engineer conclude from this?

    A. It is an acceptable practice to connect both power supplies to the same circuit.

    B. It is an acceptable practice to connect both power supplies to the same plug strip.

    C. The two power supplies should not be connected to the same circuit.

    D. The two power supplies should not be connected to the same plug strip.

60. An IT architect is proposing a plan for improving the resilience of critical data in the organization. The architect proposes that applications be altered so that they confirm that transactions have been successfully written to two different storage systems. What scheme has been proposed?

    A. Journaling

    B. Mirroring

    C. Data replication

    D. Two-phase commit

61. A department has completed a review of its business continuity plan through a moderated discussion that followed a specific, scripted disaster scenario. What kind of a review was performed?

    A. Walkthrough

    B. Simulation

    C. Parallel test

    D. Peer review

62. What is the purpose of salvage operations in a disaster recovery plan?

    A. To identify the damage to, and recoverability of, critical equipment and assets

    B. To determine the scrap value of critical equipment and assets

    C. To ensure that all personnel are accounted for

    D. To identify business processes that can be resumed

63. RAM is most used for:

    A. Secondary storage

    B. Main storage

    C. Virtual disk

    D. CPU instruction cache

64. All of the following are valid reasons for removing end users' local administrator privileges on their workstations *except*:

A. To reduce malware attack impact

B. To prevent the use of personal webmail

C. To prevent the installation of unauthorized software

D. To reduce the number of service desk support calls

65. The primary mission of data governance is:

A. To ensure the availability of sensitive and critical information

B. To ensure the integrity of sensitive and critical information

C. To control and monitor all uses of sensitive or critical information

D. To ensure compliance with applicable privacy laws

66. Many of the backout plans in the records of a change control process simply read, "Reverse previous steps." What conclusion can be drawn from this?

A. Backout plans are only relevant for emergency changes.

B. Backout plans are not a part of a change management process.

C. Backout plans are adequate.

D. Backout plans are not as rigorous as they should be.

67. The purpose of a business impact analysis (BIA) is primarily:

A. To calculate risk in a risk assessment

B. To determine the impact of a breach

C. To determine process criticalities

D. To determine process dependencies

68. The purpose for prewriting public statements describing the impact of, response to, and recovery from a disaster includes all of the following *except*:

A. During a disaster is not a good time to write such statements from scratch.

B. Key personnel who would write such statements may not be available.

C. Such public statements can be issued more quickly.

D. Prewritten public statements are required by regulation.

69. An IT analyst is searching for a solution through which documents that have been emailed to outside parties can be made to self-destruct at a certain time. What kind of a solution is the IT analyst seeking?

A. DRM

B. DLP

C. IPS

D. IDS

70. An IT service desk person is discussing a problem with an end user. The IT service desk cites the user's "personal area network." What does the IT service desk person mean by this?

  A. The network in the user's personal residence.

  B. The systems and devices the end user can access.

  C. The extent of devices in the same room as the user.

  D. The systems and devices owned by the end user.

71. All of the following are considered network-based services *except*:

  A. Print

  B. File storage

  C. Memory management

  D. Time synchronization

72. Two network engineers are discussing aspects of their organization's data network. One of the network engineers has cited the term *Layer 7*. What is the network engineer referring to?

  A. The Presentation layer of the OSI network model

  B. The Application layer of the OSI network model

  C. The Application layer of the TCP/IP network model

  D. The Transport layer of the TCP/IP network model

73. All of the following protocols are a part of the Application layer of the TCP/IP network model *except*:

  A. ICMP

  B. SNMP

  C. DHCP

  D. DNS

74. The network device that is used to connect networks together is known as:

  A. Gateway

  B. Hub

  C. Switch

  D. Router

75. An organization's IT operations manager has entered a new problem in the problem management log. What does this mean?

  A. A performance issue exists with a staff member.

  B. A security incident recently occurred.

  C. An IT incident recently occurred.

  D. Several similar incidents have recently occurred.

76. An IT manager in an organization argues that release management is unnecessary for the organization's SaaS-hosted applications. Is this position appropriate? Why or why not?

    A. Release management is necessary because the SaaS vendor regularly publishes releases and release notes.

    B. Release management is necessary because end users are using the application regardless of its location.

    C. Release management is unnecessary because the organization is not promoting newly updated code to production.

    D. Release management is unnecessary because the organization's business application is not hosted on-premises.

77. What is the relationship between configuration management and system hardening?

    A. System hardening makes systems resilient to attack, whereas configuration management is the business process of ensuring correct configuration.

    B. Ransomware attacks alter a system's hardening, which is corrected by configuration management.

    C. Configuration management procedures drive system hardening settings.

    D. The system hardening process drives configuration management settings.

78. Configuration management is concerned with all of the following *except*:

    A. OS version and configuration

    B. OS performance

    C. Hardware complement

    D. Hardware configuration

79. Are change management and release management related? Why or why not?

    A. No; they are similar, but they are not related to each other.

    B. No; change management is concerned with configuration changes, whereas release management is concerned with software release.

    C. Yes; organizations can use one or the other to release software changes to production.

    D. Yes; both are concerned with software release to production.

80. The PCI DSS requires logfile retention as follows:

    A. 3 months online

    B. 12 months online

    C. 3 months offline, 12 months online

    D. 3 months online, 12 months offline

Chapter

5

Information Asset Protection

THIS CHAPTER COVERS CISA DOMAIN 5, "PROTECTION OF INFORMATION ASSETS," AND INCLUDES QUESTIONS FROM THE FOLLOWING TOPICS:

- Information security management
- Logical access controls
- Network security
- Environmental security
- Physical security
- Privacy

The topics in this chapter represent 26% of the CISA examination.

This topic is fully covered in the companion guide, "CISA Certified Information Systems Auditor Study Guide," in Chapters 7 and 8.

Questions

You can find the answers to the questions in Appendix A.

1. A new information security manager has examined the systems in the production environment and has found that their security-related configurations are inadequate and inconsistent. To improve this situation, the security manager should create a:

    A. Jump server

    B. Firewall rule

    C. Hardening standard

    D. CMDB

2. Which US government agency enforces retail organizations' information privacy policy?

    A. National Institute of Standards and Technology

    B. Federal Trade Commission

    C. Office of Civil Rights

    D. United States Secret Service

3. Although useful for detecting fires, what is one known problem associated with the use of smoke detectors under a raised computer room floor?

    A. False alarms due to the accumulation of dust

    B. Higher cost of maintenance

    C. Lack of visual reference

    D. Lower sensitivity due to stagnant air

4. An organization is seeking to establish a protocol standard for federated authentication. Which of the following protocols is *least* likely to be selected?

    A. OAuth

    B. SAML

    C. SOAP

    D. HMAC

5. What is one distinct disadvantage of the use of on-premises web content filtering?

    A. End users can no longer inspect URLs in email messages.

    B. End users can easily circumvent it with a local IPS.

    C. Mobile devices are unprotected when off-network.

    D. It is labor-intensive to manage exceptions.

6. What is the purpose of data classification?

    A. To establish rules for data protection and use

    B. To discover sensitive data on unstructured shares

    C. To enforce file access rules

    D. To gather statistics on data usage

7. Blockchain is best described as:

    A. A cryptographic algorithm

    B. A data confidentiality technique using cryptography

    C. A popular cryptocurrency

    D. A list of records that are linked using cryptography

8. The private keys for a well-known website have been compromised. What is the best approach for resolving this matter?

    A. Change the IP address of the web server.

    B. Add an entry to a CRL for the website's TLS/SSL keys.

    C. Recompile the website's application.

    D. Reboot the web server.

9. A web application stores unique codes on each user's system to track the activities of each visitor. What is a common term for these codes?

    A. HTTP-only cookie

    B. Super cookie

    C. Session cookie

    D. Persistent cookie

10. The term *virtual memory* refers to what mechanism?

    A. The main storage allocated to a guest of a hypervisor

    B. Memory management that isolates running processes

    C. Memory that is shared between guests of a hypervisor

    D. Main storage space that exceeds physical memory and is extended to secondary storage

11. What is the effect of suppressing the broadcast of SSID?

    A. Network is not listed, but no difference in security.

    B. Only registered users are able to connect.

    C. Stronger (AES vs. TKIP) cryptography.

    D. Administrators can track users more easily.

12. What is the purpose of recordkeeping in a security awareness training program?

   A. It prevents users from repeating the training.

   B. Compliance with training provider licensing requirements.

   C. Recordkeeping is required by ISO 27001.

   D. Users cannot later claim no knowledge of content if they violate policy.

13. An attack technique in which an attacker attempts to place arbitrary code into the instruction space of a running process is known as:

   A. Cross-site scripting

   B. A time-of-check to time-of-use attack

   C. A buffer-overflow attack

   D. A race condition

14. A security analyst who is troubleshooting a security issue has asked another engineer to obtain a PCAP file associated with a given user's workstation. What is the security analyst asking for?

   A. A copy of the workstation's registry file

   B. A copy of the network traffic to and from the workstation

   C. An image of the workstation's main memory (RAM)

   D. An image of the workstation's secondary memory (hard drive)

15. A development lab employs a syslog server for security and troubleshooting issues. The information security office has recently implemented a SIEM and has directed that all log data be sent to the SIEM. How can the development lab continue to employ its local syslog server while complying with this request?

   A. Build a proxy server that will clone the log data.

   B. The development lab will have to shut down its syslog server.

   C. Export syslog data every hour, and send it to the SIEM.

   D. Direct servers to send their syslog data to the local server and to the SIEM.

16. The best time to assign roles and responsibilities for computer security incident response is:

   A. During training

   B. During tabletop testing

   C. While responding to an incident

   D. While writing the incident response plan

17. Chain of custody is employed in which business process?

   A. Internal investigation

   B. Asset management

   C. Access management

   D. Penetration testing

18. Canada's ITSG-33 is like which standard?

   A. SSAE18

   B. HIPAA

   C. NIST SP 800-53

   D. ISO/IEC 27001

19. The process of ensuring proper protection and use of PII is known as:

   A. Security

   B. Privacy

   C. Data loss prevention

   D. Data discovery

20. A CIO is investigating the prospect of a hosting center for its IT infrastructure. A specific hosting center claims to have "N+1 HVAC Systems." What is meant by this term?

   A. The hosting center has one more HVAC system than is necessary for adequate cooling.

   B. The hosting center has the "N+1" brand of HVAC systems designed for hosting centers.

   C. The hosting center has recently installed a new HVAC system.

   D. The hosting center's HVAC systems meet the N+1 reliability standard.

21. An organization has updated its identity and access management infrastructure so that users use their AD credentials to log in to the network and internal business applications. What has the organization implemented?

   A. Credential vaulting

   B. Single sign-on

   C. Federated identity

   D. Reduced sign-on

22. The primary advantage of a firewall on a laptop computer is:

   A. Laptop computers are protected when outside the enterprise network.

   B. End users have more control over their network security.

   C. Improved performance of enterprise network firewalls.

   D. Redundancy in the event the enterprise firewall is overloaded.

23. An organization's data classification policy includes guidelines for placing footers with specific language in documents and presentations. What activity does this refer to?

   A. Digital signatures

   B. Digital envelopes

   C. Document marking

   D. Document tagging

24. What technique does PGP use to permit multiple users to read an encrypted document?

   A. Key fingerprints

   B. Symmetric cryptography

   C. Digital envelope

   D. Digital signature

25. What feature permits enterprise users of Microsoft Outlook to digitally sign email messages?

   A. PGP

   B. PKI

   C. Local administrative privileges

   D. Password vaulting

26. A URL starting with HTTPS:// signifies what technology?

   A. Self-signed content

   B. Encryption with 3DES

   C. Encryption with SSL or TLS

   D. SET, or Secure Electronic Transaction

27. A recent audit of an IT operation included a finding stating that the organization experiences virtualization sprawl. What is the meaning of this term?

   A. The process related to the creation of new virtual machines is not effective.

   B. Virtual machines are contending for scarce resources.

   C. The organization has too many virtual machines.

   D. Resource requirements for virtual machines are growing.

28. Reasons for placing all IoT-type devices on isolated VLANs include all of the following *except*:

   A. Use of a different network access method

   B. Compatibility with IPv4

   C. Risks associated with unpatched and unpatchable devices

   D. Protection from malware present in end-user environments

29. What is the best reason for including competency quizzes in security awareness training courses?

   A. Quizzes are needed to improve users' knowledge.

   B. Quizzes are required by regulations such as PCI and HIPAA.

   C. It gives users an opportunity to test their skills.

   D. It provides evidence of retention of course content.

30. In the context of information technology and information security, what is the purpose of fuzzing?

   A. To assess a physical server's resilience through a range of humidity settings

   B. To assess a physical server's ability to repel static electricity

   C. To assess a program's resistance to attack via the UI

   D. To assess a program's performance

31. An attacker who is attempting to infiltrate an organization has decided to employ a DNS poison cache attack. What method will the attacker use to attempt this attack?

   A. Send forged query replies to a DNS server.

   B. Send forged query replies to end-user workstations.

   C. Send forged PTR replies to end-user workstations.

   D. Send forced PTR replies to DNS servers.

32. What is the Unix command for dynamically viewing the end of a text logfile?

   A. tail -f

   B. tail -e

   C. less -f

   D. more -f

33. In the US, what are organizations required to do when discovering child pornography on a user's workstation?

   A. Contact law enforcement after the user has admitted to viewing child porn.

   B. Contact law enforcement when the user's workstation has been retired.

   C. Contact law enforcement after terminating the user.

   D. Immediately contact law enforcement.

34. An organization suspects one of its employees of a security violation regarding the use of their workstations. The workstation is powered on and in the employee's workspace. What is the first thing the expert should do?

   A. Remove the hard drive.

   B. Photograph the laptop.

   C. Power up the laptop.

   D. Remove the RAM from the laptop.

35. Which of the following statements is true regarding the Payment Card Industry Data Security Standard (PCI DSS)?

   A. All organizations processing more than US$6,000,000 in credit card transactions annually must undergo an annual audit.

   B. Organizations using chip-and-PIN terminals are exempt from PCI requirements.

   C. Organizations processing fewer than 6 million merchant transactions annually are usually permitted to provide annual self-assessments.

   D. Organizations are permitted to opt out of low-risk controls via Compensating Control Worksheets.

36. According to the European General Data Protection Regulation (GDPR), what is the requirement for organizations when a breach occurs?

   A. All organizations are required to notify supervisory authorities within 48 hours.

   B. All organizations are required to notify supervisory authorities within 72 hours.

   C. All organizations are required to notify affected parties within 24 hours.

   D. Only organizations based in Europe are required to notify supervisory authorities.

37. What is the biggest risk associated with access badges that show the name of the organization?

   A. Someone who finds the badge may know where it can be used.

   B. An attacker can look up the organization's public key and create forged badges.

   C. An attacker would know what brand of access badge technology is being used.

   D. Someone who finds a lost badge would be able to return it to the company.

38. A user at work logs on to a website that includes links to various business applications. Once the user logs on to the website, the user does not need to log on to individual business applications. What mechanism provides this capability?

   A. Public key infrastructure

   B. Reduced sign-on

   C. Single sign-on

   D. Key vaulting

39. What is the primary advantage of cloud-based web content filtering versus on-premises web content filtering?

   A. Cloud-based web content filtering systems are less expensive.

   B. Exceptions can be processed more quickly.

   C. Off-network users are protected just as in-office users are.

   D. Users are unable to circumvent this protection.

40. An organization is investigating the use of an automated DLP solution that controls whether data files can be sent via email or stored on USB drives based on their tags. What is the advantage of using tags for such a solution?

A. Users are easily able to tag files so that they can be properly handled in email.

B. Data files are automatically processed based on tags instead of their data content.

C. Tags are a better solution than the use of digital envelopes.

D. Tags are human-readable and can be altered as needed.

41. All of the following are appropriate uses of digital signatures *except*:

A. Verification of message authenticity

B. Verification of message integrity

C. Verification of message confidentiality

D. Verification of message origin

42. The entity that accepts requests for new public keys in a PKI is known as the:

A. Reservation authority (RA)

B. Validation authority (VA)

C. Registration authority (RA)

D. Certificate authority (CA)

43. What method is used by a transparent proxy filter to prevent a user from visiting a site that has been blacklisted?

A. Proxy sends an HTTP 400 Bad Request to the user's browser.

B. User is directed to a "website blocked" splash page.

C. Proxy filter simply drops the packets, and the user's browser times out.

D. User's workstation is quarantined to prevent malware from spreading.

44. In a virtualized environment, which method is the fastest way to ensure rapid recovery of servers at an alternate processing center?

A. Copy snapshots of virtual machine images to alternate processing center storage system.

B. Provide build instructions for all servers and make master server images available.

C. Perform full and incremental backups of all servers on a daily basis.

D. Perform grandfather–father–son backups of all servers on a daily basis.

45. In an environment where users are not local administrators of their workstations, which of the following methods ensures that end users are not able to use their mobile devices as mobile Wi-Fi hotspots for circumventing network security controls such as web content filters and IPS?

   A.   Require employees to turn off their mobile devices at work.

   B.   Jam the signals of unauthorized Wi-Fi networks.

   C.   Create an allow list of permitted Wi-Fi networks.

   D.   Create a deny list of forbidden Wi-Fi networks.

46. What is the most effective method for training users to detect and delete phishing messages more accurately?

   A.   Block access to personal webmail and permit corporate email only.

   B.   Include phishing information in regular security awareness training.

   C.   Conduct phishing tests, and publicly inform offenders of their mistakes.

   D.   Conduct phishing tests, and privately inform offenders of their mistakes.

47. An attacker has targeted an organization to steal specific information. The attacker has found that the organization's defenses are strong and that very few phishing messages arrive at end-user inboxes. The attacker has decided to try a watering hole attack. What first steps should the hacker use to ensure a successful watering hole attack?

   A.   Determine which websites are frequently visited by the organization's end users.

   B.   Determine which restaurants the organization's end users visit after working hours.

   C.   Determine which protocols are blocked by the organization's Internet firewalls.

   D.   Determine the IP addresses of public-facing web servers that can be attacked.

48. Which of the following techniques most accurately describes a penetration test?

   A.   Manual exploitation tools and techniques

   B.   Vulnerability scan, with results tabulated into a formal report that includes an executive summary

   C.   Vulnerability scan, with results validated to remove any false positives

   D.   Vulnerability scan, followed by manual exploitation tools and techniques

49. A security analyst spends most of her time on a system that collects log data and correlates events from various systems to deduce potential attacks in progress. What kind of a system is the security analyst using?

   A.   SIEM

   B.   IPS

   C.   IDS

   D.   AV console

50. The general counsel receives notifications of all security incidents, including minor ones, and is becoming annoyed by these notifications. This general counsel receiving all notifications is most likely due to:

    A. Careless users clicking on too many phishing emails

    B. Ineffective defenses allowing frequent attacks

    C. Improper classification of security incidents

    D. Lack of a security incident severity scheme

51. A forensic investigator is seen to be creating a detailed record of artifacts that are collected, analyzed, controlled, transferred to others, and stored for safekeeping. What kind of a written record is this?

    A. Storage inventory

    B. Investigation report

    C. Evidence collection log

    D. Chain of custody record

52. Which controls framework is suggested by the ISO/IEC 27001 standard?

    A. ISO/IEC 27001

    B. ISO/IEC 27002

    C. NIST SP800-53

    D. Any framework that is applicable to the organization

53. The default principle in the European General Data Protection Regulation for marketing communications from organizations to citizens is:

    A. Citizens are included but cannot opt out.

    B. Citizens are included until they explicitly opt out.

    C. Citizens are excluded until they explicitly opt in.

    D. Citizens are excluded and cannot opt in.

54. The primary purpose of an access control vestibule (formerly known as a mantrap) is:

    A. To catch an individual attempting to enter a room without authorization

    B. To hold an offender in custody until charged or released

    C. To permit entry of one authorized person at a time

    D. To permit entry or exit of one authorized person at a time

55. What is the purpose of locking a user account that has not been used for long periods of time?

    A. Reduction of the risk of compromised credentials

    B. Free up space for others to use the system

    C. Avoidance of audit exceptions

    D. Recycle license keys and cost reduction

56. What is the best approach for implementing a new blocking rule in an IPS?

  A. First implement a firewall rule, and then activate the IPS rule.

  B. Use the change control process so that stakeholders are aware of the new rule.

  C. Implement a new rule during a change window.

  D. Put the rule in learn mode, and analyze the results.

57. A security leader needs to develop a data classification program. After developing the data classification and handling policy, what is the best next step to perform?

  A. Configure DLP systems to monitor and enforce compliance.

  B. Configure DLP systems to monitor compliance.

  C. Announce the new policy to the organization.

  D. Work with business departments to socialize the policy.

58. An organization wants to implement an IPS that utilizes TLS inspection. What must first be implemented so that the IPS will function?

  A. A span port on the Internet switch must be configured.

  B. A new root certificate must be pushed to all user workstations.

  C. Users must sign a consent for their personal traffic to be monitored.

  D. All end-user private keys must be refreshed.

59. In what manner does a PKI support whole-disk encryption on end-user workstations?

  A. PKI stores the bootup passwords used on each end-user workstation.

  B. PKI detects unauthorized use of data on end-user workstations.

  C. PKI stores decryption keys in the event an end-user forgets their bootup password.

  D. PKI records encryption and decryption operations.

60. A browser contacts a web server and requests a web page. The web server responds with a status code 200. What is the meaning of this status code?

  A. The user has been redirected to another URL on the same domain.

  B. The user has been redirected to another URL on a different domain.

  C. The requested page requires prior authentication.

  D. The request is valid and has been accepted.

61. For what reason would an engineer choose to use a hosted hypervisor versus a bare-metal hypervisor?

  A. There are insufficient resources available for a bare-metal hypervisor.

  B. Features available only in a host operating system are required.

  C. Guest OS monitoring is required.

  D. The hypervisor is supporting a VDI environment.

62. The laboratory environment of a pharmaceutical research organization contains many scientific instruments that contain older versions of Windows and Linux operating systems that cannot be patched. What is the best remedy for this?

A. Isolate the scientific instruments on a separate, protected network.

B. Upgrade the OSs on the scientific instruments to current OS versions.

C. Disconnect the OSs from the network.

D. Audit user accounts on the OSs periodically.

63. Which of the following is the best policy for a security awareness training course?

A. Users are not required to take competency quizzes.

B. Users are required to repeat modules when they fail competency quizzes.

C. Users are required to take competency quizzes only one time, regardless of score.

D. Users can skip training if they pass competency quizzes.

64. Guessing that an intended victim has a particular online banking session open, an attacker attempts to trick the victim into clicking on a link that will attempt to execute a transaction on the online banking site. This type of attack is known as:

A. Cross-site scripting

B. Cross-site request forgery

C. On-path attack

D. Man in the browser

65. The purpose of the DAD Triad is:

A. To model common application vulnerabilities

B. To calculate risk levels

C. To illustrate the opposites of the CIA triad

D. To calculate security event severity

66. The purpose of file integrity monitoring tools is:

A. Make changes to file permissions.

B. Detect changes to file permissions.

C. Detect changes to file contents.

D. Detect changes to file contents and permissions.

67. Which of the following correctly describes the correct sequence for computer security incident response?

A. Protect, detect, respond, recover

B. Identify, protect, detect, respond, recover

C. Evaluate, detect, eradicate, contain, recover, closure

D. Detect, initiate, evaluate, contain, eradicate, recover, remediate

68. Which of the following devices is needed for the creation of a forensically identical hard disk drive?

A. Diode

B. Bit locker

C. Read blocker

D. Write blocker

69. Which of the following statements about NIST CSF is true?

A. NIST CSF is a security controls framework.

B. NIST CSF is a policy framework for cybersecurity.

C. NIST CSF is a computer security incident response framework.

D. NIST CSF is a software development framework.

70. The "right to be forgotten" was first implemented by:

A. GDPR

B. Google

C. NYDFS

D. Facebook

71. The term *tailgating* most often refers to:

A. Personnel who prop or shim doors so that others can enter a protected facility without authentication

B. Personnel who permit others to follow them into a protected facility without authentication

C. Personnel who follow others into a protected facility without authentication

D. Personnel who loan their keycards to others to enter a protected facility

72. A security manager in a large organization has found that the IT department has no central management of privileged user accounts. What kind of a tool should the security manager introduce to remedy this practice?

A. FAM tools

B. FIM tools

C. PAM tools

D. SIEM tools

73. An employee notes that a company document is marked "Confidential." Is it acceptable for the employee to email the document to a party outside the company?

   A. Yes, but the document must be encrypted first.

   B. Yes, the document can be emailed to an outside party in plaintext.

   C. This cannot be determined without first consulting the data classification and handling policy.

   D. No, the document cannot be emailed to any inside or outside party.

74. An auditor has completed an audit of an organization's use of a tool that generates TLS certificates for its external websites. The auditor has determined that key management procedures are insufficient and that split custody of the key generation procedure is required. How might this be implemented?

   A. Of two engineers, one creates the certificate, and the other verifies its creation.

   B. Of two engineers, each performs half of the procedure used to create a new certificate.

   C. Of two engineers, each has one-half of the password required to create a new certificate.

   D. Of two engineers, one approves the creation of the certificate, and the other creates the certificate.

75. An organization that issues digital certificates recently discovered that a digital certificate was issued to an unauthorized party. What is the appropriate response?

   A. Suspend the certificate, and create a CRLF entry.

   B. Revoke the certificate, and create a CRL entry.

   C. Notify all certificate holders.

   D. Call a press conference.

76. Why is it important for a web session cookie to be encrypted?

   A. Parties that can observe the communication will not be able to hijack the session.

   B. Parties that observe the communication will not be able to view the user's password.

   C. Third parties will not be able to push unsolicited advertising to the user.

   D. The website operator will not be able to record the user's session.

77. Why would a hypervisor conceal its existence from a guest OS?

   A. To prevent the guest OS from breaking out of the container

   B. To improve the performance of the guest OS

   C. To avoid letting an intruder know that the OS is part of a virtualized environment

   D. To let an intruder know that the OS is part of a virtualized environment

78. How can an organization prevent employees from connecting to the corporate Exchange email environment with personally owned mobile phones?

   A. Implement multifactor authentication.

   B. Permit only Outlook clients to connect to the Exchange server.

   C. Encrypt OWA traffic.

   D. Put the OWA server behind the firewall and VPN switch.

79. An organization is implementing a new SIEM. How must engineers get log data from systems and devices to the SIEM?

   A. Install agents on IoT devices.

   B. Send them via Windows event.

   C. Send them via syslog.

   D. Send them via syslog and Windows events.

80. What should be the *first* step in correcting issues of SOC operators declaring incidents that turn out to be false positives?

   A. Additional training to improve their incident-handling skills

   B. Termination of employment

   C. Removal of incident declaration privileges

   D. No consequence, as false positives are a part of business as usual

Practice Test 1

1. Which area of an operating system is used to temporarily store data being sent to a hardware device?
   A. Register
   B. Buffer
   C. CPU
   D. DMA channel

2. Which of the following is a critical element during the requirements definition phase of the SDLC?
   A. Skilled developers
   B. Management commitment
   C. User involvement
   D. Adequate funds

3. What is the primary *security* advantage to switching from shared-media networks to switched networks?
   A. A node sees only packets sent explicitly to or from the node, as well as some broadcast traffic, reducing the risks of eavesdropping
   B. Elimination of collision domains
   C. Elimination of broadcast domains through the use of VLANs
   D. Improved throughput

4. An IS auditor in a government organization has been requested to advise on whether the organization should prepare an Incident Response Plan (IRP). Which of the following is the purpose of the IRP?
   A. To enable the organization to effectively respond to cyber threats
   B. To monitor the potential impact of security threats
   C. To mitigate all threats and vulnerabilities affecting the organization
   D. To assist the organization in preventing all security incidents

5. Which ISACA guideline would an auditor use to help prepare the final report for an audit?
   A. 2401, Reporting
   B. 1402, Follow-up Activities
   C. 2402, Follow-up Activities
   D. 1401, Reporting

6. Which of the following audit evidence collection methods involves the IS auditor asking management about the operation of IS controls?

   A. Inspection

   B. Reperformance

   C. Inquiries

   D. Interrogation

7. Which component of the Zachman framework is described as conceptual, logical, or physical, depending on the functional model or context?

   A. Data

   B. Functional

   C. Network

   D. Strategy

8. IS auditors are permitted by the ISACA Standards to use the work of other experts in performing their work. Which of the following is not one of the aspects to be considered when relying on the work of other experts?

   A. The financial standing of the expert

   B. The adequacy of the expert's work

   C. The independence of the expert

   D. The qualifications of the expert

9. Which overarching program includes monitoring project schedules, budgets, resource allocation, conflicts, and the preparation of status reports for senior management?

   A. Incident management

   B. IT management

   C. Program management

   D. Configuration management

10. Quality management refers to the methods by which business processes are controlled, monitored, and managed to bring about continuous improvement. It involves key activities such as software development, software acquisition, service desk, IT operations, and security. What are some of the required components to build and operate an effective quality management system?

    A. Presence of skilled personnel

    B. Sound financial planning

    C. Documented processes and key measurements

    D. Thorough customer surveys

11. Which of the following access management techniques is *single*-factor only?

    A. Fingerprint and PIN

    B. Smartcard and PIN

    C. RSA token and PIN

    D. User ID and password

12. During a systems audit review, an IS auditor seeks to determine whether an organization has defined a logical representation of detailed tasks to be undertaken to complete a software project. Which of the following describes the software development approach under review during this exercise?

    A. Work breakdown structure (WBS)

    B. Gantt chart

    C. PERT analysis

    D. Critical Path Methodology (CPM)

13. An organization has hired a CIO to build and run an IT organization. The new CIO is building a document that states the mission, objectives, roles, and responsibilities for IT. This document is commonly known as a:

    A. Charter

    B. RACI model

    C. Policy

    D. Standard

14. An IS auditor selects a web application for a penetration test. Which of the following should the penetration tester do first?

    A. Obtain permission from management

    B. Draft preliminary findings

    C. Select the tools and commence the test

    D. Identify relevant personnel to interview

15. What is the purpose of the ISACA IT Audit Framework?

    A. To define ethical behavior and required audit standards

    B. To define procedures for the audit of IT systems

    C. To define guidance on ethical behavior

    D. To define ethical behavior and optional audit standards

16. An IS auditor performing a review of the organization's infrastructure management processes notes the operation of various systems without proper vetting from the IT department. Which of the following represents an IT area that the IS auditor is reviewing?

    A. Shadow IT

    B. Bring your own device (BYOD)

    C. Unauthorized systems

    D. Systems misconfiguration

17. An organization that is interested in implementing a data loss prevention capability might consider all of the following techniques *except*:

    A. Intrusion prevention system (IPS)

    B. Control of removable storage devices

    C. Internet website access filtering

    D. Email quarantine system

18. Which of the following controls only serves to alert the organization of unwanted events but has no inherent capability to enforce any activity?

    A. Detective

    B. Preventive

    C. Deterrent

    D. Compensating

19. Who is the primary user of utility software, and what is its purpose?

    A. End user; to enhance productivity

    B. IT specialist; system development, support, or operations

    C. End user; system development, support, or operations

    D. IT specialist; to enhance productivity

20. An IS auditor is reviewing capacity management activities at a software development firm. Which of the following activities assists in predicting future capacity requirements by identifying trends in system usage?

    A. Adequate resource allocations

    B. Effective change processes

    C. Periodic measurements

    D. Timely incident logging

21. An IS auditor is examining a document that describes the required configuration components for network devices. The auditor is examining which kind of document?

   A. Control

   B. Procedure

   C. Standard

   D. Policy

22. Why should an organization classify its IT assets as part of its risk management program?

   A. To ensure proper valuation of its assets

   B. To eliminate the need for maintaining an asset register

   C. To enhance the effectiveness of risk assessments

   D. To assign and mitigate risks associated with the assets

23. Which of the following technologies is an XML-based API specification that facilitates real-time communications between applications using the HTTP and HTTPS protocols?

   A. RPC

   B. SQL

   C. XML

   D. SOAP

24. Which of the following is a crucial feature of rapid application development (RAD)?

   A. Slow, iterative development

   B. Large development team

   C. Development of prototypes

   D. Tight cost control

25. Which of the following logical access controls is designed to permit or deny network traffic based on specific type, origin, or destination?

   A. Screening router

   B. Permissions

   C. Smart cards

   D. Switch

26. IS auditors should consider new organizational initiatives in audit planning. Which of the following is the rationale for adopting this approach?

   A. Organizational initiatives are linked to the organization's objectives.

   B. It leads to a reduction in audit costs.

   C. It simplifies audit management processes.

   D. Organizational initiatives reduce audit coverage.

27. Which resilience technology is appropriate to use where the recovery point objective and recovery time objective are not as time sensitive?

    A. Server clusters

    B. Replication

    C. SAN or NAS

    D. Backup and restore from media

28. During a hiring process review, an IS auditor discovers that a prospective candidate falsified holding a graduate degree. Which steps in the background verification process could have discovered this anomaly?

    A. Credit check

    B. Certificate check

    C. Education check

    D. Employment check

29. What is the purpose of a risk analysis that is performed at the start of an audit project?

    A. To know how long the audit should take

    B. To know which staff members should perform the audit

    C. To know which areas require the greatest amount of attention

    D. To know which areas should be mentioned first in the audit report

30. Why is it essential for an IS auditor to have considerable technical expertise when auditing IT operations?

    A. To understand the technology fully and reduce reliance on interviewees.

    B. IS auditors just need minimum knowledge of IT operations.

    C. To eliminate interviews from the audit process.

    D. To impress the IT staff of the client.

31. A cybersecurity committee is discussing items in the risk register and is making decisions about their disposition. The types of decisions being made are known as:

    A. Risk dashboard

    B. Quantified risk

    C. Qualified risk

    D. Risk treatment

32. Which of the following controls should an organization implement if it desires to ensure that high-value transactions are approved by multiple managers?

    A. Segregation of duties

    B. Two-person integrity

    C. Two-person control

    D. Transaction verification

33. Which authentication method renders replay attacks ineffective?

    A. Simple password

    B. Complex password

    C. Token

    D. Cipher lock

34. The following figure illustrates a diagramming method that is used to support IS auditing. Which of the following terms refers to the diagramming method?

    A. Maturity capability diagram

    B. Audit process diagram

    C. Data flow diagram

    D. Procedure flow diagram

35. Which method of testing disaster recovery plans will enable an organization to fully exercise and evaluate its disaster recovery capabilities?

    A. Walkthrough

    B. Parallel test

    C. Cutover test

    D. Simulation

36. During an organization's systems development audit, an IS auditor discovered that the application development project lacks a business case. At which stage of the systems development life cycle is the business case developed?

A. Implementation

B. Requirements definition

C. Verification and validation

D. Feasibility study

37. Which activity represents an organization's effort to measure the effectiveness of its controls?

A. Benchmarking

B. Compliance audit

C. Control self-assessment

D. External audit

38. A large financial institution seeks to improve its IT service delivery and has approached you for specialist advice. Which of the following frameworks would you advise its management to adopt to achieve the institution's objectives?

A. COSO

B. ISO/IEC 27001:2022

C. COBIT

D. ITIL

39. Which of the following terms refers to changing each application's authentication from stand-alone to centralized and the resulting reduction in the number of user ID–password pairs that each user is required to remember?

A. Authorization

B. Reduced sign-on

C. Authentication

D. Single sign-on

40. There is a very narrow distinction between an intrusion prevention system (IPS) and an intrusion detection system (IDS), which is that an IPS:

A. Eliminates the need for a firewall

B. Performs penetration tests

C. Detects novel attacks only

D. Prevents attacks

41. The elements of the business continuity planning (BCP) process life cycle include all of the following *except*:

   A. Conduct business impact analysis (BIA).

   B. Perform criticality analysis.

   C. Establish recovery targets.

   D. Transition operations back to the original site.

42. While reviewing an organization's system conversion methods, the IS auditor notes that the organization runs both the old and new systems at the same time. Which of the following represents this form of cutover?

   A. Module-by-module

   B. All-at-once

   C. Geographical

   D. Parallel

43. Which of the following standards is applied for the protection of cardholder data?

   A. PCI DSS

   B. PA-DSS

   C. PCI

   D. FIPS 199

44. You are the IS auditor of a small financial institution, and you are reviewing the IT strategic planning process. What would you expect to find during your review?

   A. The presence of qualified IT personnel

   B. Adopted software development practices

   C. The adequacy of operational controls

   D. Vision and mission of IT

45. The period from the onset of an outage until the resumption of service is known as the:

   A. Recovery time objective (RTO)

   B. Recovery response time (RRT)

   C. Recovery point objective (RPO)

   D. Time to recovery (TTR)

46. Which of the following is the most relevant feature of a unified threat management (UTM) system?

   A. UTMs can only be operated manually.

   B. UTMs focus on intrusion detection.

   C. UTMs are expensive and difficult to maintain.

   D. UTMs perform several different security functions.

47. What factor significantly contributes to the success of malware?

    A. Password compromise

    B. Exploitable vulnerabilities

    C. False rejection rate

    D. Unencrypted traffic

48. Which of the following should project team members representing business owners review to confirm that the system design aligns with the owners' concept?

    A. Only the major components of high-level design

    B. Only the high-level design

    C. Only the low-level design

    D. Both the high-level and low-level designs

49. A financial services organization needs to solicit external auditors to perform audits of its services on behalf of its customers and would like to use the most current and relevant standard. Which type of audit should the organization choose?

    A. ISO 27001

    B. SAS 70

    C. SSAE 18

    D. AUP

50. An IS auditor reviewing coding practices at a pharmaceutical firm discovers that the organization sends a vendor's electronic copy to a third-party organization for safekeeping in case the vendor goes out of business. Which of the following terms does this practice represent?

    A. Code review

    B. Code storage

    C. Source code subcontract

    D. Source code escrow

51. HTTP is generally associated with which layer in the TCP/IP model?

    A. 3

    B. 7

    C. 6

    D. 4

52. An IS auditor performing a systems development review encounters the widespread use of sprint retrospectives in a software development project that follows the Scrum methodology. Which of the following is the purpose of a sprint retrospective?

   A. To formulate new sprint objectives

   B. To define the backlog sprint

   C. To approve the just-completed sprint

   D. To reflect on the recently completed sprint

53. An organization may elect to voluntarily undergo an annual ISO 27001 audit for any of the following reasons *except*:

   A. To compensate for poor PCI audit results

   B. To improve its market competitiveness

   C. To give business customers greater confidence in the organization's security controls

   D. For the prestige value

54. Which of the following features of cloud computing allows users to pay only for those resources they consume at any given time?

   A. Scalability

   B. Convenience

   C. Ubiquitous

   D. Measured service

55. An IS auditor is examining an organization's third-party risk management (TPRM) process and has found that the 600+ vendors were assessed with the same questionnaire during onboarding. No assessments are conducted after onboarding. What should the auditor conclude from this?

   A. The TPRM process should be outsourced.

   B. The TPRM process is properly designed.

   C. Critical service providers should be audited annually.

   D. Multiple questionnaires should be used.

56. Which of the following is the reason an IS auditor may recommend that an organization benchmark its key IT processes?

   A. To reduce the cost of procuring IT equipment

   B. To copy competitors' strategies

   C. To compare its processes with those of competitors and determine methods to maintain these processes

   D. To compare how similar organizations solve challenges and determine improvements

57. Which of the following is a verification of system specifications and technologies as performed by individual developers?

    A. Design review

    B. User acceptance testing (UAT)

    C. Quality assurance testing (QAT)

    D. Unit testing

58. The IS auditor seeks to analyze digital evidence while avoiding the alteration of the original evidence. Which of the following methods will assist the IS auditor in achieving this goal?

    A. Document the evidence collection process.

    B. Use original evidence for analysis.

    C. Prepare original evidence work papers.

    D. Use a copy of the original evidence for analysis purposes.

59. All of the following are attack methods that can be used to bypass physical security controls and cause conditions such as tailgating and piggybacking *except*:

    A. Disabled video surveillance equipment

    B. Stolen access card

    C. Social engineering

    D. Bribery

60. Which of the following should the IS auditor recommend for inclusion in restoration procedures after a disaster has occurred?

    A. Closing the primary site

    B. Keeping IT operations permanently at the disaster recovery site

    C. Training employees for future disasters

    D. Transitioning IT operations back to the primary site

61. Which kind of testing ensures that data is being formatted properly as it moves from one application to another?

    A. Unit testing

    B. Integration testing

    C. Regression testing

    D. Functional testing

62. Encapsulation is a key aspect of object-oriented (OO) system development. Which of the following represents the main purpose of encapsulation?

A. To eliminate the need for code reuse

B. To increase code complexities

C. To improve inheritance

D. To hide the internal details of an object

63. An IS auditor sends a questionnaire to the Finance Director to investigate the circumstances surrounding unreconciled sales accounts. After a week of thorough review, the auditor discovers that the Finance Department did not have a policy in place to guide sales reconciliation. What is the most appropriate next step for the IS auditor in this scenario?

A. Expand the scope of audit testing to obtain sufficient evidence.

B. Issue a report stating that the controls in the Finance Department are inadequate.

C. Request a written management representation from the Finance Director regarding the unreconciled accounts.

D. Abandon the audit until the sales policy is in place.

64. During the verification of digital certificates, which of the following is one of the crucial steps that the IS auditor must perform?

A. Confirm the date the certificate was issued.

B. Confirm whether a registration authority (RA) was involved in certificate issuance.

C. Check whether the certificate contains the organization's name.

D. Confirm the certificate was issued by a trusted certificate authority (CA).

65. A new CISO has observed that personnel in the organization are not using the specific safeguards that should be followed to protect a particular information type found in the company's sensitive documents and email. What is the organization apparently missing?

A. Document shredders

B. Security policy

C. Data classification

D. Acceptable use policy

66. The key purpose of initial access provisioning for new employees in an organization is:

A. To assess employees' technical skills

B. To review employee access

C. To provide employee training

D. To provide the appropriate access privileges

67. An auditor is performing an audit of a company's financial operations, including the outsourced expense management service. The expense management service has an SSAE 18 audit report. Can the auditor use this audit report?

   A. The auditor may rely on the SSAE 18 report but will have to confirm whether it covers all areas of interest.

   B. The auditor may rely on the SSAE 18 report, which will cover all areas of interest.

   C. The auditor may not rely on the SSAE 18 report but instead must audit the outsourced expense management service directly.

   D. The auditor does not need to audit the expense management service because it is outsourced.

68. Which of the following training techniques can assist users to better recognize and respond appropriately to phishing attacks?

   A. On-the-job training

   B. Role-based training

   C. Targeted training

   D. Phishing simulations

69. The international standard for standard IT service management processes is known as:

   A. ISO 9000

   B. SABSA

   C. ITIL

   D. ISO 27001

70. An IS auditor carried out a review of a recently implemented application and discovered that many design changes were made after implementation. Which of the following should the IS auditor conclude?

   A. The application was subjected to inadequate testing.

   B. The application met its performance targets.

   C. Application testing was properly conducted.

   D. The application had inadequate requirements.

71. Which of the following auditing standards provides guidance to ensure that all IS audit tasks are performed within the required competence levels?

   A. Due Professional Care

   B. Performance and Supervision

   C. Organizational Independence

   D. Proficiency

72. What is the term used to describe the audit strategy and audit plans that include scope, objectives, resources, and procedures used to evaluate a set of controls and deliver an audit opinion?

A. An audit program

B. An audit system

C. An external audit

D. An internal audit

73. During the review of the business continuity plan (BCP), the IS audit team discovers a missing critical hardware component. Which of the following issues represents this scenario?

A. Syntax error

B. Recovery delay

C. Resumption effect

D. Walkthrough error

74. An IS auditor is reviewing the classification levels at a financial institution. Which of the following would the IS auditor not expect to find?

A. Tags

B. Public

C. Confidential

D. Secret

75. An organization needs to prevent users from being able to access Internet sites whose contents violate organization policy. What should be implemented to accomplish this?

A. Intrusion prevention system

B. Cloud access security broker

C. Web content filtering

D. Advanced antimalware

76. During a recent audit review, the IS audit team discovered that one individual could create supplier accounts, request payments, and make payments. Which of the following principles was being violated?

A. Aggregation of duties (AODs)

B. Segregation of duties (SODs)

C. Dual control

D. Process workflow

77. An auditor is auditing a user account management process and has noted that access requestors are able to approve their own access requests. How should the auditor proceed?

    A. Notify audit client management immediately.

    B. Note the audit exception that requestors may approve their access requests in some cases.

    C. Examine business records to see whether there have been any instances of managers approving their own access requests.

    D. Continue with auditing, because there is no finding here.

78. An IS auditor reviewing an organization's information security practices discovers that vulnerabilities are not being formally tracked and assigned for remediation. Which of the following processes should the organization implement to address this finding?

    A. Penetration testing

    B. Vulnerability management

    C. Patch management

    D. Change management

79. What is the business purpose of a configuration management database?

    A. Provide information about the configurations of IT systems

    B. Create a record of approvals for changes made to a system

    C. Create a record of every configuration change made to IT systems

    D. Create a record of the most recent change made to IT system components

80. Various reasons are often cited for why organizations implement IT governance frameworks, such as the Control Objectives for Information and Related Technologies (COBIT). Which of the following is the most important aim of implementing an IT governance framework for a pharmaceutical firm?

    A. Improving transparency

    B. Increasing sales and profitability levels

    C. Aligning IT strategy with business strategies

    D. Improving managerial performance

81. Which of the following parts of a BIA includes a qualitative or quantitative description of the consequences of an incapacitated process or system?

    A. Criticality analysis

    B. Inventory of key processes and systems

    C. Statement of impact

    D. Risk analysis

82. As part of its security practices, an organization configured a device that has the primary purpose of ensuring that only authorized traffic enters the network from the Internet. It can perform application-layer inspection of all traffic entering the network. What term best describes this device?

    A. Web application firewall

    B. Intrusion detection system

    C. Next generation firewall

    D. Intrusion prevention system

83. An IT leader who wants to build IT processes according to a standard model should adopt which standard?

    A. ISO/IEC 27701

    B. ISO/IEC 27002

    C. ISO/IEC 20000

    D. NIST 800-53

84. An auditor is auditing a purchase order process and needs to select individual purchases to audit. There is a small number of high-value purchase orders. Which sampling technique is best suited for this audit?

    A. Stratified sampling

    B. Statistical sampling

    C. Variable sampling

    D. Discovery sampling

85. A collection of servers that appear as a single server and provide high availability is known as (a):

    A. Resilience

    B. Backup

    C. Cluster

    D. Virtualization

86. What is the most compelling security reason for isolating IoT devices from other systems on a network?

    A. IoT devices communicate via an insecure multicast protocol.

    B. Many IoT devices cannot be patched in the field.

    C. Many IoT devices generate excessive syslog messages.

    D. IoT devices cannot be field upgraded.

87. During an audit review, an IS auditor recommends that the organization develop a policy to provide guidance regarding its handling of personally identifiable information (PII). Which of the following policies should the organization develop?

   A. Strategic

   B. Operations

   C. Privacy

   D. Personnel

88. An IT operations manager has observed that a specific application server chronically exhausts its available memory space. What should the IT operations manager do next?

   A. Open a new incident.

   B. Open a new problem.

   C. Reboot the server.

   D. Report a security incident.

89. Which of the following types of tools is best for reading PCAP files?

   A. Web application scanner

   B. Password cracker

   C. Fuzzer

   D. Network sniffer

90. Which of the following testing methods ensures that the individual software modules work properly?

   A. Integration

   B. Unit

   C. System

   D. Penetration

91. An auditor has audited a business process and its business records. After performing sampling, the auditor has determined that the confidence coefficient is 70%. How should the auditor proceed?

   A. The auditor should select more samples.

   B. The auditor may stop sampling.

   C. The auditor should switch to judgmental sampling.

   D. The auditor should start over.

92. Why is it important for the IS auditor to examine user account lockout settings during a review of identity and access management practices?
    A. To assess the locking and unlocking of accounts after unsuccessful login attempts
    B. To remove all unlocked accounts
    C. To determine the complexity of passwords
    D. To determine the sharing of passwords among users

93. Which is usually the best argument for a CISO not reporting to a CIO?
    A. Personality conflict
    B. Conflict of interest
    C. Separation of duties
    D. Regulation

94. Analysis of competitive information normally takes place during which phase of the systems development life cycle?
    A. Testing phase
    B. Design phase
    C. Requirements definition phase
    D. Feasibility study

95. Why would an IS auditor advise an organization to have a functional contingency plan in place during a cutover test?
    A. To provide guidance for personnel involved in the cutover process
    B. To speed up the cutover process
    C. To ensure rapid recovery of primary systems in the event of a cutover failure
    D. To enhance the organization's ability to identify system bottlenecks

96. In order to meet the BIA objective of creating a detailed list of all identifiable processes and systems, which method is usually used to gather process and system information?
    A. Network diagram review
    B. Documentation review
    C. Criticality analysis
    D. Questionnaire or intake form

97. Which of the following entities retains ownership of internal IS audit engagements?
    A. Management
    B. Internal auditors
    C. Chief audit executive
    D. External auditors

98. Which of the following should be the final authority for notifying law enforcement in the event of a security breach?

   A. Chief information security officer

   B. General counsel

   C. Chief privacy officer

   D. Internal audit

99. Which of the following is out of scope for media management and destruction?

   A. Main memory

   B. Hard drive

   C. Hard copy

   D. Optical media

100. The CIS Benchmarks are an example of what kind of a document?

   A. Encryption standards

   B. Incident case history

   C. Hardening standard

   D. Maturity standard

101. A network-based DLP should be deployed to prevent the loss of sensitive organizational information during email transmission through:

   A. Applying labels to information

   B. Monitoring all hosts for attack attempts

   C. Automatically applying encryption

   D. Allowing unencrypted transmissions to pass through

102. The design of a database is known as its:

   A. Index

   B. View

   C. B-tree

   D. Schema

103. Which of the following IT risk assessment methods should an IS auditor employ if the goal involves the analysis of IT risk based on specific dollar figures?

   A. Critical path analysis

   B. Qualitative risk analysis

   C. Quantitative risk analysis

   D. Business impact analysis

104. What is the minimum standard interval for the retention of video surveillance data at a data center?

   A. 28 days

   B. 7 days

   C. 30 days

   D. 90 days

105. Which of the following is an important reason an IS auditor should recommend that the organization establish the maximum tolerable downtime (MTD) for each of its critical processes?

   A. To set the maximum level of tolerable risk

   B. To set the maximum acceptable data loss

   C. To ensure the continued survival of the organization during a disaster

   D. To assist in coordinating recovery efforts

106. Which of the following is the best method for recovering a server whose root file system has become corrupted?

   A. Full restore

   B. Data restore

   C. Transaction log restore

   D. Rebuild from scratch

107. Which of the following is one of the primary goals of a digital signature?

   A. To encrypt the message in transit

   B. To ensure fast arrival of the message

   C. To assure nonrepudiation by the sender

   D. To prove message ownership

108. Why would an auditor contact an audit client months after an audit has been completed?

   A. To inform the audit client that it is time for another audit

   B. To remind the audit client to complete its audit remediation

   C. To ask the audit client for a reference

   D. To show concern for the audit client and an interest in its success

109. Why would an organization decide to discontinue using an older information system?

   A. The system has serious incompatibilities with new applications.

   B. The system complies with new laws and regulations.

   C. The system has recently been updated.

   D. The system has sufficient data storage space.

110. An auditor has observed that a process that lacks procedure documentation is performed by five persons and is performed consistently. What should the auditor conclude from this?

    A. Minor finding due to lack of process documentation

    B. Major finding due to lack of process documentation

    C. No finding

    D. Material weakness due to lack of process documentation

111. DWT Limited seeks to ensure that its internal IS auditor can act independently when conducting audits. Which of the following ISACA standards addresses the IS auditor's placement within the organizational structure to achieve this independence?

    A. Organizational independence

    B. Audit charter

    C. Reasonable expectation

    D. Objectivity

112. An employee is reading a document that describes levels of protection for information, along with handling guidelines. What kind of a document is the employee reading?

    A. Information security policy

    B. Data classification policy

    C. Data privacy policy

    D. Data disposal procedure

113. As an IS auditor, which of the following do you expect to find from a review of an organizational chart?

    A. Lines of reporting and responsibility

    B. Key risk indicators

    C. Audit objectives

    D. Key performance indicators

114. The protocol data unit for the UDP protocol is:

    A. Datagram

    B. Checksum

    C. MTU

    D. Header

115. Which of the following cryptosystems uses a single shared secret key to enforce confidentiality?

    A. Symmetric cryptosystems

    B. Asymmetric cryptosystems

    C. Quantum cryptosystems

    D. Homomorphic cryptosystems

116. The CMMI is an example of what kind of a model?

   A. Control

   B. Risk

   C. Maturity

   D. Infrastructure

117. Which of the following is the reason for validating the length of input data in each field?

   A. To prevent buffer-overflow attacks

   B. To spell-check the data

   C. To ensure accurate totals

   D. To produce hash totals

118. The types of quality assurance methods involving IT personnel instead of end users include all of the following *except*:

   A. System testing

   B. Functional testing

   C. User acceptance testing (UAT)

   D. Quality assurance testing (QAT)

119. Which category of government data classification requires data to have the highest degree of protection due to the potential for exceptionally grave damage if the data is disclosed?

   A. Top secret

   B. Secret

   C. Private

   D. Confidential

120. A systems engineer is asserting to an auditor that patching a specific vulnerability in a base operating system also protects guest operating systems from the same vulnerability. How should the auditor respond?

   A. Agree, because only host OSs listen on the network

   B. Agree, because hypervisors pass immunity to their guests

   C. Disagree, because closing host OS vulnerabilities does not close guest OS vulnerabilities

   D. Disagree, because host OSs are not patched; only guest OSs are

121. During an audit, an IS auditor needs to verify that only authorized systems can establish communication with APIs. Which of the following safeguards is least relevant to this objective?

A. Data controls

B. Interface controls

C. Access controls

D. Firewalls

122. An IT department has started performing a new procedure during which the IT manager reviews the central identity management system to review and approve privileged users. What kind of a control is this procedure?

A. Detective

B. Preventive

C. Administrative

D. Recovery

123. An IS auditor in a large multinational mining company wishes to apply a risk-based auditing approach to all audits across various companies located around the globe. What is the *first* step the IS auditor should take in rolling out this program?

A. Understand existing internal controls.

B. Gather relevant information.

C. Identify potential risks.

D. Develop a risk-based audit program.

124. What is the purpose of requiring a third-party service provider to provide detailed metrics of its services?

A. To ensure compliance with GDPR

B. For purposes of reporting to regulator

C. To understand how much to pay the service provider every month

D. To ensure the third-party service provider meets quality standards

125. Network devices can sometimes be identified based on the layer of the Open Systems Interconnection (OSI) Model at which they operate. Which of the following network devices typically operates at Layer 2?

A. Firewall

B. Switch

C. Proxy

D. Repeater

126. During which phase of the infrastructure development life cycle are systems verified for correct operation?

   A. Testing

   B. Maintenance

   C. Design

   D. Implementation

127. The balanced scorecard (BSC) is used to measure how well an organization fares in meeting its objectives. Which of the following is *not* one of these perspectives?

   A. Internal processes

   B. External processes

   C. Financial

   D. Customer

128. A security architect is developing a network design wherein end-user computers are regarded the same as end-user devices on the Internet. The security architect is using which model?

   A. Least privilege

   B. VDI

   C. Implicit trust

   D. Zero trust

129. An IS auditor has completed a security posture review in an organization and discovered incidents of identity theft. After further investigation, the auditor discovers that those attacks were primarily the result of credential theft. Which of the following is effective in mitigating this risk?

   A. CASB

   B. MFA

   C. IPS

   D. IDS

130. An auditor has found that servers in the DMZ are using the RIP protocol. What should the auditor conclude from this?

   A. The server is dual-homed.

   B. The network is using archaic protocols.

   C. There are multiple paths to the Internet.

   D. The server's NICs are operating in promiscuous mode.

131. The key difference between business continuity planning (BCP) and disaster recovery planning (DRP) is that the DRP focuses more on:

    A. Less critical business functions

    B. Restoring of systems after a disaster

    C. Operational functions

    D. Human resources aspects of a recovery effort

132. What is the essential minimum practice for administering security awareness training?

    A. At the time of hire

    B. Annually

    C. At the time of hire and quarterly thereafter

    D. At the time of hire and annually thereafter

133. An IS auditor would like to gain an understanding of a client's operating procedures. Which of the following should the IS auditor perform to realize this goal?

    A. Review available instruction manuals.

    B. Conduct walkthroughs.

    C. Review management procedure documentation.

    D. Utilize control checklists.

134. What is the purpose of assigning severity levels to security incidents?

    A. To apply an appropriate level of reporting

    B. To determine the method of evidence collection

    C. To apply an appropriate level and type of response

    D. To determine the method of evidence protection

135. An employee at a large retail organization receives an unexpected email requesting them to update their account details. A link is also included in the email. Which of the following represents the *best* approach the employee should take in this scenario?

    A. Open the email link.

    B. Report to ICT, and delete the mail.

    C. Forward the email link to ICT.

    D. Store the link in the email archive.

136. An auditor is conducting a walkthrough of security configurations on production servers. Flat files are not available because the configuration data exists in an encrypted file. Which of the following is the best method for collecting evidence of security configurations?

    A. Ask the engineer to take screenshots during the walkthrough, which are given to the auditor during the session.

    B. Ask the engineer to take screenshots during the walkthrough, which can be sent via email.

    C. Ask the engineer to take screenshots after the walkthrough, which can be sent via email.

    D. Ask the engineer to write a narrative that lists the requested security configurations.

137. As an IS auditor, which of the following would you consider the *most* critical determinant in allocating resources for an audit engagement?

    A. The availability of skilled personnel

    B. The purpose and scope of the audit

    C. The extent of the organization's geographic footprint

    D. The availability of automated audit tools

138. A new IT leader in an organization wants to introduce quality management into the IT organization. Which is the best standard to use as a reference?

    A. ISO 9000

    B. ISO 27001

    C. ISO 27002

    D. IT BSC

139. Which of the following represents a key component in commencing a program?

    A. Appointing a nontechnical program manager

    B. Development of a program charter

    C. Appointing the CEO as the program sponsor

    D. Setting a tight program timeline

140. Which of the following is a process model *not* developed by ISACA?

    A. COBIT

    B. The Risk IT Framework

    C. Val IT

    D. CMMI

141. An organization plans to establish terms and conditions in its use of external audit services. Which of the following is the primary consideration for establishing audit terms on turnaround time for requests from external auditors?

- **A.** Schedule of IT upgrades
- **B.** Availability of key personnel
- **C.** Availability of the CEO
- **D.** Terms for payment of audit fees

142. A security manager has implemented hidden-camera video surveillance at the data center ingress and egress points. What type of control is this surveillance?

- **A.** Stealth
- **B.** Deterrent
- **C.** Preventive
- **D.** Detective

143. Which of the following is the primary purpose of migration testing during the IT system testing phase of the SDLC?

- **A.** To validate system functionalities
- **B.** To verify that data is properly imported from an old system onto the new system
- **C.** To verify whether user requirements were met
- **D.** To verify that individual modules interface properly

144. All of the following are considered risks to a software development project *except*:

- **A.** Delivered software not adequately meeting business needs
- **B.** Delays in software escrow
- **C.** Purchased software not meeting efficiency needs
- **D.** Key design personnel resigning from the organization

145. Which of the following is the main reason for an organization to implement a "gate process" approach in its systems development life cycle (SDLC) processes?

- **A.** To remove the need for project reviews
- **B.** To review and approve each phase before proceeding
- **C.** To address project challenges during each phase
- **D.** To assess the amount of funds utilized at each phase

146. An auditor is performing a walkthrough of a server environment. Regarding a set of production servers, the systems engineer has told the auditor that the systems are operating in an "active-active" configuration. What can the auditor conclude from this?

   A.   The servers occupy different VLANs.

   B.   The servers are part of a cluster.

   C.   The servers employ multiple power supplies and NICs.

   D.   These are database management systems.

147. Why would an IS auditor perform qualitative risk analysis before undertaking quantitative risk analysis?

   A.   To be precise on the financial impacts of threats

   B.   To identify the most critical risks quickly before undertaking risk quantification

   C.   To reduce the extent of risk analysis

   D.   To measure risk in numerical terms

148. What is the purpose of an MDM platform?

   A.   Active management and protection of smartphones, tablets, and laptop computers

   B.   Monitoring of data exfiltration

   C.   Prevention of data exfiltration

   D.   User self-service password reset

149. An IS auditor is evaluating the procedures used to set up and manage systems in an organization. They are most concerned about ensuring that security settings are properly deployed on various systems. Which of the following items would be most appropriate to examine?

   A.   Systems operations procedures

   B.   Systems configuration standards

   C.   Disaster recovery procedures

   D.   Systems update processes

150. Which form of attack always involves the exploitation of a previously unknown vulnerability?

   A.   Evil twin attack

   B.   Zero-day attack

   C.   DDoS attack

   D.   Social engineering attack

Practice Test 2

1. Which of the following is used to illustrate the flow of information, in business terms, between IT applications?

   A. Zachman model

   B. OSI model

   C. Data flow diagram (DFD)

   D. Clark-Wilson model

2. An IS auditor has observed that the software development team and the operations team are often involved in conflict, leading to the development of insecure software. Which of the following is effective in resolving such conflicts and ensuring the development of secure software?

   A. DevSecOps

   B. Agile

   C. Scrum

   D. DevOps

3. In the context of routers and firewalls, which of the following best describes the use of access control lists (ACLs)?

   A. Access control lists audit network traffic for certain characteristics but allow it to pass unfiltered.

   B. Access control lists are packet-filtering rules that make allow/deny decisions based on IP address, port, service, and other criteria.

   C. Access control lists determine who has administrative access to the router or firewall.

   D. Access control lists filter inbound network traffic only.

4. An IS auditor provides advice to management to apply for cyber-risk insurance coverage in response to some of its cyber risks. Which of the following forms of risk treatment does this advice represent?

   A. Risk transference

   B. Risk avoidance

   C. Risk acceptance

   D. Risk mitigation

5. All of the following are top-level processes in the PRINCE2 project management framework *except*:

   A. Defining Requirements (DR)

   B. Starting Up a Project (SU)

   C. Directing a Project (DP)

   D. Managing Product Delivery (MP)

6. Which of the following artifacts is not part of effective IT governance?

- **A.** Audit program
- **B.** Resource management
- **C.** Standards
- **D.** Policy

7. What is a technique used to distribute a problem or task to several computers at the same time, taking advantage of the processing power of each, to solve the problem or complete the task in less time?

- **A.** Server clusters
- **B.** Grid computing
- **C.** Cloud computing
- **D.** Network-attached storage

8. Which of the following situations is most likely to impair an IS auditor's independence and internal audit objectivity?

- **A.** The IS auditor operated a payroll system subject to audit in the past month.
- **B.** The IS auditor provides advice on the implementation of an ERP system.
- **C.** The IS auditor does not hold the CISA qualification.
- **D.** The IS auditor did not report CPE credits in the past year.

9. Which of the following does *not* describe ethical standards for auditors?

- **A.** 2005, Due Professional Care
- **B.** 1207, Irregularities and Illegal Acts
- **C.** 1204, Performance and Supervision
- **D.** ISACA Code of Professional Ethics

10. During an exit meeting, the IT audit director reported that the requirements specification document did not include all the security requirements. All of the following should form part of the security requirements *except*:

- **A.** IT value delivery
- **B.** Encryption
- **C.** Authentication
- **D.** Authorization

11. Which software development methodology is characterized by small, highly experienced development teams; integrated development tools; and frequent design sessions with end users?

- **A.** Data-oriented system development (DOSD)
- **B.** Rapid application development (RAD)
- **C.** Object-oriented (OO) system development
- **D.** Component-based development

12. Which of the following represents a valid reason for hiring contractors or consultants during seasonal periods?

    A. Varying demand

    B. Financial discipline

    C. Lack of skills

    D. High labor turnover

13. In a risk-based audit:

    A. Auditors perform a risk assessment while performing an audit.

    B. The results of a risk assessment determine which areas warrant additional audit scrutiny.

    C. Auditors determine which audit findings constitute the highest risks.

    D. Management determines which areas warrant additional audit scrutiny.

14. Which of the following categories of utility software encompasses tools that are used to manipulate, query, and import and export data in an organization?

    A. Data management

    B. Data manipulation

    C. Systems health

    D. Software testing

15. Which network device uses only physical (hardware) addresses to forward traffic?

    A. Gateway

    B. Router

    C. Switch

    D. Firewall

16. You have been requested to perform an application vulnerability analysis. Which of the following strategies would you deploy to effectively manage a large number of applications?

    A. Prioritize the analysis of critical applications.

    B. Analyze each application individually.

    C. Perform a single analysis for all applications.

    D. Prioritize the analysis of all intangible assets.

17. Which mode must be used by IPsec to establish a secure connection between networks?

    A. Encryption mode

    B. Authentication mode

    C. Transport mode

    D. Tunnel mode

18. Which of the following sections of an IS audit engagement letter addresses invoicing for services rendered in the IS audit?

  A. Scope of non-audit work

  B. Executive summary

  C. Report distribution list

  D. Confidentiality and nondisclosure

19. The ISACA model for enterprise risk management is known as:

  A. Zachman

  B. NIST 800-30

  C. COBIT

  D. The Risk IT Framework

20. Which of the following is the primary objective of availability management in IT systems?

  A. Sustaining IT services to support organizational objectives

  B. Allocating skilled human resources to the IT program

  C. Increasing monitoring of IT systems performance

  D. Ensuring that IT assets are properly safeguarded

21. Which of the following is true regarding how application software is managed in terms of recovery site planning?

  A. Application software must already be running at a cold site.

  B. Application software should be installed at the hot site.

  C. Application software is not normally installed at a cold site.

  D. Application software is not normally installed at a warm site.

22. Which of the following represents the effect of mergers and acquisitions on IS audit programs?

  A. They introduce business integration, which increases audit complexities.

  B. They create a stable environment for IS audit operations.

  C. They reduce the audit budget.

  D. They increase the need for more skilled IS auditors.

23. What is the purpose of a preaudit?

  A. To permit an audit client to prepare for an upcoming initial audit

  B. To provide the client with examples of evidence it will request in an upcoming audit

  C. To coach the client on answering questions in a way that will prevent auditors from discovering unfavorable information

  D. To provide training to new auditors

24. Why is it critical for an organization to notify its key stakeholders, including authorities, during a disaster?

   A. To inform them of the disaster status and any changes in operations

   B. Professional courtesy

   C. To ensure that they stop the processing of transactions for the organization

   D. To comply with laws and regulations

25. All of the following are considered good password protection measures *except*:

   A. Using passwords meeting complexity requirements

   B. Using default passwords

   C. Using unique passwords in each environment

   D. Using electronic password vaulting

26. After completing a vulnerability analysis, an IS auditor needs to rank the severity of the identified vulnerabilities. Which of the following is a key factor used to determine vulnerability severity?

   A. Likelihood of threat realization

   B. The duration of time the vulnerability has existed

   C. Effectiveness of IT controls implemented

   D. Cost of mitigating the vulnerabilities

27. An organization's HR department is writing a job description for a new CRO position. Which of the following best describes the CRO's role?

   A. Build and manage the ERM program

   B. Build and manage the information security program

   C. Build and manage IT governance

   D. Build and manage product development

28. In an audit of IS problem management operations, which of the following represents the importance of examining IT problem management records?

   A. To determine the effectiveness of problem management activities

   B. To rectify all problems

   C. To enhance media control

   D. To improve the effectiveness of recovery efforts

29. What is the reason an organization might use internal firewalls in addition to its border firewalls?

   A. To create separate zones of trust within the network

   B. To prevent communication between two departments

   C. To assist border firewalls in stopping external threats

   D. To prevent malware from propagating throughout the network

30. Which of the following is the purpose of implementing an employee policy manual in an organization?

   A. To specify the terms and conditions of employment

   B. To train employees

   C. To advertise internal vacancies

   D. To train employees in controls

31. Management in an organization is considering making changes to enhance the ownership in the quality of its processes. What new activity would most effectively achieve this?

   A. Control self-assessment

   B. Internal audit

   C. External audit

   D. Balanced scorecard

32. Which of the following is the *main* purpose of data minimization in the early stages of the information life cycle?

   A. To collect the least amount of data necessary to meet business requirements

   B. To ensure that data is collected for multiple purposes

   C. To maximize the extent of data sources

   D. To speed up the data collection process

33. Which of the following wireless network attacks enables attackers to steal logon credentials and redirect traffic?

   A. MAC address spoofing

   B. Rogue access point

   C. Wireless sniffing

   D. MAC address filtering

34. Which of the following describes the hybrid model for end-user computing?

   A. The organization provides some computing resources, with employees permitted to access certain resources on their personal devices.

   B. The organization provides all computing resources.

   C. The organization restricts the use of personal end-user devices.

   D. Employees provide all computing devices and software.

35. Which of the following tools will enable an organization to better understand the depth and performance capabilities of its business processes?

   A. Control framework

   B. Risk assessment

   C. Maturity model

   D. Clark-Wilson model

36. Which of the components of the ISACA Information Technology Audit Framework (ITAF) is optional?

   A. IT audit and assurance guidelines

   B. IT audit standards

   C. Code of Ethics

   D. All of them are optional.

37. A business user is creating a document that will describe a new system and the benefits that will be realized. This document is better known as a:

   A. Business case

   B. Financial stability

   C. Budget request

   D. Migration plan

38. During which of the following BCP stages does an organization implement architecture improvements?

   A. Development

   B. Analysis

   C. Training

   D. Testing

39. An IS auditor is auditing firewall change records, which contain the date of the change, the type of configuration change, and the name of the person who performed the change. What conclusion should the auditor draw from this observation?

    A. Records are incomplete, as they do not contain the change approval.

    B. Records are complete.

    C. Records are incomplete, as they do not contain a business reason for the change.

    D. Records are incomplete, as they do not contain the backout plan.

40. An organization is considering connecting its systems to facilitate online transactions. Which of the following firewalls would protect this arrangement?

    A. Stateless firewall

    B. NGFW

    C. Stateful firewall

    D. Packet filtering firewall

41. Which of the following is an email security protocol that provides sender and recipient authentication and encryption of message content and attachments?

    A. POP

    B. S-HTTP

    C. S/MIME

    D. HTTPS

42. Which of the following is classified as a natural disaster?

    A. Theft

    B. Volcanic eruption

    C. Hacking attempts

    D. Insider threat

43. In the context of a business impact analysis, a statement of impact:

    A. Outlines how much downtime the organization could suffer before production is affected

    B. Details the expense in resources an organization would have to spend to recover from a particular disaster

    C. Is a qualitative or quantitative description of the impact if the process or system were incapacitated for a defined period

    D. Is used to determine financial losses in the event of a natural disaster

44. Which of the following types of tests is used to confirm that the application is communicating effectively with other applications?

A. Regression

B. Interface

C. Unit

D. Functional

45. The practice of managing budgets, equipment, and personnel is collectively known as:

A. Capacity planning

B. Internal audit

C. Benchmarking

D. Resource management

46. According to ISACA, all of the following documents are critical to the operation of the IS audit function *except*:

A. Audit charter

B. Management representations

C. Audit objectives

D. Audit scope

47. What is the term used for a section of code in a program that permits someone to bypass access controls and access data or functions?

A. Trojan horse

B. Bot

C. Logic bomb

D. Back door

48. Which of the following RAID approaches splits data evenly across two or more disks with the objective of improving performance?

A. RAID-1

B. RAID-0

C. RAID-2

D. RAID-10

49. Who are the most appropriate personnel to perform control self-assessments?

A. Process owners

B. Internal auditors

C. External auditors

D. Chief Audit Executive

50. An IS auditor should provide assurance that processes for a quality management system are periodically monitored and measured to ensure that they are designed properly and operating effectively. Why is management review of key measurements an important step in quality management?

    A. It helps to identify data leakages in the organization.

    B. It allows management to assess performance expectations.

    C. It encourages the organization to focus on developing new quality processes.

    D. It helps the organization to prevent the development of poor-quality products.

51. A company performing due diligence on a cloud-based service provider has requested an audit report. The service provider provided an audit report for its data center hosting provider. How should the company proceed?

    A. Thank the service provider for providing the audit report.

    B. Examine the audit report for significant deficiencies and material weaknesses.

    C. Request an audit report for the service provider's own operations.

    D. File the report in its due diligence recordkeeping.

52. A recent IS access management review at a bank revealed a high incidence of identity theft, with fraudsters accessing customers' financial transactions through a mobile application platform. Which of the following is the *best* solution the organization should adopt to protect against this threat?

    A. Regularly rotating passwords

    B. Implementing multifactor authentication (MFA)

    C. Enforcing the use of ATMs

    D. Conducting staff training and development sessions.

53. The least intrusive type of disaster recovery test is the:

    A. Cutover test

    B. Walkthrough

    C. Documentation review

    D. Parallel test

54. Which of the following is a visual representation tool that can be used to depict IT project tasks, timelines, and dependencies in a left-to-right time sequence?

    A. Project timeline

    B. Gantt chart

    C. Program evaluation and review technique (PERT)

    D. Critical path analysis (CPA)

55. A method where the first personnel involved in a disaster begin notifying others in the organization to inform them of the developing disaster and to enlist their assistance is called a:

A. Direct notification

B. Call tree

C. Conference call

D. Wide-area alert

56. Which of the following models would you recommend to a client seeking to determine the level of maturity of its governance processes?

A. Capability maturity model integration (CMMI)

B. COBIT 2019

C. Agile methodology

D. Val IT

57. How much unscheduled downtime is permitted for an IT organization that commits to 99.9% uptime?

A. 88 hours

B. 8.76 hours

C. 52 minutes

D. 52 seconds

58. Which of the following represents the impact of capacity issues on IT systems service-level agreements (SLAs)?

A. Reduce system response times

B. Lead to SLA violations due to overutilized IT systems

C. Optimize system performance

D. Reduce the need for incident monitoring

59. Integrity can be ensured by which type of cryptographic process?

A. Session encryption

B. Symmetric encryption

C. Asymmetric encryption

D. Hashing functions

60. Which of the following entities is responsible for starting the first phase of the systems development life cycle (SDLC)?

A. Functional users

B. Management

C. Developers

D. IS auditors

61. An IT service desk is planning an implementation of BitLocker for corporate desktop computers. What should be implemented that will provide the service desk with a method to access the contents of computers when users forget their passwords or leave the organization?

A. Key escrow via Active Directory

B. Password hints

C. Back doors

D. Password recovery

62. During an audit of the user access provisioning process, which of the following should the IS auditor examine regarding access request processes?

A. Whether access requests are always denied or approved

B. Whether access requests are consistent

C. Whether access requests are encrypted

D. Whether all users have requested access

63. Which of the following make up the best selection of members for an IT steering committee?

A. Senior executives and department heads

B. Board members

C. End users

D. Customers

64. An IS auditor reviewing an organization's risk management processes encounters a statement of impact on the documentation provided for the audit. What is the rationale for including this statement as part of the impact analysis?

A. To show the results of risk analysis

B. To clearly present business impact in relatable terms

C. To show threats that have no impact on operations

D. To ensure that risk analysis addresses all impacts

65. Which of the following areas is business continuity operations most concerned with?

A. Business processes

B. IT operations

C. Disaster recovery

D. Data restoration

66. Don would like to digitally sign a message he is sending to Zara. What key should he use to sign the message?

A. Don's public key

B. Don's private key

C. Zara's private key

D. Zara's public key

67. Advantages of control self-assessment (CSA) include all of the following *except*:

A. Risks can be detected earlier.

B. Process owners have more of a stake in the effectiveness of their processes.

C. Improvements can be made more quickly.

D. CSA is a viable substitute for internal audit.

68. During the development of an online registration form, a systems developer would like to ensure that each field accepts only valid dates within a specific range. Which of the following types of input validation should the systems developer implement?

A. Typing checking

B. Value and range checking

C. Validity checking

D. Check digit

69. A systems analyst is troubleshooting a chronic batch program malfunction, where the software application is aborting because alphanumeric data is being copied to a numeric date field. What kind of solution would resolve these incidents?

A. Range and value checking

B. Type checking

C. Spell checking

D. Batch totals

70. Which of the following is the immediate action an IS auditor should recommend to an organization that has suffered a data breach?

A. Disconnect all network connections and devices.

B. Activate the incident response plan.

C. Notify law enforcement agents.

D. Evacuate people from the premises.

71. An organization has just completed the implementation of a new business system. The CIO wants to measure and report on the new system's business benefits. Why should the CIO not report on business benefits right away?

A. To provide time to collect and measure meaningful data.

B. Benefits will improve after the shakedown period.

C. Benefits will improve after post-implementation issues are resolved.

D. Metrics will improve after external resources have rolled off.

72. During an IS security review, you note that your client organization experienced ransomware during the period under review. Which of the following types of threat actors is *most* likely behind this attack?

A. Nation-states

B. Criminal syndicates

C. Hacktivists

D. Script kiddies

73. Which of the following methods is most suitable for monitoring the performance of servers in a server farm?

A. Egress filtering

B. Network monitoring

C. Event logging

D. Hardware monitoring

74. The following diagram shows the steps that are ordinarily performed by IS auditors in the determination of the audit scope. Which of the following represents the initial input into the process as represented by the letter X?

A. Management input

B. Risk assessment

C. Prior audit reports

D. Strategic plan

75. Which term describes the time frame for the audit, geography, technology involved, business process to be audited, and portion of the organization affected by the audit?

A. Charter

B. Scope

C. Audit program

D. Audit plan

76. An IS auditor has developed an audit plan to review the BCP processes as shown in the following diagram. Which of the following represents the next step after specifying the business objectives, indicated by the letter X?

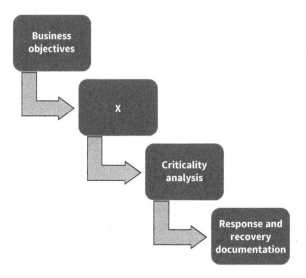

- **A.** Risk analysis
- **B.** Business impact analysis (BIA)
- **C.** Testing
- **D.** Maintenance

77. Which of the following approaches is best regarding virtualization security?
- **A.** Patch the base OS only.
- **B.** Patch the hypervisor only.
- **C.** Patch the base OS and hypervisor.
- **D.** Patch the base OS, the hypervisor, and all guest OSs.

78. During an audit review, the IS auditor seeks to collect sufficient evidence in preparation for legal proceedings. Which of the following types of IS audits is the IS auditor undertaking?
- **A.** Operational audit
- **B.** Financial audit
- **C.** Forensic audit
- **D.** Legal audit

79. An IT document describes the technique used to set up and manage a new firewall. What type of document is this?

    A. Procedure

    B. Standard

    C. Process

    D. Policy

80. As an IS auditor, you have been asked to advise on a device to purchase to solve the issue of signal attenuation. Which of the following network devices would you recommend?

    A. Firewall

    B. Switch

    C. Repeater

    D. Router

81. A customer of an SaaS company has claimed that the SaaS company has violated the SLA. What does this mean?

    A. The SaaS company's software is not functioning properly.

    B. The SaaS company's sales have not met agreed-on levels.

    C. The SaaS company's services are not meeting minimum performance targets.

    D. The SaaS company is overcharging for its services.

82. Which of the following protocols is insecure and should not be used for sensitive communications?

    A. SFTP

    B. TLS

    C. HTTP

    D. SSH

83. An auditor is auditing a retail store chain and needs to select individual stores to audit. There are newer stores with newer technology and older stores with older technology. Which sampling technique is best suited for this audit?

    A. Statistical sampling

    B. Judgmental sampling

    C. Attribute sampling

    D. Discovery sampling

84. The Transport Layer Security (TLS) provides message confidentiality capabilities through:

    A. Asymmetric encryption only

    B. Symmetric encryption only

    C. Both symmetric and asymmetric encryption

    D. Neither symmetric nor asymmetric encryption

85. An auditor is auditing an employee termination process. The auditor wants to select groups of samples until an exception is found. What type of sampling should be used?

    A. Stratified sampling

    B. Statistical sampling

    C. Variable sampling

    D. Discovery sampling

86. Which of the following is a statement by the IS auditor confirming the results of an audit?

    A. Audit program

    B. Interim report

    C. Attestation

    D. Audit test results

87. What is the best evidence for determining the effectiveness of security awareness training?

    A. Attendance records

    B. Competency quiz results

    C. Length of time spent in training

    D. Gartner MQ rating of content

88. Performance optimization entails the continual improvement of IT processes and systems. Which of the following is the main objective of performance optimization?

    A. To enhance the complexity of the organization's IT processes

    B. To develop new systems in a cost-effective way

    C. To obtain maximum benefit from the use of IT services with minimum resources

    D. To enhance employee productivity

89. In the context of logical access controls, how are the terms "subject" and "object" related?

    A. "Subject" refers to the data being accessed, and "object" refers to the file that contains the data.

    B. "Subject" refers to a person or thing that is accessing the data, and "object" refers to the resource being accessed.

    C. "Subject" refers to the security context, and "object" refers to the data.

    D. "Subject" refers to a person who is accessing the data, and "object" refers to the person who created the data.

90. Watermarking is a key method used in DLP systems to prevent data loss. How does the practice of watermarking in DLP systems assist in preventing data losses in an organization?

A. Detecting data corruption

B. Identifying and blocking the exfiltration of encrypted information

C. Identifying and blocking the exfiltration of unencrypted information

D. Serving as a honeypot

91. A central antivirus system console is preferred by organizations for all of the following reasons *except*:

A. Smaller agent footprint

B. Centralized monitoring and reporting

C. Consistent agent configuration

D. Bulk scan and update capabilities

92. Which of the following is the primary reason an organization should have an IT disaster declaration procedure in place?

A. To train employees for the disaster recovery process

B. To provide guidelines for evacuation efforts

C. To clarify conditions for declaring a disaster

D. To eliminate the need for disaster recovery plan testing

93. An information security analyst who is trained in forensics is continuing an investigation into a possible criminal act by an employee through the use of a computer. The analyst is retrieving a hard drive from the evidence locker to examine it some more. What business record should the analyst update to ensure the integrity of the hard drive?

A. Chain of custody

B. Evidence log

C. Hash file

D. Time sheet

94. An IS auditor is assigned to review the effectiveness of unit testing procedures at a software development firm. During which of the following phases of software development would the IS auditor expect unit testing to have been performed?

A. Migration phase

B. User acceptance testing phase

C. Coding phase

D. Design phase

95. A security steering committee consisting of senior executives has refused to consider a risk recently added to the risk register by the CISO. What risk treatment has been taken?

   A. Risk acceptance

   B. Risk avoidance

   C. Residual risk

   D. Risk transfer

96. Which of the following techniques should an IS auditor recommend an organization use in recovering deleted files from a physical disk?

   A. Live analysis

   B. Hardware analysis

   C. Media analysis

   D. Network analysis

97. When auditing a business process, what types of evidence should the auditor examine?

   A. Written process documents and business records

   B. Written process documents and interviews of process owners

   C. Written process documents, interviews of process owners, and business records

   D. Business records and interviews of process owners

98. Which of the following is least directly related to IT governance from the perspective of an IS auditor?

   A. IS risk management

   B. IS strategic planning

   C. IS skills development

   D. IS laws and regulations

99. Hardware monitoring can be used for all of the following purposes *except*:

   A. Resource availability

   B. OS patch levels

   C. System health

   D. CPU utilization

100. Why would an IS auditor use a standard report template from similar engagements?

   A. To reduce the length of the report

   B. To avoid having to rewrite the report

   C. To ensure consistency in audit reporting

   D. To include client responses in the report

101. An auditor has observed that a systems engineer does not possess the necessary qualifications for the position. What is the auditor's best course of action?

    A. Train the systems engineer in the basics of the job.

    B. Recommend that the systems engineer receive training.

    C. Note this as a finding in the audit report.

    D. Immediately notify audit client management.

102. An IS auditor reviewing an organization's systems development methodologies is informed of the use of data-oriented system development (DOSD). Which of the following serves as the central focus around other development activities in DOSD?

    A. Information

    B. People

    C. Data

    D. Evidence

103. The unauthorized collection and aggregation of data is a concern of the:

    A. Chief risk officer

    B. Chief information security officer

    C. Data protection officer

    D. Chief marketing officer

104. Once an organization has received a digital certificate, steps should be taken to verify its authenticity. Which of the following is essential to verify a digital certificate?

    A. The last date the certificate was audited

    B. The registration authority's (RA) signature

    C. The certificate authority's (CA) signature

    D. The certificate's encryption algorithm

105. The act of asserting one's identity is known as:

    A. Authorization

    B. Authentication

    C. Identification

    D. Logging

106. When the transaction count and control totals do not match the expected values, an application should:

    A. Reprocess the entire batch.

    B. Accept the entire batch and create an error report.

    C. Reject the entire batch.

    D. Accept the entire batch and create a warning.

107. The purpose of load balancers is:

    A. To ensure a balanced load across process threads

    B. To ensure a balanced load across servers

    C. To measure network utilization

    D. To test network utilization

108. You are an IS auditor at an external auditor firm, and you need to track your evidence collection. Which of the following evidence collection methods would you adopt?

    A. Inspection

    B. Email

    C. PBC list

    D. Document review

109. A security manager has noted that a recent security scan shows two devices not present in the asset inventory system. What should the security manager do next?

    A. Remove the two devices from the vulnerability scan database.

    B. Keep the two devices in the vulnerability scan database but stop scanning them.

    C. Reconcile the vulnerability management and asset management databases.

    D. Wait until asset inventory agents true up the asset inventory system.

110. During an IS security review, an IS auditor discovers that an attack was carried out by an individual using automated tools, targeting various vulnerable organization systems indiscriminately. Which of the following types of threat actors does this describe?

    A. Hacktivists

    B. Advanced persistent threat (APT) actors

    C. Script kiddies

    D. Insiders

111. The advantage of cloud-based web content filtering versus on-premises web content filtering is:

    A. Laptops are protected while off-premises.

    B. Laptops are protected while on-premises.

    C. GDPR compliance.

    D. End users cannot circumvent cloud-based web content filtering.

112. The following diagram shows the Systems development life cycle, which is subject to review by an IS auditor. Which of the following is represented by X in the diagram?

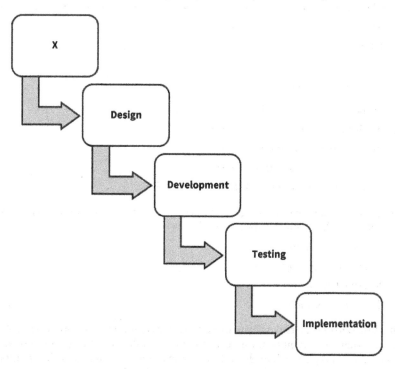

A. Project charter

B. Project plan

C. Requirements development

D. Risk assessment

113. The GDPR is an example of:

A. Maturity model

B. OSI model

C. US State privacy regulation

D. International privacy regulation

114. An organization is planning to implement an information security management system (ISMS) to improve its IT security governance posture. Which of the following frameworks should the IS auditor recommend as the most appropriate for this exercise?

A. TOGAF

B. COBIT 2019

C. NIST CSF

D. ISO/IEC 27001:2022

115. The purpose of an encrypted session cookie is:

A. To distinguish users from each other

B. To encrypt responses sent to a user

C. To encrypt queries sent by a user

D. To comply with credit card security standards

116. Which of the following sampling techniques involves the use of professional expertise by the IS auditor to select a sample for testing?

A. Systematic sampling

B. Discovery sampling

C. Stratified sampling

D. Judgmental sampling

117. ABC Ltd. outsources its data center to a third-party cloud service provider (CSP). The IS auditor wants to determine the extent of the CSP's adherence to agreed-on service-level agreements (SLAs). Which of the following engagements would be the *most* appropriate to assess whether the CSP is adhering to the stipulated SLAs?

A. Operational audit

B. Compliance audit

C. Quality audit

D. Integrated audit

118. Which of the following standards is a highly effective non-law standard widely adopted by financial institutions across the world?

A. CSF

B. ISO/IEC 27001:2022

C. NIST

D. PCI DSS

119. Test plan development is key to which phase of the SDLC?

   A. Requirements definition phase

   B. Maintenance phase

   C. Deployment phase

   D. Testing phase

120. Which of the following is the first stage in the incident response process?

   A. Incident response

   B. Incident analysis

   C. Incident detection

   D. Incident preparation

121. What is the purpose of using a non-exportable digital certificate on a company-owned workstation in the context of a VPN?

   A. It permits personally owned devices to connect to the VPN.

   B. It prevents personally owned devices from connecting to the VPN.

   C. It encrypts all traffic over the VPN.

   D. It hashes all traffic over the VPN.

122. Which of the following is the *most* important objective behind the implementation of an IT governance framework in an organization?

   A. To enhance productivity

   B. To enforce accountability

   C. To reduce operating costs

   D. To ensure IT alignment with the business strategy

123. Which monitoring processes take place after the implementation phase of the SDLC?

   A. Maintenance management and change management

   B. Service management and configuration management

   C. Problem management

   D. Event management and capacity management

124. You have been requested by the CEO of your organization to advise on the differences between a vulnerability assessment and a penetration test. You should explain that the main difference is that a vulnerability assessment:

   A. Requires the scanner to have a valid security certification

   B. Is similar to a penetration test

   C. Is only applicable to physical assets

   D. Only detects vulnerabilities and does not exploit them

125. Performing a bare-metal restore of a production server is an example of what type of control?

A. Compensating

B. Restorative

C. Recovery

D. Automatic

126. Which of the following represents a vital step that should be considered after the design reviews to ensure that the design phase remains stable?

A. Performing a requirements analysis

B. Developing system test plans

C. Conducting storyboarding sessions with all staff

D. Implementing a design freeze

127. A new CIO is finding it difficult to understand the effectiveness of IT processes in the organization. What should the CIO implement to provide better visibility?

A. Zachman scorecard

B. Balanced scorecard

C. Benchmarks

D. Control self-assessments

128. An IS auditor has recommended that an organization consider implementing a control to warn and discourage unauthorized persons from accessing sensitive information. Which of the following types of controls is the IS auditor referring to?

A. Logical

B. Preventive

C. Detective

D. Deterrent

129. The most effective method of deploying patches to a large server farm is:

A. A software distribution system

B. Gold images

C. Hardened images

D. Auto-update

130. A major advantage of cloud computing compared to traditional computing is that in cloud computing, multiple users can share resources without their knowledge or interaction. This is referred to as:

    A. Scalability

    B. Measured service

    C. On-demand access

    D. Multitenancy

131. A CIO is finding it difficult to align the IT group with the greater organization. What should the CIO implement to resolve this?

    A. Control self-assessments

    B. Benchmarking

    C. IT steering committee

    D. Balanced scorecard

132. Which of the following should IS auditors consider a critical component in functional testing?

    A. Each functional requirement must be resilient.

    B. Each functional requirement must be recent.

    C. Developers must test each functional requirement.

    D. Each functional requirement must be verifiable.

133. An auditor is performing a walkthrough with the director of software development, who says that developers use the Burp Suite tool. What is the purpose of this tool in this environment?

    A. Stress testing

    B. User acceptance testing

    C. Functional testing

    D. Security testing

134. During a review of an organization's disaster recovery processes, an IS auditor discovers that the disaster recovery procedures are not updated. Which of the following is the main purpose of disaster recovery procedures?

    A. To train staff in new emergency procedures

    B. To create new procedures

    C. To eliminate the need for a disaster recovery plan

    D. To bootstrap services supporting critical business functions

135. An auditor is examining the physical configuration of production servers and has observed that they employ dual NICs and dual power supplies. What is the most likely reason for the servers having dual NICs?

    A. They occupy multiple VLANs.

    B. NICs are unreliable.

    C. System resilience.

    D. The servers are connected to a supernet.

136. Why should IS auditors engage in audit planning?

    A. To avoid external audits

    B. To comply with legal requirements

    C. To reduce the amount of workload

    D. To determine the amount of audit resources required

137. The purposes of a dynamic DLP platform are all of the following *except*:

    A. Passive monitoring of database schema changes

    B. Automatic enforcement of data classification policy

    C. Data exfiltration prevention

    D. Identifying instances of sensitive data on file shares

138. Client management should be allowed to respond to the results of an IS audit. Which of the following represents an acceptable way for client management to respond to IS audit findings?

    A. Rewrite the audit report

    B. Deny the findings

    C. Approve the report

    D. Remediate the issues

139. An auditor wants to audit an IT department's change control process. What is the best source of information to determine the total population of changes?

    A. Approved changes from the change control process

    B. Logfile containing all changes to a system

    C. Systems events stored in the SIEM

    D. Number of administrator logins

140. Component-based development environments typically structure their applications as:

    A. A set of unrelated modules

    B. Monolithic systems

    C. Standalone applications

    D. Several components working together

141. What is the primary purpose of a SIEM?

    A. Server farm session management

    B. Aggregation of log data

    C. Aggregation of log data and alerting

    D. Protection of privacy encryption keys

142. An IS auditor is planning an audit review of an organization's identity and access management (IAM) solution and is contemplating the adoption of a risk-based approach to determine the controls and activities to audit. Which of the following ISACA standards outlines this requirement?

    A. Audit Charter

    B. Audit Planning

    C. Risk Assessment

    D. Risk Assessment in Planning

143. Which party approves feasibility studies to support a business case?

    A. CTO

    B. Project manager

    C. IT steering committee

    D. CISO

144. The *main* reason for conducting a simulation test in the context of business continuity and disaster recovery plans is to:

    A. Assess the effects of the disaster

    B. Respond to the current disaster

    C. Simulate a disaster scenario and ignore the response

    D. Simulate a disaster scenario and evaluate the response

145. An IT architect has developed and published a document describing the protocols to be used for multifactor authentication. What kind of a document did the IT architect publish?

    A. Process

    B. Architecture

    C. Standard

    D. Policy

146. Which of the following indicates to an IS auditor that numerous emergency changes were made to an application?

  A. Inadequate test cases

  B. Absence of a change management policy

  C. Well-documented change management process

  D. Numerous back-out procedures

147. An auditor is performing a walkthrough of a manufacturing organization's information security management program and has asked what controls framework is in use. The auditee replied that no international standard is used, but instead the organization implemented its own framework based on the ISO/IEC 27001 standard. What can the auditor conclude from this?

  A. Material weakness

  B. Major deficiency

  C. No conclusion can be drawn at this time.

  D. Minor deficiency

148. The ISACA COBIT 2019 is an important tool that can be used by IS auditors in assessing IT governance processes in a variety of organizational environments. The following diagram shows the COBIT 2019 Goals Cascade. Which of the following does the X represent?

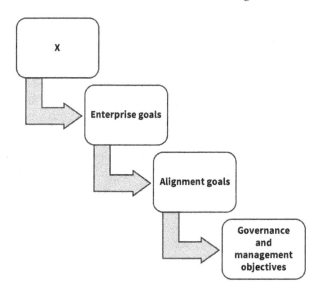

  A. Environmental scanning

  B. Board of directors directives

  C. Chief executive officer's strategic plans

  D. Stakeholder drivers and needs

149. An auditor is auditing a server environment and has noted that backup media are stored in locked cabinets adjacent to the primary storage system. The auditor has been told that a second set of backup media is stored at an offsite media storage center. For what reason would an organization employ two sets of backup media for servers?

A. Business continuity purposes

B. Disaster recovery purposes

C. Because backup media cannot be trusted

D. Rapid data recovery and disaster recovery purposes

150. What type of interface is commonly used to allow applications to interact with a web service without going through the normal user interface?

A. Graphical user interface (GUI)

B. User interface

C. System interface

D. Application programming interface (API)

Appendix

Chapter 1

1. C. The IT Assurance Framework is an ISACA publication that includes the ISACA Code of Professional Ethics, IS audit and assurance standards, IS audit and assurance guidelines, and IS audit and assurance tools and techniques. It does not contain the ISACA Audit Job Practice.

2. B. The CAB should discuss emergency changes made since the last CAB meeting. Although the changes have been made already, they should go through a similar approval process to ensure that all stakeholders are aware of the changes and agree that they were appropriate.

3. A. A video surveillance system is considered a detective control because it only records events without actually preventing events, unlike preventive controls such as locked doors and other barriers. A video surveillance system, when its components are conspicuous, is also considered a deterrent control because its presence serves as a visible deterrent to persons considering an intrusion into a building.

4. C. A risk assessment is the primary means for determining which controls may represent greater organizational risk.

5. C. A service provider audit, such as an SSAE18, SOC 2, ISO 27001 certification, or AUP audit, is designed for service providers that want to provide objective assurance of the integrity of their control environments.

6. A. Although any of these answers are plausible, the first thing that should be examined is whether the audit is being effectively project managed so that all parties understand the audit's objectives, schedule, resources required, and regular status reporting.

7. D. In an audit where an auditor needs to select a portion of events to test, statistical sampling is the best approach.

8. B. An auditor will generally examine process documentation first to understand how a process is supposed to be performed. This will be followed by a walkthrough, observation, examination of records, and corroborative inquiry (and often in that sequence).

9. C. The task of auditing a large number of transactions needs to be automated with one or more computer-assisted audit techniques (CAATs). Manually testing a large number of transactions would be onerous and costly.

10. D. There is rarely a valid reason why the audit client should not be notified immediately of an audit exception. That said, the auditor will often need to reserve the final audit opinion until all the testing has been completed and all the audit exceptions analyzed. Still, notifying the audit client of individual exceptions during the audit provides the audit client with opportunities to begin remediation.

11. A. ISACA Audit Standards are mandatory for all audit professionals – compliance with ISACA Audit Standards is a requirement for earning and retaining the CISA certification.

12. D. The problem with the existing business process can be partly remedied by a frequent user access review, which will partly compensate for the control failures. However, the organization should seek to identify and correct the root cause(s) of the control failures so that fewer exceptions are identified in the monthly user access reviews and subsequent audits.

13. C. The best and first approach to unwanted events is prevention. Where prevention is difficult or expensive, detection is the next best approach.

14. B. An auditor can use a risk assessment performed by a qualified external party to develop a risk-based audit plan, resulting in areas of higher risk being examined more closely than areas of lower risk.

15. D. The payroll services organization should undertake an SSAE18 audit. This type of audit is designed for financial services providers so that the auditors of the customers of the payroll services organization can rely on the payroll services organization's SSAE18 audit report while auditing financial controls.

16. D. The auditor should select which servers are to be sampled (by whatever sampling methodology) and view the configurations during a walkthrough with a systems engineer. Walkthroughs are the most reliable method for ensuring the integrity of the evidence.

17. A. The auditor wants to examine the population and select specific high-risk transactions. Strictly random selections may not include enough privileged access requests; judgmental sampling is needed to pick enough privileged access request transactions to satisfy the auditor's needs.

18. C. A control owner describing a process is known as a walkthrough. Here, each step of a process is described in detail to the auditor.

19. B. The staff auditor should first notify their supervisor, who may notify others in the audit firm. Depending on the nature of the illegal content, it may be appropriate for the audit firm to notify law enforcement, the auditee, or senior officials in the auditee organization, such as audit committee members. Local laws and regulations may influence this decision.

20. A. The QSA auditor signing the audit report as compliant would violate the ISACA Code of Professional Ethics. If ISACA were to learn about this matter, the auditor could lose their ISACA certifications.

21. D. Control self-assessments (CSAs) force control owners to focus on the effectiveness of their controls. For the most part, control owners will self-regulate and improve their control procedures to ensure that their controls are more effective.

22. A. A video surveillance system would record all persons entering and leaving the data center. A security manager could examine the video contents from time to time to understand whether specific persons violate the policy.

23. C. An ISAE3402 audit is the international version of the SSAE18 audit.

24. C. There is little hope that the ROC can be completed in four weeks. After being notified by the audit firm, the merchant organization should request an extension from its acquiring bank.

25. B. Stratified sampling involves selecting samples based on some quantified value in each sample (in this case, the payment amount). Stratified sampling is useful for situations like this, where auditors want to examine very high- or very low-value samples that might not be selected in random sampling.

26. D. Management's comments will appear in the report discussing the specific findings.

27. A. ISACA audit standard 1002, "Organizational Independence," states, "The IS auditor's placement in the command-and-control structure of the organization should ensure that the IS auditor can act independently." This helps to avoid the possibility that the auditor is being coerced into providing a favorable audit opinion.

28. B. The absence of risk assessments (or their omission as an input to the risk management process) constitutes an ineffective process. Risk assessments are among the most important inputs to the risk management process.

29. D. Restoration of a server from backup media is known as a recovery control.

30. C. The PCI audit is not risk-based, and the presence or absence of a risk assessment will not alter the audit plan. This is despite the fact that PCI (as of version 4.0.1) requires an organization to conduct a risk assessment, although this has no bearing on the organization's obligation to implement all controls in the standard.

31. A. A SOC 1 audit is specifically intended for financial service providers in payroll, general accounting, expense management, and other financial services.

32. A. Auditees sometimes take a long time to search for and provide requested evidence to auditors. By providing this request list at the beginning of the audit, auditors will obtain evidence earlier than if they wait until their walkthrough meetings.

33. D. This methodology captures transactions throughout the entire audit period. In a period of this length, there could be personnel changes and other changes that could result in periods of acceptable or unacceptable performance throughout the period.

34. B. This evidence request will provide enough information for the auditor to understand whether background checks are performed for all positions requiring them, as well as whether any no-hire decisions are made.

35. C. The total population is the total set of configuration changes present in the DBMS.

36. B. It is entirely sufficient for the service provider to provide the signed attestation of compliance (AOC) to any merchant, customer, or other entity requesting evidence of PCI DSS compliance.

37. D. ISACA Audit Guidelines are suggested implementation guidelines and are not required of ISACA-certified personnel.

38. A. The TPRM process could be more efficient if the organization stratified its vendors based on risk. The highest-risk vendors would be assessed annually with the most rigorous questionnaire, whereas vendors at lower-risk tiers would be assessed with shorter questionnaires or not at all.

39. C. This is the correct definition of SSAE18 Type I and Type II audits.

40. A. Although the auditee's desire to select the stores to audit may seem proactive, the auditor needs to better understand the nature of each store's information systems before overruling the auditee. For instance, the systems in all stores may be identically configured, and the nearby store operators may be better equipped to explain audit processes. On the other hand, if store systems are not identically configured and operated, the client's desire to select samples may have to be overruled so the auditor retains independence.

41. D. An auditor discussing a business process with additional personnel outside the process is known as corroborative inquiry. This helps to give the auditor more confidence in the veracity of the evidence obtained from control owners and operators.

42. A. An auditor is free to contact an auditee after an audit to show concern for the auditee and be sure that the auditee is proceeding properly by working to resolve any findings identified by the auditor.

43. B. All types of risks should be considered when planning an audit of a business process or system.

44. B. The service desk is performing a monthly review of user account provisioning to make sure that all such account provisioning activities were, in fact, requested.

45. D. Visible notices announcing its presence are an example of a deterrent control.

46. C. A penetration test reveals a limited view of risks, and a full risk assessment is still needed if the audit is to be truly risk driven.

47. D. A reconciliation of all user account changes with approved requests in the ticketing system ensures that all such changes were actually requested and approved.

48. A. It is necessary to identify control owners to send evidence requests to the right personnel. Next, walkthroughs are performed, and finally, corroborative interviews are held.

49. B. Discovery sampling is used when an auditor is examining samples in the search for at least one exception.

50. B. A secure file transfer portal is the best choice because sensitive information will be encrypted in transit, end to end, and the portal can handle volumes of evidence that may be too large to email.

51. D. The best way to deliver an audit report is face-to-face so that the auditor can explain the audit project, provide the audit report, and answer any questions that the audit client might have. An in-person meeting provides the auditor with valuable body language cues from the audit client to better understand the audit client's response to the audit report and its description of findings.

52. D. An ISACA member violating the ISACA Code of Professional Ethics "can result in an investigation into a member's or certification holder's conduct and, ultimately, in disciplinary measures," including loss of certifications.

53. A. The auditor has discovered a separation-of-duties (sometimes known as segregation-of-duties) issue. Payment requests and approvals should be handled by separate persons in accounts payable.

54. C. This is a preventive control and also an automatic control. The workflow prevents a single individual from performing the review and approval steps.

55. A. This is a reperformance audit because the auditor will essentially repeat the steps performed in the review.

56. B. This is statistical sampling, where the auditor has requested 10% of the population, effectively random and spread throughout the audit period. This assumes, of course, that change-control requests are serialized sequentially.

57. C. The DBA is an independent party from the asset process owner and should have little or no interest in the audit's outcome.

58. D. The auditor has no choice but to stand by the audit report as is, particularly after a review upholds all findings.

59. A. The auditor should first report the matter to their manager, who will, in turn, decide how to handle the matter. More than likely, the audit manager will notify the audit client's audit committee, which can decide whether to refer the matter to regulatory authorities.

60. D. The change-control process lacks a step where requested changes are reviewed, discussed, and approved. As it stands, it appears that engineers unilaterally decide what changes to make.

61. C. This is a detective control. The system is not a deterrent control because the video surveillance system is not visible.

62. B. This is stratified sampling, where an auditor selects samples from various classes or values – in this case, higher-risk privileged accounts.

63. A. This is an example of the discovery sampling technique, where an auditor examines samples until an exception is found.

64. D. Stop-or-go sampling is performed when an auditor believes the overall risk is low and wants to sample as few records as possible.

65. A. This is an example of the discovery sampling technique, where an auditor examines samples until an exception is found.

66. C. In the US, auditors (as well as IT and cybersecurity) are generally required to notify law enforcement when child pornography is detected. However, in many (if not most) cases, a staff employee is not authorized to notify external parties; instead, the staff employee should notify their supervisor, who will follow audit firm policy to determine who is authorized to notify law enforcement.

67. A. None of these items should be excluded from the archive of the audit; all should be retained.

68. C. Staff auditors should always notify their supervisors when they detect a potential conflict of interest situation. Audit management can then decide how to proceed.

69. A. Generally, the requestor and approver in a business process should be two different people or roles. When the requestor and approver are the same person, an issue with segregation of duties exists.

70. C. A security scan of a vendor's website is just one of many ways the vendor should be assessed for risk, but by itself it is inadequate. Other means of assessing risk include issuing detailed questionnaires, reviewing audit reports, and obtaining information about the health of a vendor's business from business intelligence bureaus.

71. D. In SOC 1 and SOC 2 audits, the auditee can issue comments that will appear in the report, explaining their perspective regarding the findings. Often, management will state that the business process will be fixed or has been fixed.

72. B. An organization's Internal Audit department will typically perform a risk assessment every year or two to see for itself where important risks exist in the organization, helping Internal Audit develop its audit plan for the year, including paying more attention to those higher-risk activities and areas.

73. A. Control self-assessments (CSAs) are a good way of instilling ownership and quality on the part of control owner–operators because they will be asked to demonstrate the soundness of their controls.

74. A. Confidential information should not be uploaded to a public LLM AI service such as ChatGPT or Bard, as this may result in the compromise and exposure of that information.

75. C. The use of contractors in an Internal Audit department is considered the outsourcing of internal audit.

76. A. Audit planning requires that the scope, purpose, and schedule of an audit be determined. Findings will be identified during the audit.

77. D. Organizations obligated to comply with multiple control frameworks should first identify the scope of each and then map those controls in common where they overlap, helping to identify activities that are common to two or more controls and control frameworks.

78. C. Video surveillance is often considered both a deterrent control (because cameras and perhaps even monitors are plainly visible, thus deterring any wrongdoing for fear of detection) and a detective control (because the system will permit observation of activities). This is common in control classification, where a control can have one or more classifications.

79. A. The organization is still required to comply with PCI DSS because its own website directs customers to the third-party payment gateway for processing payments. The organization will not be required to comply with specific PCI DSS controls related to the storage of credit card numbers, but many other controls will still apply.

80. B. Favorable results in control self-assessments are not likely to alter the scheduling of audits. Instead, CSAs help identify control issues before audits occur and instill ownership on the part of control owners.

Chapter 2

1. C. ISACA defines governance as a set of processes that "Ensures that stakeholder needs, conditions, and options are evaluated to determine balanced, agreed-on enterprise objectives to be achieved; setting direction through prioritization and decision-making; and monitoring performance and compliance against agreed-on direction and objectives."

2. B. The best way to align an IT department to the business is to find and understand the organization's vision statement, mission statement, goals, and objectives. Many organizations develop and publish one or more of these statements. Others take a simpler approach and develop strategic objectives for a calendar or fiscal year. Whatever can be found is valuable: once an IT manager understands these statements, they can prioritize resources and activities in the IT department to support the vision, mission, goals, or other strategic statements.

3. A. The best first step in aligning an IT department to the organization's strategic objectives is to better understand those objectives, including the resources and activities that will be employed to achieve them.

4. C. A risk appetite statement (sometimes known as a risk tolerance statement or risk capacity statement) provides guidance on the types of risk and the amount of risk an organization may be willing to accept versus what risks an organization may instead prefer to mitigate, avoid, or transfer. Risk appetite statements are most often created in financial services organizations, although they are seen in other types of organizations as well. They help management seek a more consistent approach to risk treatment decisions. In part, this can help management avoid the appearance of being biased or preferential through the use of objective or measurable means for risk treatment decisions.

5. C. The department head (or division head or business owner, as appropriate) associated with the business activity regarding the risk treatment decision should be the person making the risk treatment decision. This is because a risk treatment decision is a business decision that should be made by the person responsible for the business function. Many organizations employ a cybersecurity steering committee to discuss such matters, but the final decision often rests with the business unit head.

6. A. The ultimate responsibility for everything in an organization, including its cybersecurity program, lies with its board of directors. Various laws and regulations define board member responsibilities, particularly in publicly traded organizations in the United States and other countries.

7. D. In most US publicly traded companies, the CIO will report the state of the organization's IT function to members of the board of directors. Although this is the best answer, in some organizations, the CIO or COO may instead report on the IT function.

8. B. An IT steering committee, consisting of senior executives, business unit leaders, and department heads, when properly facilitated by the CIO, can discuss organization-wide issues related to IT and make strategic decisions about the allocation of resources.

9. C. The cybersecurity steering committee, which should consist of senior executives, business unit leaders, and department heads, should openly discuss, collaborate, and decide on most risk treatment issues in an organization. If decisions are made by an individual such as the CISO or CRO, business leaders may be less likely to support those decisions as they may not have had as large a role in decision-making.

10. D. The persons who are responsible for business activities should review users' access to applications that support their business activities. All too often, however, access reviews are performed by persons less qualified to make decisions about which persons should have access (and at what levels or capabilities) to systems and applications critical to their business processes. Commonly, IT personnel perform these reviews as a proxy for business owners, but often, IT personnel do not have as much knowledge about relevant business operations and are therefore less qualified to make quality decisions about user access.

11. A. As the parties responsible for the ongoing operations and success of business operations and business processes, business department heads are best suited to determine the behavior of business applications supporting business processes.

12. D. A custodian is charged with a potentially wide range of decisions regarding the care of an asset. Decisions are based on the customer's defined interests. A germane example is an IT department that builds and maintains information systems on behalf of internal customers; the IT department will make various decisions about the design and operation of an information system so that the system will best meet customers' needs.

13. C. IT personnel tend to focus their thoughts on the technology supporting business departments and do not focus enough on the business operations occurring in the business departments they support. Often, IT departments are observed to make too many assumptions about the needs of their customers and do not work hard enough to understand their users' needs to ensure that business applications will support them properly.

14. B. The CRO (chief risk officer) is responsible for managing risk for multiple types of assets, commonly information assets, as well as physical assets and/or workplace safety. In financial services organizations, the CRO will also manage risks associated with financial transactions or financial asset portfolios.

15. D. The chief privacy officer (CPO) is the best title for a position in which the executive ensures that the organization's policies, practices, controls, and systems enforce policies that address the proper collection, use, and protection of personally identifiable information (PII).

16. D. A data architect is the best position title for someone who is responsible for the overall relationships and data flows among a company's information systems. Database administrator (DBA) is the best position title for someone who is responsible for maintaining the systems containing information (often, database management systems [DBMSs]) throughout the organization.

17. A. A network engineer is primarily involved with networks and internal network media (including cabling and internal wireless networks such as Wi-Fi), whereas a telecom engineer is primarily involved with networks and external (carrier) network media such as MPLS, Frame Relay, and dark fiber.

18. C. Any Internal Audit function should not design or implement controls or procedures other than those in its own department. Internal Audit may, however, opine on the design of controls for their suitability to achieve control objectives and auditability. Internal Audit cannot play a design role in any process or control that it may later be required to audit.

19. B. Personnel who design and manage information systems are more likely to be familiar with the nature of alerts, as well as procedures for responding to them.

20. A. The purpose of metrics is to manage the performance and effectiveness of security controls. The meaning and usefulness of specific metrics will depend upon the context and measurement method of specific controls.

21. D. There is a strong correlation between the absence of security patches and the likelihood and success of attacks on systems. Information systems patched soon after patches are available are far less likely to be successfully attacked, whereas systems without security patches (and those where the organization takes many months to apply patches) are easy targets for intruders.

22. A. This is the best metric that serves as a leading indicator. This metric portrays the average time that critical servers are potentially exposed to new security threats. A metric is considered a leading indicator if it foretells future events.

23. C. An "installation completion" metric is most likely associated with a strategic goal; in this case, the installation of advanced antimalware on systems. This metric could, arguably, be a KRI as well because this may also indicate risk reduction on account of an improved capability.

24. C. The most suitable metric is a key risk indicator (KRI). Still, this will be a challenge because high-impact events usually occur rarely.

25. B. SMART, in the context of metrics, stands for Specific, Measurable, Attainable, Relevant, and Timely.

26. D. "Complete migration of flagship system to latest version of vendor-supplied software" is a statement of a strategic objective.

27. A. The best way to manage an IT department is to align it with the business it is supporting. When creating an IT department mission statement, a good start is to look at the overall organization's mission statement; this way, the IT department's mission is more likely to align with the overall organization. If the overall organization lacks a mission statement, the CIO can use what he knows about the organization's purpose to build an IT department mission statement that is sure to support the organization.

28. B. The purpose of risk management is to identify threats that, if they occurred, would cause some sort of harm to the organization.

29. D. The number of patches applied is not a metric that indicates risk management program effectiveness or even the effectiveness of a vulnerability management program.

30. C. The time required to perform security scans is *not* a good example of a security program performance metric.

31. A. A merger of two organizations typically results in the introduction of new practices that are not always understood. The CIO may specify directives to the new, combined IT department that could result in an increase in one or more risks. For example, the combining of two different organizations' device configuration standards could result in a new standard that leads to new, unforeseen problems.

32. A. Value delivery metrics are most often associated with long-term reductions in costs in proportion to other measures, such as the number of employees and assets.

33. D. The balanced scorecard is a well-known framework that is used to measure the performance and effectiveness of an organization. The balanced scorecard is used to determine how well an organization can fulfill its mission and strategic objectives and how well it is aligned with overall organizational objectives.

34. B. The Business Model for Information Security (BMIS) describes the dynamic interconnections between the four elements of an organization: people, process, technology, and the organization itself. The dynamic interconnections describe the relationship between each of the relationship pairs. For example, the dynamic interconnection known as "human factors" describes the relationship between people and technology.

35. C. This is a depiction of the Business Model for Information Security (BMIS), which was developed by ISACA to help individuals better understand the nature of the relationships between people, process, technology, and the organization itself.

36. B. The deficiency was identified in the vulnerability management process. The CISO would see what dynamic interconnections (DIs) are connected to the process element. They are emergence (connecting to people), enabling and support (connecting to technology), and governing (connecting to organization). A description of the deficiency in the vulnerability management process should lead Jacqueline to one of the dynamic interconnections: emergence, enabling and support, or governing. In this case, the process deficiency is related to the frequency of scans, which is most likely the governing DI. Further investigation reveals that policy permits vulnerability scans only during small service windows, which is not enough time for scans to be completed. The solution to this deficiency is likely a process or policy change so that scans will be permitted to run through to completion.

37. D. Zachman is an IT enterprise framework that describes IT systems at a high level and in increasing levels of detail, down to individual components.

38. A. The IT architect needs to develop data flow diagrams, which are visual depictions showing information systems (and information system components, optionally) and the detailed nature of data flowing among them. DFDs are sometimes accompanied by documents that describe metadata, such as system specifications and descriptions.

39. C. *Controls* is the best term describing the mechanisms designed to ensure desired outcomes in business processes.

40. A. Starting with a standard control framework is the best approach, particularly if an appropriate business-relevant framework is selected. In a proper risk management framework, risk assessment and risk treatment will result in adjustments to the framework (removing, improving, and adding controls) over time.

41. D. COBIT is an IT process framework with security processes that appear throughout the framework. Developed by ISACA and now in its fifth major release, COBIT's four domains are Plan and Organize, Acquire and Implement, Deliver and Support, and Monitor and Evaluate. IT and security processes are contained in each of these domains.

42. A. Single copies of the ISO 27001 standard (as well as virtually all other ISO standards) cost over US $100 each. This prevents widespread adoption of the standard, as organizations are somewhat less likely to implement it because the standard costs hundreds of dollars to download and understand. Further, students are unlikely to learn about the standard in school because of its cost. Contrast this with most other standards, such as NIST SP 800-53 or CIS, which are free to download and use.

43. B. ISO 27001's main focus is the body of requirements that describe all of the required activities and business records needed to run an information security program. ISO 27001 also includes an appendix containing a framework of information security controls. The controls here are described briefly; the ISO 27002 standard contains the same control framework but with extensive descriptions for each control.

44. B. HIPAA is the Health Insurance Portability and Accountability Act, which is composed of a "Privacy Rule" and a "Security Rule."

45. D. NIST SP 800-53, also known as NIST 800-53, is the security controls framework developed by the US National Institute for Standards and Technology and published in its 800-series Special Publication library. NIST SP 800-53 is required for all branches of the US federal government and has also been widely adopted by other government agencies and private industry in the US and around the world.

46. C. Although the CSF states that Implementation Tiers are not strictly maturity levels, they are very similar to maturity levels.

47. D. As a service provider for the US federal government, Jeffrey's organization is required to adopt the NIST SP 800-53 controls framework.

48. A. The systems that are in scope for PCI DSS are all those that store, process, or transmit credit card numbers, as well as all other systems that can communicate with those systems.

49. B. All applicable controls are required for all organizations. Additional controls are required for service providers.

50. B. PCI DSS was developed by a consortium of the major credit card brands in the world: Visa, MasterCard, American Express, Discover, and JCB. PCI DSS is enforced through credit card brands' operating rules, as well as by acquiring banks – all enforced through contracts.

51. D. When a risk manager is developing a long-term strategy for an information security program, the best three factors are risk levels, operating costs, and compliance levels. One of these factors may be more important than others in any given organization and for a variety of reasons. Generally, a long-term strategy is being developed to improve the state of one of these: reduction of risk, reduction of cost, or improvement of compliance.

52. D. A primary role of the CISO is the facilitation of an organization's cybersecurity program and the risk management process. With few exceptions, the CISO should facilitate discussions and decisions on risk treatment but should not be the final decision maker on such matters.

53. B. Zachman is an enterprise architecture framework used to depict the layers of an IT environment in increasing levels of detail.

54. A. A data flow diagram (DFD) visually depicts the flow of information between systems and/or entities.

55. C. Zero trust is an architectural philosophy wherein one or more portions of an environment are considered untrusted by default.

56. B. A site classification policy can be used to define various classifications with respective protective measures to drive consistency to site protection.

57. D. A public information officer (PIO) should be the person or role authorized to represent the organization on social media. Similar titles include social media manager and corporate communications director.

58. B. A guideline is a document containing information to help personnel understand how to comply with a policy or standard.

59. D. The four options for risk treatment are Accept, Mitigate (or Reduce), Transfer, and Avoid. Defer is not a valid risk treatment option.

60. A. In the context of risk management, assets include buildings and property, equipment, IT systems and devices, supplies and materials, records, information, intellectual property, personnel, and more.

61. A. The most effective method for building a reasonably complete asset inventory requires acquiring data from multiple sources, including but not limited to network discovery scans, financial asset inventory, and endpoint management system data.

62. C. The best next step is the development of one or more risk mitigation options for each identified risk. This often includes the development of multiple risk mitigation strategies, with risk analysis performed on each to determine whether there are any clear favorites.

63. B. After identifying potential threats, the best next step is the identification of vulnerabilities. Only when threats and corresponding vulnerabilities are identified can risks then be identified.

64. D. It is relatively easy to quantify the impact of a threat event in terms of recovery costs, lost revenue, and other costs. However, the probability of threat events is far more difficult to quantify, in part because there are so many risk factors.

65. B. Missing patches, non-expiring passwords, and incorrect configuration settings are all vulnerabilities. These conditions could make it easier for threat events to occur.

66. B. Exposure factor, expressed as a percentage, represents the financial loss that occurs when a threat is realized. A threat does not always completely destroy an asset, hence the expression of exposure factor as a percentage of the total value of an asset.

67. A. Annualized rate of occurrence (ARO) is an estimate of the number of times that a threat event will occur in a single year.

68. C. Annualized loss expectancy (ALE), defined as the annualized loss of asset value due to threat realization, is calculated by multiplying single loss expectancy (SLE minus the financial loss of a single instance of a threat event) times annualized rate of occurrence (ARO minus an estimate of the number of times that a threat event will occur in a year).

69. B. Cyber insurance policies – as well as other types of insurance policies – represent risk transfer, where another organization accepts certain risks in exchange for a fee.

70. D. Generally, when a risk treatment decision for avoidance is made, this means that the activity associated with the risk will be discontinued.

71. A. An employee policy manual, sometimes known as an employee handbook, is a collection of policies, expectations, benefits, compensation, and other employer–employee matters.

72. D. In financial services and other industries, mandatory vacations provide an extended block of time that can be used to carefully examine an employee's activities, including the existence of wrongdoing.

73. A. Accumulation of privileges occurs in organizations when access rights are granted to long-time employees, particularly those who transfer from department to department. This is exacerbated in organizations where access rights are seldom or never reviewed.

74. B. Accumulation of privileges occurs most frequently with personnel who stay in one organization for many years, slowly accumulating access to more systems and information. Organizations that lack periodic access reviews are less likely to detect this.

75. B. Segregation of duties issues more often arise in smaller organizations that lack enough personnel to separate roles in critical processes. One remedy is to increase the frequency and/or rigor of periodic transaction reviews to detect and deter wrongdoing.

76. A. A key risk indicator is a metric that depicts an important measure of cyber risk.

77. C. Vulnerabilities in application source code are potential entry points for attackers who intend to compromise a system.

78. D. Compliance risk is the risk of an organization being found out of compliance with any applicable law, regulation, standard, or other legal obligation. In some instances of compliance risk, there is no appreciable cyber risk, meaning that the probability or impact of a related threat event is low.

79. C. In risk treatment, when a risk is accepted, the risk should be reviewed again in the future to determine whether the risk should continue to be accepted or another risk treatment option selected. A risk that is acceptable today may not be acceptable in the future because of changes in threats, vulnerabilities, business practices, and risk appetite.

80. A. Risk managers and CISOs should not be routinely making risk treatment decisions; instead, business leaders should be making these decisions because those decisions have an operational impact on business operations. Additionally, there may be independence issues because the risk manager works for the CISO.

Chapter 3

1. C. The system being evaluated is too complex to evaluate in a walkthrough or by analyzing its specifications.

2. B. An RFP is a formal process used to publish the organization's requirements to several vendors, who will then reply formally with proposals that will meet those requirements.

3. A. An organization that wishes to acquire a new IT system or service that it already fully understands should issue a request for proposals (RFP). If the organization does not yet understand the IT products or services it wants to acquire, it should first issue a request for information (RFI) to learn more about them.

4. C. The repeatable level of the SEI CMM five-level model states that there is some consistency in the ways that individuals perform tasks from one time to the next, as well as some management planning and direction to ensure that tasks and projects are performed consistently.

5. C. Requirements should be developed early in the systems development/acquisitions life cycle. The best answer here is prior to writing the test plan, but ideally, requirements will be developed far earlier than that – even before the solution is designed.

6. A. It is not the project manager's job to design and test the system but instead to coordinate those activities as performed by others.

7. D. After a system has been put into production, the maintenance phase involves activities relating to incident management, problems, defects, changes, and configuration.

8. B. The post-implementation phase of the SDLC is carried out by the change management and configuration management processes.

9. C. Change management and configuration management are essential operational processes in the maintenance phase of the SDLC.

10. D. Quality assurance testing is a formal verification of system specifications and technologies. Users are usually not involved in QAT; instead, this testing is typically performed by IT or IS departments.

11. A. A software vendor's choice of source code languages is of lesser concern when selecting and evaluating software vendors.

12. D. User acceptance testing (UAT) should consist of a formal, written body of specific tests that permits application users to determine whether the application will operate properly.

13. C. Termination of the project manager is not an anticipated risk in a software development project.

14. B. Changes in business conditions, including market changes and regulations, take place during the feasibility study, prior to requirements definition, design, and testing.

15. D. A typical Scrum project consists of several "sprints," which are focused efforts to produce some portion of the total project deliverable. A sprint usually lasts from two to four weeks.

16. D. In an Internet-based financial application, it may be useful to record the IP address of each user who logs in. Although it may be infeasible to restrict access by IP address (especially for traveling users), recording IP address at the time of login can be useful later if there is a reason to believe that a user's account has been hijacked.

17. A. The terms *subject* and *object* are used in the context of access management. *Subject* refers to a person (or program or machine), and *object* refers to data (or other resource) being accessed.

18. C. The correct definition of *fail closed* in an access control mechanism is one in which all requested accesses will be denied.

19. B. A good example of an access control that fails open is the case of building access controls, which would need to permit the evacuation of personnel in an emergency.

20. A. The three levels of the COCOMO method for estimating software development projects are Basic, Intermediate, and Detailed.

21. D. An organization that is developing requirements for an RFP (request for proposals) for products or services from vendors needs to develop these requirements internally.

22. A. The best development methodology in a situation where the organization is unable to determine (in the design phase) how end-user interaction will work in a system is to build prototypes of various kinds until the most suitable one can be chosen.

23. C. A PERT chart shows the project status and critical path for a given project.

24. C. Testing is the phase of a development process where functionality and design are verified in the test plan.

25. B. When one application is replacing another, data from the old application is often imported into the new application to eliminate the need for both old and new applications to function at the same time. Migration testing ensures that data is being properly formatted and inserted into the new application. This testing is often performed several times in advance of the real, live migration at cutover time.

26. D. An IT steering committee formally commissions the feasibility study, approves the project, assigns IT resources to the project, and approves the project schedule.

27. A. A configuration management database (CMDB) stores all changes made to a system. This makes it possible for system managers to know the precise configuration of every component at any point in time. This often proves useful during system troubleshooting.

28. B. The best time to measure the business benefits of a new system is after implementation and when enough time has passed for business measurements to be collected and measured.

29. D. An OBS is a visual or structural representation of the system, software, or application in a hierarchical form, from high level to fine detail.

30. C. Data integrity testing is used to confirm whether an application properly accepts, processes, and stores information. Data integrity tests will determine whether there are any failures or errors in input, processing, or output controls in an application.

31. A. Sizing for software projects has traditionally relied on source lines of code (SLOC) estimates. A similar measuring unit is kilo lines of code (KLOC). The advantage of SLOC and KLOC is that they are quantitative and somewhat repeatable for a given computer language, such as COBOL, FORTRAN, or BASIC. However, these methods are falling out of favor because many of the languages in use today are not textual in nature.

32. A. Developers usually perform unit testing during the coding phase of the software development project. When each developer is assigned the task of building a section of an application, the specifications that are given to the developer should include test plans or test cases that the developer will use to verify that the code works properly.

33. D. Software escrow ensures that the customer organization will be able to continue using and maintaining an application even if the vendor goes out of business.

34. B. The requirements definition phase and the system requirements developed during this phase are continually referenced throughout the SDLC to ensure that the system meets the requirements that were agreed on.

35. C. Post-phase reviews are used to ensure that any project deliverables due at the end of each phase meet requirements. These reviews are sometimes called *gate reviews* because they represent a gating process where a project is not permitted to progress to a later phase until an earlier phase is reviewed and approved by management.

36. B. Benefits realization is the result of strategic planning, process development, and systems development, which all contribute toward the launch of business operations to reach a set of business objectives.

37. A. A program is an organization of many large, complex activities and can be thought of as a set of projects that work to fulfill one or more key business objectives or goals. A program is generally a multiyear effort that consists of many complex projects, each with its own project manager, project schedule, budget, and participants.

38. D. A charter is a formal document that defines the objectives of a program, its main timelines, the sources of funding, the names of its principal leaders and managers, and the names of the business executive or executives who are sponsoring the program.

39. A. A feasibility analysis defines the business problem and describes potential solutions.

40. C. The organization should have first conducted a business case, a formal document that includes a definition of the business problem, the results of a feasibility analysis, a high-level project plan, a budget, metrics, risks, and success criteria.

41. D. Organizations should not conduct business benefit measurements immediately after implementing a new business application; it can take some time – even several calendar quarters – for IT and business users to learn how to fully utilize a new system.

42. A. A distinct advantage of departments having their own project managers is that those PMs will inherently be more familiar with their departments' operations, personnel, and practices. When centralizing a PMO, the project managers will be less familiar with each department's practices.

43. C. In matrix management, staff members are organized by subject matter or domain expertise and also by project or program.

44. B. The figure is an example of an object breakdown structure (OBS), which represents the components of the project in graphical or tabular form.

45. C. The figure is an example of a work breakdown structure, a logical representation of the high-level and detailed tasks that must be performed to complete the project.

46. A. Project managers are generally *not* in a position to approve changes in a project, such as scope, cost, or resources.

47. C. A large, multiyear project that is over time and over budget requires a department head to make the kinds of changes needed to get the project back on track. A program manager, project manager, and ScrumMaster are likely not sufficiently empowered to make these changes, although they may play a significant role in figuring out what changes need to be made.

48. C. An IT Steering Committee sets priorities and addresses IT department issues, thus ensuring improved business alignment for the IT department.

49. D. In the absence of any particular stipulations regarding the reporting of exceptions and risks, a project manager should immediately inform a project sponsor of a project delay of this magnitude.

50. C. An organization's cybersecurity team should be responsible for developing standardized (for all projects) and bespoke (for specific projects) cybersecurity requirements.

51. D. Software engineers and any others who are developing and configuring system components should be responsible for complying with cybersecurity requirements.

52. A. Unit testing consists of tests on software modules and other system components and should be performed by software developers.

53. A. An ARCI model, more often known as a RACI model, depicts the parties responsible, accountable, informed, and consulted for each task and activity in a project.

54. C. A RACI (Responsible, Accountable, Consulted, Informed) chart defines the four types of responsibilities of each party for every activity in a project. A RACI chart can also be used to define responsibilities in a business or technology operation.

55. B. A project manager is responsible for tracking the start and completion of each task so that project sponsors, department heads, and others can be kept informed of a project's status and progress.

56. A. SLOC, or source lines of code, has been traditionally used to estimate the level of effort required to develop the code.

57. A. The chart shown is a Gantt chart, a visual representation of a project in which individual tasks occupy rows on a worksheet and horizontal time bars depict the time required to complete each task relative to other tasks in the project. A Gantt chart can also show schedule dependencies and the percentage of completion of each task.

58. C. Function point analysis (FPA) is a time-proven estimation technique for larger software projects. Developed in the 1970s, it looks at the number of application functions and their complexity. FPA is not hindered by specific technologies or measuring techniques (such as lines of code).

59. D. The diagram is a PERT chart, which shows project tasks from left to right in time sequence, with connectors signifying dependencies.

60. A. A timebox is a period in which a project (or a set of tasks within a project) must be completed.

61. B. Scrum is an iterative and incremental process most commonly used to manage an agile software or system development effort.

62. C. The ScrumMaster is the role filled by a project manager or team leader who facilitates the scrum process.

63. D. The product backlog is the list of required deliverables for the entire project (not just the current sprint).

64. B. The diagram depicts the scrum process.

65. A. The greatest strength of Kanban is its visual display of planned tasks, work in progress, and completed tasks – shown on a Kanban board.

66. A. The diagram is a Kanban board, a visual display of planned tasks, work in progress, and completed tasks.

67. C. Organizations often employ a gate-process approach to their SDLC by requiring that a formal review be held at the conclusion of each phase before the next phase is permitted to begin. The review is usually a formal meeting where project managers and other participants describe the status of the project; management, if satisfied that the current phase of the project has been completed successfully and that all requirements have been met, will permit the project to proceed to the next phase.

68. D. Requirements traceability is the ability to trace a requirement back to the project team member who added it to the project. Requirements traceability is essential for larger projects containing hundreds of requirements.

69. B. This figure, originally found in a textbook from the 1970s, depicts the fact that user requirements are often not stated clearly and with sufficient detail.

70. B. In the waterfall process, each phase of the project must be fully completed (sometimes with formal management approval) before the next phase is permitted to begin.

71. A. Source code escrow involves the vendor delivering an electronic copy of its source code to a third-party software escrow firm, which keeps control of the software. If, however, the software vendor goes out of business, the organization will be able to obtain a copy of the vendor's software for support purposes.

72. D. Effective segregation of customer data so that any individual customer is unable to access the data of other customers is one of the greatest challenges that SaaS companies face.

73. C. For a significant RFP project, it's often wise to begin contract negotiations with more than one finalist. Contract negotiations sometimes do not go well; if an organization begins negotiations with only a single vendor and the negotiation breaks down, more time is consumed than if two or three are begun simultaneously.

74. A. In a general sense, Secure SDLC is applicable to IT projects in which new business applications are being developed in-house, developed by an outsider, or acquired in the form of COTS or SaaS. Any organization implementing COTS or SaaS software should still develop requirements, design (to the extent relevant), and testing to ensure that all requirements – security and otherwise – are met.

75. A. Source code repositories do not typically compile code on check-in. Instead, a continuous integration (CI) system will perform code compilation that is separate from (but may be triggered by) check-in.

76. D. Usually performed by software developers and utilizing their integrated application development environment (IDE), unit testing is a test of individual software modules to identify and resolve defects in individual modules.

77. C. Even when all earlier phases of application testing go well, parallel testing in a parallel cutover is prudent and considered an essential practice to further ensure that a new system processes transactions and arrives at the same results as the former application.

78. B. DevSecOps is a DevOps environment with automated security scanning and other safeguards integrated with the automated development platform. For instance, a DevSecOps environment might include a source code scanner that examines recently checked-in code, as well as dynamic security scanning executed as a part of the daily build cycle.

79. A. Web-based application development is the development of web-based applications and not a characteristic of the tools used in such development.

80. C. The figure is a cloud responsibility model; specifically, this model is from Amazon Web Services.

Chapter 4

1. C. A router is a network device that forwards packets toward their destination.

2. B. The best option to confirm that a vulnerability scan is catching all known assets is to compare it with a well-managed configuration management database (CMDB). In organizations lacking a CMDB, reconciliation of the scan results can be performed against other tools, such as configuration management tools, antimalware tools, or network management tools.

3. A. A storage system snapshot is nearly instantaneous and is the best method for producing a "point-in-time" backup of a large database.

4. C. WSDL is a protocol used to describe the functionality of a web service, not for authentication.

5. C. If malware is introduced by the end user in a phishing or watering hole attack, the malware will run as an administrator, which is the highest privilege level on the system. Malware would have access to all files, data, and devices on the machine.

6. A. The customer service manager is the best available choice because a business leader is almost always more familiar with business processes than IT and information security personnel. Further, because the customer service manager is responsible for customer service, this is the person who should be specifying which persons in the organization are permitted to access customer service data.

7. D. The best choice here is to build a prototype system that closely resembles the network, computing, and database activities and perform load testing. This will give the organization an idea of the capacity of the planned system. However, because this technique is imperfect, load tests should be performed throughout the development process.

8. B. The definition of a problem in ITIL is a recurrence of the same type of incident. This indicates that there is something wrong with a business process or information system that needs to be corrected.

9. C. The best use of vulnerability scanning is its function as a quality assurance activity to ensure that security patching and system hardening are being performed effectively.

10. D. A service-level agreement (SLA) is used to define the quantity and quality of service to be provided by a service provider to its customers. An SLA can cover issues such as transaction volume, service quality, issue resolution, and service availability.

11. A. A business impact analysis (BIA) defines the most critical business processes in the organization. The BIA reveals which business processes warrant the development of emergency contingency planning and disaster recovery planning.

12. D. A redundant power supply only addresses the problem of a power supply failure but does not address other failures, such as storage or CPU.

13. C. Storage system snapshots effectively store the state of a storage system from time to time; if ransomware destroys files in the storage system, the system can be rolled back to a recent snapshot, effectively restoring damaged files.

14. B. A business continuity plan is a document that describes procedures to be followed when events such as local and regional disasters prevent normal business operations.

15. D. A business impact analysis (BIA) is used to determine which business processes are most critical, and this leads to the development of recovery objectives, which in turn lead to the development of DR capabilities that meet those objectives.

16. D. Legal holds in most organizations are manual processes and involve the cessation of data purging for arbitrary sets of information. A better approach would be a manually initiated data purging process that is started only after it is determined that no legal holds exist for the data to be purged.

17. A. Automated patching, together with giving end users some control over restarts, is most likely to be successful, as this gives users an option to defer restarts (for a while) so that important work is not interrupted.

18. A. In the short term, removing the offending files is the best first step. In the long run, in most organizations, few people truly need to write to the organization-wide readable share (for example, HR, legal, and IT). This will drive users to use department shares to save sensitive data, which will result in lower risk to the business because sensitive data will then be readable only by personnel in their respective departments instead of the entire organization. Further improvement opportunities may be found after that.

19. B. Applications that need to access the database need to be able to access the SQL listener on a database server, as do DBAs who need to perform maintenance on the database management system.

20. A. Problem management is the correct ITIL process to be invoked when similar incidents are recurring.

21. D. Repeated implementation failures should first call for more rigorous testing in a test or staging environment to iron out any issues that may occur when changes are applied in production environments.

22. A. DDL (Data Definition Language) is commonly used to change the schema (or architecture of a database) in a database management system.

23. C. A *view* provides the appearance of virtual tables that are parts of real tables.

24. C. DR capabilities need to align with the results of the BIA, including established recovery objectives.

25. B. The term *hot-pluggable drives* refers to the ability to remove and replace drives in a storage system while the system is still running. Together with RAID capabilities, there would be no interruption in the storage system's ability to read and write data to the drives.

26. D. Restoration testing proves that data is actually being written to backup media. It also demonstrates that personnel know how to restore data.

27. A. Senior business executives should approve RTO (recovery time objective) and RPO (recovery point objective) targets. As business leaders, senior executives are in the best position to decide how much downtime the organization will tolerate in the event of a minor or major disaster. Further, senior executives are going to be in the best position to fund and provide resources for IT to implement DR capabilities to meet these objectives.

28. B. The best choice here is for participants to walk through the plan and discuss all of the steps in detail.

29. D. A hypervisor, whether running in an OS or on bare metal, is used to create, manage, and run virtual machines.

30. C. A relational database is one with structured tables containing rows and columns, with indexes, primary keys, and foreign keys.

31. A. The biggest risk of using a vulnerability scanning tool as a tool for tracking assets is that these tools are generally configured to scan a list of IP networks. If a network engineer creates a new network and does not inform the personnel who manage the scanning tool, the tool won't detect the new network or any systems and devices that reside in it.

32. A. The hypervisor is the system that manages the creation and use of virtual machines in an environment where virtual machines are created dynamically to support workload.

33. D. Ninety days is the most typical interval for checking for dormant user accounts.

34. B. POSIX is the system interface standard that includes several components, such as process control, interprocess communication (IPC), named pipes, and files and file systems.

35. C. A virtual desktop infrastructure (VDI) consists of one or more centralized servers that run end-user desktop operating systems that display on users' computers.

36. B. The most prudent move is for the data privacy officer to investigate the files that were found, to better understand why they are there. Possibly, some are part of vital business processes (which, in many cases, would need to be adjusted to avoid exposing the information).

37. A. Analysis of repeated incidents is known as problem management.

38. C. The IT manager is making improvements to the configuration management process.

39. C. A repository containing the configuration of systems is known as a configuration management database (CMDB).

40. B. A system and device hardening standard specifies the configurations to be used to make systems and devices more resistant to attack.

41. C. A service-level agreement (SLA) defines terms of responsiveness to various types of services and service issues.

42. C. A stored procedure is computer code that is stored in a database and executed when called.

43. B. A business impact analysis (BIA) is used to enumerate business processes and their dependencies on other processes, assets, personnel, and service providers.

44. A. A system with redundant power supplies will be more resilient if the power supplies are connected to separate electrical circuits (and even more resilient if the circuits lead to separate PDUs, UPSs, electrical feeds, and generators). In the event of a failure in any of these components, the others will still supply power to the system.

45. C. A virtual tape library (VTL) is a storage system that emulates a tape library system. A VTL is used when an organization wishes to retain its tape backup software platform while modernizing the actual backup storage.

46. D. E-vaulting is the process of backing up data to a cloud storage provider using backup software created for that purpose.

47. A. The procedure developed is a business continuity plan, which is an emergency operations procedure to be followed when one or more critical assets required for the business-as-usual procedure are unavailable.

48. D. The procedure created is a disaster recovery plan.

49. A. The safety of personnel should always be the highest priority in any disaster recovery plan.

50. D. Solid-state drives (SSDs) are mostly used as secondary storage. Prior to SSDs, hard disk drives (HDDs) were used as secondary storage.

51. D. Asset management is a critical process that other processes, such as vulnerability management, patch management, and license management, depend on. It is the author's opinion that asset management is the #1 control objective in the CIS Critical Controls for this reason.

52. B. SOAP (Simple Object Access Protocol) is a network API for exchanging data between systems over a network.

53. C. Restrictions of USB storage often address leakage of intellectual property or personally sensitive information, malware infection, and personal uses of a workstation. Restricting USB has little or nothing to do with system capacity management.

54. D. The main purpose of dynamic DLP (data loss prevention) is the unauthorized movement of sensitive information. For example, a dynamic DLP solution can prevent sensitive information from being stored on an external USB-attached storage device or transmitted through email.

55. A. A SIEM (system information and event management system) is a general-purpose system used to ingest log data from systems and devices and to create alerts when specific types of log entries are received. There is no limit to the types of log data and alerts that can be employed in a SIEM.

56. D. In ITIL terminology, a problem is an incident that keeps occurring. This means that there is some root cause for these incidents that needs to be investigated, and a plan needs to be developed to eliminate the root cause so that the incidents no longer occur.

57. D. The best remedy when a database cannot be directly backed up is the creation of an export, which itself can be backed up.

58. B. A BIA identifies critical business processes in an organization, including the organization's dependencies on IT systems and its data sets. Critical processes can be mapped to the systems they depend on, which can contribute to system classification.

59. C. The main issue at stake here is that the power supplies are both connected to the same electrical circuit. If the electrical circuit fails, the system will be powered down. A better practice is to connect the two power supplies to separate circuits.

60. D. A two-phase commit is the act of writing a transaction to separate storage systems and not completing the transaction until confirmation of successful write operations has been received.

61. B. A simulation is a type of review where a moderator reveals a realistic scenario, and test participants talk through the steps they would be taking should an actual disaster of this type occur. A simulation is more realistic than a walkthrough, as it helps to bring a disaster to life.

62. A. The primary purpose of salvage is to determine the extent of damage to critical business equipment and to determine what is still functional, which assets can be repaired, and which are damaged beyond repair.

63. B. RAM (random-access memory) is the primary technology used for a computer's main storage.

64. B. Removing local administrator access from an end user would not impact a user's ability to access personal webmail in most cases.

65. C. The primary mission of data governance is the control and monitoring of all uses of sensitive and/or critical information in an organization, in both structured and unstructured storage.

66. D. "Reverse previous steps" is wholly inadequate for most changes, as this represents unpreparedness for situations where changes are unsuccessful.

67. D. The purpose of a business impact analysis (BIA) is to determine the dependencies of business processes – what assets, staff, and outside parties are required to sustain a process. Subsequent to a BIA is the criticality assessment (CA), which determines the criticality of business processes analyzed in the BIA.

68. D. Few, if any, regulations require organizations to prewrite their public statements describing a disaster and the details about impact, response, and recovery.

69. A. The IT analyst is looking for a digital rights management (DRM) solution, which includes the ability for a document to "expire" or "self-destruct" after a specific date or time.

70. C. A personal area network (PAN) is generally used by a single individual. Its reach ranges from a few centimeters up to 3 meters, and it is used to connect peripherals and communication devices for the user.

71. C. Memory management is not a network-based service but instead is a component of an operating system and/or a CPU.

72. B. The term *Layer 7* refers to the Application (topmost) layer of the OSI network model.

73. A. ICMP (Internet Control Message Protocol) is a part of the Internet layer of the TCP/IP network model.

74. D. A router is a device used to connect networks together.

75. D. According to ITIL, a problem is defined as a cause of one or more incidents. In this case, several similar incidents have occurred, which is an indication of a problem.

76. A. Release management is essential, even when using an SaaS-based application, particularly when the SaaS provider makes regular software changes and publishes release notes describing the changes.

77. A. Configuration management is a business process used to track the configuration settings of systems and devices. Often, configuration management tools are employed to automate the configuration and monitoring of system configuration settings. System hardening is the science of making configuration changes to systems and devices to make them more resilient to attack and compromise.

78. B. Configuration management is concerned with hardware complement, hardware configuration, OS version and configuration, and software versions and configurations.

79. D. Change management is concerned with all forms of changes to production IT environments, whereas release management is concerned with the promotion of new software releases to production.

80. D. PCI DSS (Payment Card Industry Data Security Standard) requires logfiles to be retained for at least 3 months online and at least 12 months offline.

Chapter 5

1. C. A hardening standard will define the security-related configurations applicable to information systems and devices. Note that automation may also need to be implemented if there are large numbers of servers.

2. B. The US Federal Trade Commission (FTC) has historically enforced retail organizations' information privacy policies and has brought legal suits against organizations knowingly violating these policies.

3. A. Dust can accumulate under the raised floor in a computer room environment. Changes in airflow can cause the dust to circulate in the air, causing false-positive smoke detection.

4. C. SOAP is a protocol used for distributed object instantiation and communication.

5. C. On-premises web content filtering protects devices on the internal network, as well as remote devices when they have established VPNs without split tunneling. Mobile devices connected to the Internet without a VPN receive no protection from on-premises web content filtering systems.

6. A. The purpose of a data classification program is to define the classes, or categories, of data and define usage guidelines for data at each classification level. This helps personnel to understand and follow handling guidelines, which results in improved data protection.

7. D. A blockchain is a series of records that are linked using cryptography. Specifically, each successive record in a blockchain contains a hash of the previous record; this makes data in a blockchain resistant to alteration.

8. B. Adding an entry to the certificate revocation list (CRL) is the most effective solution. The certificate authority (CA) that issued the original TLS/SSL keys would perform this action. Subsequent attempts to connect with the compromised keys would be unsuccessful – at least for all software that checks the CRL first.

9. C. A session cookie is used to uniquely identify each visitor to a website and to manage user sessions.

10. D. Virtual memory is the technique of creating memory space that exceeds the physical main memory of a system; memory is extended onto secondary storage.

11. A. Suppressing the broadcast of SSID in a Wi-Fi network makes little difference in terms of the network's security. Some believe that suppressing SSID is better for security, but there are numerous tools available that show all available networks, whether they are broadcasting SSID or not.

12. D. When a user completes security awareness training and there is evidence of this completion in business records, the user cannot easily refute knowledge of the training content if they later are found to violate policy. Competency quizzes as a part of security awareness training help even more in this regard.

13. C. A buffer-overflow attack is a technique where the attacker attempts to overflow a running program's input buffer, resulting in arbitrary code overwriting other instructions in the program. Successful exploitation of a buffer-overflow vulnerability gives the attacker complete control over the target program.

14. B. A PCAP (packet capture) file is a file containing a copy of network traffic associated with one or more devices on a network.

15. D. Servers and devices can send syslog data to multiple destinations.

16. D. The best time to establish and assign roles and responsibilities for computer security incident response is at the time of incident response plan development.

17. A. Chain of custody is employed whenever there is an investigation, including forensics and security incidents, where evidence needs to be collected and retained for later legal proceedings.

18. C. Canada's ITSG-33 is effectively a clone of the US standard NIST SP 800-53.

19. B. Privacy is primarily concerned with the protection of PII (personally identifiable information), as well as its uses in and by an organization.

20. A. N+1 refers to any of several critical systems, including incoming power, HVAC, and Internet connectivity, where at least one additional component is available so that the failure of one component will not interrupt hosting center services.

21. D. Reduced sign-on is the result of integrating a central identity store such as Active Directory (AD) with applications and networks. The term *reduced sign-on* refers to the reduction in the number of login credentials users need to access networks and systems.

22. A. The firewall on a laptop computer will provide some network protection in cases where the laptop is connected to the Internet at a location outside of the enterprise and its firewalls.

23. C. Document marking is the process of placing human-readable text in a document that advises a reader of its sensitivity.

24. C. PGP uses a digital envelope to encapsulate multiple public keys that permit multiple users to read an encrypted document.

25. B. The PKI capabilities in Active Directory facilitate the use of digital signatures and encryption of email messages in Outlook.

26. C. HTTPS:// signifies the use of the TLS/SSL protocol to encrypt transmissions between the browser and the web server.

27. A. Virtualization sprawl is the phenomenon whereby new virtual machines are created without adequate management control. Because new servers can be created in a virtual environment without requiring the purchase of server hardware, organizations without effective controls will find that they have far more virtual machines than management intends.

28. B. Compatibility with IPv4 is rarely, if ever, a reason for isolating IoT devices onto a separate VLAN.

29. D. Quizzes help to reinforce learning and provide evidence that users learned the content. Some online courses can require users to pass quizzes with an arbitrary minimum score to complete the course. Finally, a user accused of policy violation cannot rightfully claim their lack of understanding of policies if quiz scores demonstrate they did understand them at the time of their training.

30. C. Fuzzing refers to techniques where numerous iterations of data input combinations are offered to input fields to assess the presence and exploitability of security vulnerabilities.

31. A. A DNS poison cache attack works by sending forged DNS query replies to a DNS server in an attempt to plant false information in the server's cache. The purpose of this attack is to direct users to the wrong server when their workstations query the DNS server in attempts to obtain IP addresses for target servers. When the attacker has successfully poisoned the DNS server's cache, the DNS server provides falsified replies, and users are sent to imposter servers.

32. A. The "tail -f" command will dynamically display the end of a text logfile. When new entries appear in the logfile, "tail" will automatically show the new entries with no user intervention required.

33. D. Organizations in the US are required to contact law enforcement immediately on discovery of child porn on any computer or workstation.

34. B. Prior to performing any action on the laptop, the forensic expert should first photograph the laptop to show its state prior to the start of the forensic analysis.

35. C. Merchant organizations with fewer than 6 million credit card transactions annually are usually permitted to complete annual self-assessment questionnaires.

36. B. According to Article 33 of the GDPR, organizations are required to notify the supervisory authority within 72 hours of a breach.

37. A. An access badge bearing the name of the organization would give someone finding the badge valuable information about where the badge may be used. If the organization does not use multifactor access controls, anyone finding a badge may be able to enter buildings, parking garages, and even data centers.

38. C. The user has logged on to a single sign-on (SSO) portal, which provides easy access to many business applications without the user having to log on to each one.

39. C. The primary advantage of cloud-based web content filtering is that all users are protected, whether they are on the organization's internal network or off-network, either at home or traveling.

40. B. Automated systems can take action based on the tags in a file. However, this is only as good as the mechanism used to apply tags in the first place, which could be accurate or inaccurate.

41. C. Verification of message confidentiality is *not* a use of digital signatures, as digital signatures do not provide confidentiality of a message by themselves.

42. C. A registration authority (RA) is the entity that receives and accepts requests for new public keys or digital certificates in a PKI, such as an SSL certificate issuer, to secure website communication.

43. B. A transparent proxy server will usually direct a user to a "splash page," informing the user that their request to access a forbidden website has been blocked. Some organizations include information on the splash page that can direct the user to make a request to unblock access to the desired site.

44. A. Copying snapshots of actual server images ensures that recent server images are available at the alternate processing center for rapid restoration.

45. C. The best workable solution is to create an allow list (formerly known as a whitelist) of Wi-Fi networks that workstations are permitted to connect to. These networks would include all corporate Wi-Fi networks, as well as any trusted noncorporate networks.

46. D. Well-managed phishing testing campaigns can help employees learn how to spot phishing messages. Providing "I think this is a phish" capability gives end users the ability to affirm that test messages are phishing tests, and it's also a good method for reporting actual phishing messages.

47. A. To conduct a successful watering hole attack, the attacker must first determine which websites are frequently visited by employees in the organization. This will include cloud-based applications used for primary business processes such as accounting, sales, human resources, and file storage.

48. D. A penetration test most commonly begins with a vulnerability scan that enumerates assets and provides a big-picture attack profile. This is followed by an array of manual attack techniques that attempt to exploit vulnerabilities in the systems and services identified by the security scan.

49. A. The security analyst is using a SIEM, or security information and event management system. A SIEM collects log data from devices throughout the environment and then correlates seemingly disparate events to deduce potential attacks. When such attacks are discerned, the SIEM will produce an alert that directs the security analyst to investigate the matter further and take possible action.

50. D. The most likely reason the general counsel is being notified of minor incidents is the lack of an incident classification scheme in the organization's security incident response plan. Without a severity classification scheme, all incidents are treated as equal, regardless of their actual severity. In this case, the result is executives being notified of minor incidents that should be of little or no concern to them.

51. D. The recordkeeping described is a chain of custody record, which provides a detailed account of each artifact collected and analyzed.

52. B. ISO/IEC 27001 suggests the use of the ISO/IEC 27002 standard for controls. Annex A of ISO/IEC 27001 contains a summary list of the controls found in the ISO/IEC 27002 standard. However, organizations following (or being certified to) ISO/IEC 27001 are free to select any control framework they want or build one of their own.

53. C. Under the GDPR, organizations are not permitted to market to individual citizens unless the citizens first opt in.

54. D. An access control vestibule (formerly known as a mantrap) is a special controlled entrance or exit that permits only one person at a time to enter or exit an area.

55. A. If a user has not logged in to an application for long periods of time, then perhaps the user account for that application can be locked. This would reduce the impact of compromised credentials by preventing an unauthorized party from logging in to a system.

56. D. The best approach is to first create the rule in learn mode, where the rule will detect and log rule activations but not actually block traffic. Analysis of the log will help analysts understand whether the new rule would inadvertently block legitimate traffic and disrupt system operation. If no such interference is observed, the rule can be safely put into block mode.

57. D. The best next step is to work with various business departments to discuss the new policy and handling guidelines to understand the potential impact of the policy. A badly implemented data classification program can cause business disruption and erode goodwill.

58. B. Unless the organization creates a root certificate and pushes it to all end-user workstations, users' browsers will throw certificate errors.

59. C. Although a PKI is not required to implement whole-disk encryption on end-user workstations, a PKI can be used to store administrative keys that can be used to unlock a workstation if the user has forgotten their bootup password.

60. D. A response code of 200 means the request is valid and has been responded to.

61. B. An engineer would select a hosted hypervisor (that is, a hypervisor that runs on an operating system like Windows, Linux, or macOS) because one or more features or functions found only on the operating system are required.

62. A. The presence of older and/or unpatchable OSs on scientific equipment is a common problem that is not easily solved. Most often, the best approach is to isolate those systems through network segmentation and security controls to ensure that all attempts to attack those systems will be automatically detected and blocked.

63. B. When a user fails to achieve the minimum passing grade on a competency quiz, the user should be required to repeat the learning module and then take the quiz again.

64. B. A cross-site request forgery (CSRF) attack is one in which an attacker attempts to trick a victim into performing a transaction on another website (for example, a banking transaction in which the victim transfers money to the attacker).

65. C. The DAD triad – Disclosure, Alteration, and Denial – portrays the opposites of the CIA triad – Confidentiality, Integrity, and Availability.

66. D. File integrity monitoring (FIM) tools are used to detect changes to the contents and access permissions to files in a file system. FIM tools are commonly used to detect intrusions and unauthorized changes to systems.

67. D. The correct sequence for organizing computer security incident response is detect, initiate, evaluate, contain, eradicate, recover, and remediate. This is often followed by a post-incident review.

68. D. A write blocker is a device used to read data from a hard drive whose contents are being evaluated. The write blocker makes it impossible for data to be written to the hard drive.

69. B. NIST CSF is a policy framework for cybersecurity that provides guidance for organizations that want to improve their cybersecurity capabilities.

70. A. The "right to be forgotten" is a concept that has been codified in the European General Data Protection Regulation (GDPR). A European citizen can make requests of online service providers and ask that records associated with them be anonymized or expunged.

71. C. Tailgating refers to people who follow others into a protected facility without themselves authenticating with their keycard or other device.

72. C. Privileged access management (PAM) tools are used to centrally control the use of privileged accounts, both for administrative personnel and for service accounts.

73. C. A simple marking on a document such as "Confidential" does not by itself reveal what handling is permitted. An employee would need to consult a data classification and handling policy to see what actions are permitted.

74. C. Split custody refers to the concept of splitting knowledge of a key task, such as two halves of a safe combination or two halves of a password. This requires that both parties cooperate to complete a sensitive task.

75. B. Creating an entry in the certificate revocation list (CRL) is the appropriate response. In the future, when any party attempts to verify the integrity of the certificate, its presence in the CRL will render it invalid.

76. A. When a user's session cookie is encrypted, another party that can observe the communication will not be able to hijack the user's session.

77. C. Concealing the existence of the virtualized environment hides the fact of its existence. Hence, an intruder may be led to believe that the OS is running on bare metal. This is a security-by-obscurity tactic that does not prevent an intruder from attempting to break into the hypervisor.

78. D. By putting the OWA server behind the firewall and the VPN switch, the organization prevents personally owned mobile devices from reaching the OWA server – provided the VPN switch is configured to permit only company-managed devices to connect.

79. D. Any SIEM can accept log entries sent via syslog and Windows events.

80. A. If SOC operators chronically declare incidents where none exist, this suggests that they need additional training to better recognize and distinguish real incidents from false positives. A false positive now and then should not be a big deal.

Practice Test 1

1. B. A buffer is a temporary storage area designed to hold a small amount of data while it is being processed by the CPU or other hardware device such as a printer.

Register is incorrect because a register is a storage area within a CPU for short-term storage of instructions and variables. CPU is incorrect because a CPU is the main processor of a computer. DMA channel is incorrect because a DMA channel facilitates the transfer of data between the CPU and RAM.

2. C. User involvement is crucial during the requirements definition phase of the SDLC because it ensures that the system being developed aligns with the users' actual needs and requirements. Direct participation from users facilitates a more accurate and comprehensive understanding of the necessary functions and features, leading to a more successful system implementation. Management commitment, although important for project support and direction, is not specific to accurately defining requirements. Skilled developers are necessary for building a quality system, but their expertise does not guarantee that the system will meet user requirements without proper input. Adequate funds are essential for project completion but do not impact the accuracy and completeness of the requirements themselves. Without user input, even the best-funded project with skilled developers might not meet the intended objectives.

3. A. Although these choices are all advantages to moving to a switched environment, the real security advantage is the reduction of eavesdropping; switched networks are difficult to sniff.

    Elimination of collision domains is incorrect because this is not a security concern. Elimination of broadcast domains is incorrect because this is not a significant security concern. Improved throughput is incorrect because this is not a security concern.

4. A. The purpose of an Incident Response Plan (IRP) is to enable the organization to effectively respond to cyber threats. An IRP provides a structured approach for identifying, managing, and recovering from incidents, which is crucial for minimizing damage and ensuring a swift return to normal operations. Monitoring the potential impact of security threats is not the primary focus of an IRP, although impact assessment is part of the response process. Mitigating all threats and vulnerabilities is unrealistic and not the aim of an IRP, as its main goal is to manage and respond to incidents when they occur, rather than eliminating them entirely. Assisting the organization in preventing all security incidents is also not feasible; while elements of prevention are included in a comprehensive security strategy, the IRP is specifically focused on response and recovery efforts once an incident has occurred.

5. A. An auditor would use ISACA guideline 2401, Reporting. Although the standards and guidelines listed for the other answer options may give some information on audit reporting, ISACA guideline 2401 describes how an IS auditor should comply with ISACA auditing standards on the development of audit findings, audit opinion, and audit reports.

    The answers mentioning Follow-up Activities are incorrect because follow-up activities do not assist with final report preparation but instead are involved with post-audit activities. 1401, Reporting is incorrect because it is one of the ITAF required standards – not an optional guideline.

6. C. Inquiries are the appropriate audit evidence collection method that involves an IS auditor asking management about the operation of IS controls, as it specifically denotes a verbal or written request for information. Inquiries allow auditors to gain understanding, clarification, or explanations regarding the control environment directly from those who manage or understand it best. Reperformance involves the auditor independently executing the controls to ascertain their design and operational effectiveness, rather than seeking information from management. Inspection refers to examining records or tangible assets, which is more about

verifying evidence than asking questions. Interrogation implies a more confrontational or adversarial form of questioning, which is not typical in standard audit evidence collection where professional and cooperative communication is maintained.

7. A. Within the Zachman framework, the data component is described as conceptual, logical, or physical, depending upon the functional model used (enterprise, systems, or technology).

    "Functional (application)," "network (technology)," and "strategy" are not Zachman framework components.

8. A. Evaluating the financial standing of the expert is not a relevant consideration when relying on their work. IS auditors must focus on aspects directly related to the quality and reliability of the expert's work, such as the adequacy of the work, the independence of the expert, and their qualifications. These aspects directly impact the credibility and impartiality of the expert's contribution to the audit process. The financial standing of the expert, however, does not inherently affect their ability to perform quality work or maintain independence, and thus, it is not considered a significant factor by ISACA Standards in this context.

9. C. Program management is the oversight of several projects and project teams. A program manager oversees project managers, who manage individual projects in a program that contributes to an organization's objective. The program manager's oversight includes monitoring project schedules, budgets, resource allocation, conflicts, and the preparation of status reports for senior management.

    Incident management is incorrect because it is concerned with the detection and handling of operational or security incidents. IT management is incorrect because it is concerned with the management of the overall IT department mission and operations (including programs). Configuration management is incorrect because it is concerned with the configuration of systems and devices.

10. C. Documented processes and key measurements are critical components of an effective quality management system because they provide a clear framework for how tasks should be performed and allow for the tracking and analysis of performance against established benchmarks. This aids in identifying areas for improvement and supports continuous improvement efforts by providing a consistent method to measure success. Sound financial planning, while important for overall business operations, is not specific to quality management systems and does not directly impact how processes are controlled or improved. The presence of skilled personnel is essential for implementing and executing quality management processes, but without documented processes and measurements, skilled personnel may not be able to effectively contribute to improving quality. Thorough customer surveys provide valuable feedback but are just one tool among many in understanding customer needs and do not encompass the full scope of process control and monitoring inherent in quality management systems.

11. D. User ID and password combinations are single-factor only, whereas the other listed methods are multifactor forms of access management.

    Fingerprint and PIN, smartcard and PIN, and RSA token and PIN are all examples of multifactor authentication.

12. A. The software development approach under review is a work breakdown structure (WBS) because it provides a logical representation of detailed tasks, breaking the project into manageable components and tasks necessary to complete the software project. A Gantt chart visually represents the schedule and timelines of tasks but does not focus on task decomposition. PERT analysis emphasizes identifying task dependencies and estimating project duration using probabilistic time estimates. Critical Path Methodology determines the sequence of tasks that cannot be delayed without affecting the project timeline but does not specifically detail all tasks like a WBS does.

13. A. A charter defines a program and its mission, objectives, roles, and responsibilities.

RACI is incorrect because RACI is a responsibility matrix. Policy is incorrect because a policy defines business rules of expected behavior. Standard is incorrect because standards define technologies and techniques to be employed.

14. A. Obtaining permission from management is crucial before beginning a penetration test to ensure that the testing is authorized and legal. This step is essential for ensuring that the penetration tester has documented approval to assess the security of the web application, which helps prevent any legal issues or misunderstandings about the activities to be performed. Drafting preliminary findings cannot be done effectively until the test is conducted. Selecting tools and commencing the test jumps ahead without ensuring proper authorization and scope, potentially creating legal and ethical issues. Identifying relevant personnel to interview might be a useful part of understanding the application environment but is secondary to ensuring that necessary permissions are in place before any testing begins.

15. A. The ITAF, published by ISACA in *ITAF. A Professional Practices Framework for IT Audit*, consists of the entire set of ISACA Auditing Standards, the Code of Professional Ethics, Audit Standards, Audit Guidelines, and IS Audit and Assurance Tools and Techniques. Compliance with the Code of Professional Ethics and Audit Standards is required. Audit Guidelines and IS Audit and Assurance Tools and Techniques provide further optional guidance to IS auditors.

16. A. Shadow IT is the area being reviewed by the IS auditor because it involves the use of information technology systems, devices, software, applications, and services without explicit organizational approval. The issue highlighted in the scenario reflects systems operating without proper vetting from the IT department, a classic characteristic of Shadow IT. Bring Your Own Device (BYOD) is about the personal devices employees bring into the workplace, which may or may not be aligned with IT policies but are not inherently unauthorized or unvetted systems themselves. Unauthorized systems simply refer to any systems that are not authorized, but this doesn't specifically address the process or involvement of IT in their operation, lacking the nuance of operation without IT knowledge. Systems misconfiguration pertains to technical errors in system setup, unrelated to whether or not the systems were approved by the IT department.

17. A. An organization that wants to implement data loss controls would consider implementing tools to control the use of removable devices (for example, USB drives), Internet website access filtering, and an email quarantine system. An IPS would likely not be considered.

The control of removable storage devices, Internet website access filtering, and email quarantine are all DLP capabilities that organizations may consider using to provide visibility and/or control of the transfer of sensitive information.

18. A. Detective controls are designed to identify and alert an organization to unwanted or unauthorized activities after they have occurred. They do not have the capacity to prevent or enforce any activity but rather serve to notify the organization so that corrective actions can be taken. Preventive controls are intended to stop unwanted events before they happen, actively enforcing security measures to prevent errors or incidents. Deterrent controls aim to discourage potential threats or unauthorized actions through the display of consequences but do not actively detect or prevent specific actions once attempted. Compensating controls are established to mitigate risks when primary controls are not adequate, providing alternatives to reduce risk levels but not merely alerting to occurrences. Thus, only detective controls simply alert organizations without enforcing activities.

19. B. Utility software is primarily used by IT specialists whose responsibilities include some aspect of system development, support, or operations. End users, on the other hand, most often use software applications instead of utilities.

    Answers mentioning the end user are incorrect because end users do not typically use utilities. The answer stating that the IT specialist used the software to enhance productivity is incorrect because IT specialists do not typically use utilities solely to enhance productivity.

20. C. Periodic measurements assist in predicting future capacity requirements because they involve the collection and analysis of data over time, allowing patterns and trends in system usage to be identified and thereby informing future capacity planning. Effective change processes ensure that changes are implemented smoothly but do not directly focus on identifying usage trends. Adequate resource allocations address current needs but do not predict future demand, as they are about managing the present load effectively rather than forecasting. Timely incident logging is crucial for troubleshooting and corrective actions, but it does not provide a view into future capacity needs or usage patterns.

21. C. A standard is a document that describes required protocols, configurations, architectures, vendors, methodologies, or technologies to be used in an organization.

    "Control" is incorrect because a control is a means for achieving a specific desired outcome. "Procedure" is incorrect because a procedure is a sequence of steps to be followed to accomplish a task. "Policy" is incorrect because a policy is a statement of business rules.

22. C. Enhancing the effectiveness of risk assessments is the correct answer because classifying IT assets helps identify their criticality, vulnerabilities, and associated risks, enabling targeted and efficient risk management. Eliminating the need for maintaining an asset register is incorrect, as classification complements, not replaces, the asset register. Ensuring proper valuation of assets is not the primary goal of classification, as valuation focuses on financial worth rather than risk. Assigning and mitigating risks associated with assets is a subsequent step in risk management that relies on classification but is not the direct purpose of the classification itself.

23. D. SOAP, or Simple Object Access Protocol, is an XML-based API specification that facilitates real-time communications between applications using the HTTP and HTTPS protocols. Functionally, SOAP operates similarly to RPC (Remote Procedure Call), wherein one application transmits a query to another application, and the other application responds with a query result. SOAP messages are based on the XML (eXtensible Markup Language) standard.

RPC is incorrect because it is a specification used for inter-process communications between computers. SQL is incorrect because it is a database query language. XML is incorrect because it is a markup language for encoding documents.

24. C. Development of prototypes is a crucial feature of Rapid Application Development (RAD) because RAD focuses on quickly developing software through iterative prototyping and user feedback. This process allows for rapid adjustments in response to user input and changing requirements, ensuring the final product is closely aligned with user needs. Unlike traditional methodologies, a large development team is not a defining characteristic of RAD; rather, the approach prioritizes small, efficient teams to facilitate fast decision-making and rapid prototyping. Since RAD emphasizes speed, slow, iterative development does not align with its principles, which aim for fast completion through multiple iterations. Additionally, while controlling costs is desirable in any development process, RAD is primarily focused on speed and flexibility, with cost control being a secondary benefit of reduced development time rather than a core feature.

25. A. A screening or border router is designed to permit or deny messages of specific types (and possibly will also permit or deny based upon origin and destination) to pass. A firewall can also make pass/block decisions based upon the type of traffic, origin, and destination.

Permissions is incorrect because access permissions are not likely to be associated with network traffic filtering based on type, origin, or destination. Smart cards is incorrect because smart cards have little or no association with the filtering of network traffic based on type, origin, or destination. Switch is incorrect because a switch is not typically deployed as a network ingress/egress filter as described in the question.

26. A. Organizational initiatives are directly related to the organization's objectives, which is why considering these initiatives is crucial in audit planning. These initiatives often signify changes or developments in the organization that could impact the risk profile and audit priorities. Auditors need to be aware of these to ensure that their audit efforts are aligned with the current goals and potential risk areas of the organization. Reducing audit costs is not the primary reason for incorporating organizational initiatives into audit planning, as the focus is more on relevance and risk coverage rather than cost efficiency. Simplifying audit management processes is not a direct result of considering organizational initiatives; the process might require additional complexity to accommodate new objectives. Additionally, organizational initiatives do not inherently reduce audit coverage; instead, they might necessitate broader or more focused coverage to address emerging risks and objectives effectively.

27. D. Server clusters and replication technologies would be used when the RTO and RPO values are extremely time sensitive or do not allow for significant data loss. Backing up and restoring from media require time and may result in data loss since the last backup and therefore may be used when the RTO and RPO values allow.

The answers giving server clusters and replication are incorrect because these are performed when recovery time objectives are more time sensitive. The answer mentioning SAN and NAS technologies is incorrect because these technologies are used to store data that can be accessed over a network.

28. C. An education check is specifically designed to verify the authenticity of a candidate's educational background, which directly addresses the issue of falsified academic credentials. The education check involves directly contacting institutions to confirm degrees or certifications claimed by the candidate. A certificate check could encompass verifying professional certifications but may not cover general educational history unless specifically directed. A credit check focuses on the candidate's financial history and does not reveal discrepancies in education claims. An employment check verifies past job experiences and roles, which, although important, do not directly address discrepancies in educational qualifications. Therefore, only the education check is directly aligned with identifying falsifications in a candidate's educational background.

29. C. A risk analysis will generally not be used to determine the level of effort in an audit, or which staff members should perform the audit. It plays no role in determining the sequence of findings in the audit report. Instead, a risk analysis helps auditors understand which controls and processes have higher risk, which are the areas that require greater attention.

The answer mentioning duration is incorrect because a risk analysis does not determine the length of the audit. The answer specifying staff members is incorrect because a risk analysis does not determine who performs an audit. The answer specifying the order of different areas is incorrect because other factors such as findings, or the control framework organization, will determine the sequence of findings in the audit report.

30. A. Possessing considerable technical expertise is crucial for an IS auditor during IT operations audits because it enables the auditor to understand the technology thoroughly and reduces reliance on interviewees. This knowledge allows auditors to independently verify information, assess risks, and evaluate controls effectively without solely depending on information received from others, which might be biased or incomplete. Relying solely on interviews can be risky if auditors lack the necessary technical understanding to fully comprehend and verify the responses they receive. Having just a minimum knowledge of IT operations is insufficient because audits require a deep and comprehensive understanding to identify potential issues properly. Eliminating interviews altogether from the audit process is impractical, as auditors must still engage with personnel to gather insights and contextual information; interviews supplement the auditor's technical knowledge. Additionally, impressing the IT staff of the client should not be a goal for auditors; their primary objective is to accurately assess IT operations and ensure compliance with standards and practices.

31. D. The decisions about items in the risk register and the follow-on activities are together known as risk treatment.

    "Risk dashboard" is not a type of decision. "Quantified risk" and "qualified risk" are not types of risk decisions but instead risks that are calculated that may *lead* to risk decisions.

32. C. Two-person control is the correct answer because it requires two or more individuals to approve or authorize high-value transactions, ensuring an added layer of oversight and reducing the risk of fraud or error. Two-person integrity focuses on ensuring data accuracy and integrity by requiring collaboration but does not specifically mandate approval for high-value transactions. Segregation of duties involves dividing responsibilities to prevent a single individual from controlling all aspects of a process but does not necessarily require multiple approvals. Transaction verification involves checking the accuracy of transaction details but does not enforce multiple levels of managerial approval.

33. C. Tokens display one-time values used during authentication. The advantage of tokens is that the displayed value will change frequently, making a "replay attack" more difficult to conduct.

    The answers referring to simple or complex passwords are incorrect because password quality does little, if anything, to block a replay attack. Cipher lock is incorrect because a cipher lock is a hardware device and is not relevant to the question.

34. C. The diagramming method referred to in the figure is a data flow diagram because it visually represents how data flows through a system, highlighting the inputs, processes, and outputs in a structured format that supports IS auditing. This method is commonly used to understand and audit information systems by providing a clear depiction of data processes and identifying potential security and process inefficiencies. The term "audit process diagram" is incorrect because it generally refers to diagrams that map out the auditing process steps rather than data interactions. A "maturity capability diagram" is incorrect as it represents the maturity level of processes or capabilities within an organization, unrelated to data flows. A "procedure flow diagram" typically depicts business or system procedures rather than the specific flow of data, distinguishing itself from the specific purpose of a data flow diagram.

35. C. A "cutover test" also known as a "full interruption test" is the most intrusive type of disaster recovery test. It will also provide the most reliable results in terms of answering the question of whether backup systems have the capacity to shoulder the real workload properly.

    "Walkthrough" is incorrect because a walkthrough does not exercise recovery systems at all but is instead a facilitated discussion about a recovery effort. "Parallel test" is incorrect because a parallel test is less rigorous than a cutover test in that it continues operations at the primary site rather than requiring that all operations take place at the alternate facility. "Simulation" is incorrect because a simulation is little more than an orchestrated discussion of a disaster scenario for incident responders.

36. D. The business case for an application development project is created during the feasibility study phase of the systems development life cycle. This stage involves assessing the viability, risks, costs, and benefits of a project to determine if it makes sense to proceed. Therefore, a business case is typically developed here to justify moving forward with the project. The requirements definition stage, in contrast, focuses on gathering and analyzing the needs and

specifications for the system rather than justifying its existence. Verification and validation occur later in the process to ensure the system meets its requirements and functions as intended, not to develop planning documents such as the business case. Finally, the implementation stage involves deploying the system into a live environment, which occurs long after the justification for the project has been established.

37. C. Control self-assessment (CSA) is the activity undertaken by organizations that want to measure the effectiveness of their own controls. Although the activities listed in the other answer options can be beneficial for an organization, they serve other purposes or are performed by other parties.

Benchmarking is incorrect because it is used to compare an organization's costs (or other factors) with that of other organizations. Compliance audit is incorrect because this is generally performed by an external entity. External audit is incorrect because this is performed by an external entity.

38. D. To improve IT service delivery processes, ITIL is the most suitable framework because it is specifically designed to provide a comprehensive set of best practices for IT service management, focusing on aligning IT services with the needs of the business and improving efficiency and effectiveness. ISO/IEC 27001:2022 is focused on information security management systems and is not specifically tailored for improving IT delivery processes. COBIT is a framework for developing, implementing, monitoring, and improving IT governance and management practices, but it is broader and more governance-focused rather than delivery-focused. COSO deals with enterprise risk management and internal control, not specifically with IT service delivery processes. Therefore, ITIL is the most appropriate framework for improving IT delivery.

39. B. Although single sign-on is centralized, it also includes the ability to manage user sessions across applications. Reduced sign-on does not manage user sessions using a user's logged-on state, but it does allow a user to authenticate to an application using the same logon credentials, which are verified centrally.

Authorization is incorrect because it refers to the access rights associated with a user account. Authentication is incorrect because this refers to the process of asserting a user ID and password (and potentially other steps associated with multifactor authentication) to gain access to a system. Single sign-on is incorrect because single sign-on, while closely related to reduced sign-on, extends reduced sign-on by permitting participating applications to share a user's logged-in state with each other or with a central authority.

40. D. An intrusion prevention system (IPS) is designed to not only detect potential threats like an intrusion detection system (IDS) but also take proactive steps to prevent those threats from causing harm, which is why it prevents attacks. Both systems may detect known and unknown threats, but prevention is the key function that differentiates IPS from an IDS. Performing penetration tests is unrelated to the direct functionality of IPS or IDS; penetration tests are controlled, authorized attacks used to evaluate security systems. Detecting novel attacks is not exclusive to an IPS; both IDS and IPS can potentially identify anomalies or new threats using heuristic methods. Finally, an IPS does not eliminate the need for a firewall, as firewalls and IPS serve different roles in a layered security strategy; firewalls primarily control traffic based on pre-established rules, whereas an IPS focuses on analyzing traffic for malicious activity.

41. D. Transitioning operations back to the original site is a part of disaster recovery and not a part of the BCP life cycle.

BIA, criticality analysis, and establishing recovery targets are all incorrect because these processes *are* all part of the BCP life cycle.

42. D. Running both the old and new systems simultaneously represents a parallel cutover, as this approach allows for comparison of outputs from both systems to ensure the new system is functioning correctly before fully decommissioning the old one. All-at-once refers to an immediate switchover from the old system to the new system without overlap. Geographical refers to implementing the system in specific locations or regions in stages. Module-by-module involves implementing the system one component or module at a time, rather than running both systems in their entirety concurrently.

43. A. PCI DSS, or Payment Card Industry Data Security Standard, is an international standard concerned with the protection of cardholder data (CHD).

PA-DSS is incorrect because it is a standard for the security of payment applications. PCI is incorrect because it is an organization, not a standard. FIPS 199 is incorrect because it is a standard for security categorization.

44. D. During the review of the IT strategic planning process at a small financial institution, it is essential to find the vision and mission of the IT department. This is because the strategic planning process should align the IT objectives with the broader organizational goals, making the vision and mission central components. The adopted software development practices, while important for IT process effectiveness, are more relevant to operational or tactical planning rather than the broader strategic vision. The adequacy of operational controls focuses on specific procedures and measures to manage day-to-day IT operations, rather than the strategic direction of IT within the organization. The presence of qualified IT personnel is crucial for implementing the strategy effectively, but it does not directly pertain to the process of strategic planning, which should outline the high-level aims and direction before considering resource allocation.

45. A. The RTO is a key target that is the period from the onset of an outage until the resumption of service, usually measured in hours or days.

RRT is incorrect because "recovery response time" is not a standard recovery target. RPO is incorrect because "recovery point objective" is an expression of the maximum data loss, not the time to restore service. TTR is incorrect because "time to recovery" is not a standard recovery target.

46. D. UTMs perform several different security functions, combining tools like firewalls, intrusion prevention systems, antivirus, and content filtering into one platform, making them highly effective for comprehensive threat management. They do not focus solely on intrusion detection but cover a broader range of security functions. They are typically cost effective compared to deploying multiple separate solutions, contrary to the idea that they are expensive and difficult to maintain. UTMs often include automation and centralized management features, so they do not rely solely on manual operation.

47. B. Unpatched systems can allow known vulnerabilities that can be exploited, which is what most malware targets.

Password compromise is incorrect because although it is a factor that can aid the success and spread of malware, it is not as significant a factor as is exploitable vulnerabilities. False rejection is incorrect because FRR, the measure of a biometric system's failure to recognize legitimate subjects' biometrics, does not contribute to malware success. Unencrypted traffic is incorrect because although it is a poor practice because of adversaries being able to eavesdrop, it does not significantly contribute to the success of malware.

48. D. Both the high-level and low-level design documents are crucial for project team members representing business owners to review. The high-level design provides an overview of the system architecture and addresses the major components that align with the business objectives. At the same time, the low-level design delves into the technical and detailed aspects, ensuring that the implementation of the system aligns with the business owners' needs and future requirements. Not considering both levels of design can lead to discrepancies between the conceptual understanding of the system and its technical implementation. Reviewing only the high-level design or only its major components might miss critical implementation details that could affect the system's functionality. Just reviewing the low-level design without understanding the overarching goals and architecture would leave gaps in ensuring the system functions as desired by the business.

49. C. The SSAE 18 audit standard is used for audits of financial service organizations. Audit reports can be delivered to the customers of those organizations. The other types of audits fulfill other purposes.

ISO 27001 is incorrect because it is not as applicable for financial services as SSAE 18. SAS 70 is incorrect because it has been superseded by SSAE 18. The answer mentioning an AUP audit is incorrect because an AUP audit is not as good a choice as SSAE 18.

50. D. The practice of sending a vendor's electronic copy to a third-party organization for safekeeping in case the vendor goes out of business is known as source code escrow. Source code escrow is a critical practice in software development and procurement that ensures the customer continues to have access to the source code if the vendor can no longer provide support. This helps in business continuity and risk management associated with vendor lock-in. Code storage, in this context, would generally refer to the practice of saving code securely within a company or project but doesn't imply a third-party is involved for business continuity reasons. The source code sub-contract suggests that a secondary vendor is engaged in working with the code, which is not the scenario described where safeguarding is the primary motive. Code review is the process of systematically examining source code to identify bugs and improve quality, which is unrelated to the practice of preparing for potential vendor failure.

51. D. HTTP is a part of the TCP/IP Application layer, which is Layer 4.

3 is incorrect because HTTP is not a part of the TCP/IP Transport layer, which is Layer 3. 7 and 6 are incorrect because the TCP/IP model has only four layers.

52. D. The purpose of a sprint retrospective is to reflect on the recently completed sprint, allowing the team to review what went well, what didn't, and how processes can be improved in future sprints. It does not involve defining the backlog, as that is handled during backlog refinement or sprint planning. It is not about approving the completed sprint, which is the focus of the sprint review, where stakeholders evaluate the deliverables. Formulating new sprint objectives happens during sprint planning, not the retrospective.

53. A. An ISO 27001 audit would do little to compensate for poor PCI audit results.

The answers mentioning market competitiveness, confidence in controls, and prestige are all reasons for undertaking ISO 27001 audits.

54. D. Measured service is the feature of cloud computing that allows users to pay only for the resources they consume, as it inherently involves monitoring and optimizing resource usage, enabling clients to be charged based on their actual consumption. Convenience refers to the ease of access or use of cloud services, which does not directly relate to the cost structure or billing. Ubiquitous implies that cloud services can be accessed from anywhere, emphasizing availability and accessibility rather than billing models. Scalability refers to the ability of cloud services to increase or decrease resources as needed; while it relates to resource management, it does not specifically address the pay-as-you-go billing aspect that measured service offers.

55. C. The biggest problem with the process is that no service providers are assessed after onboarding.

Outsourcing the TPRM process is not necessarily the best remedy. The TPRM process is not necessarily designed properly (it may be properly designed and improperly implemented). The use of multiple questionnaires is not the most significant defect in this process.

56. D. An IS auditor may recommend an organization to benchmark its key IT processes to compare how similar organizations solve challenges and determine improvements. Benchmarking allows an organization to assess its performance against industry standards or peers, providing insights into areas that require enhancements or innovations. Copying competitors' strategies is not the primary intent of benchmarking, as it focuses on adopting best practices rather than direct imitation, which might not suit an organization's unique operational context. Comparing processes solely to maintain them neglects the potential for identifying areas that require improvement and can lead to stagnation rather than growth. Finally, benchmarking is about performance improvement rather than directly reducing the cost of procuring IT equipment, which involves different strategies such as negotiating with vendors or optimizing asset management.

57. D. Unit testing is performed by individual developers, to verify correct options of the sections of code they are developing.

Design review is incorrect because it is permitted by a development team (along with customers or users), not by individual developers. User acceptance testing (UAT) is incorrect because it is performed by end users, not individual developers. Quality assurance testing (QAT) is incorrect because it is performed by test personnel, not individual developers.

58. D. Using a copy of the original evidence for analysis is the best method to ensure that the original evidence remains unaltered. This approach allows the IS auditor to perform all necessary examinations and manipulations on the duplicate rather than risking changes to the primary source, thereby preserving its integrity for subsequent verifications or legal inquiries. Using the original evidence for analysis increases the risk of accidental alteration, compromising the evidence's integrity. Preparing original evidence work papers involves creating documentation based on the evidence, but this does not prevent alteration during the analysis itself. Documenting the evidence collection process is crucial for maintaining a chain of custody and understanding context but does not inherently protect the original evidence from alteration during analysis.

59. A. Disabled video surveillance equipment is not a method that can be used to bypass physical security controls.

Stolen access cards, social engineering, and bribery are all incorrect because they are methods that *can* be used to bypass physical security controls.

60. D. Transitioning IT operations back to the primary site should be included in restoration procedures after a disaster. This step ensures that the organization returns to its normal operating environment and maximizes the efficiency and resource allocation initially intended for the primary site setup. Keeping IT operations permanently on the disaster recovery site is not advisable since disaster recovery sites are typically designed for temporary use and might not support long-term operations with the same efficiency. Training employees for future disasters, while important, is a proactive measure rather than a restoration procedure. Similarly, closing the primary site is not a feasible option unless it is completely irreparable, as it contradicts the purpose of restoring operations to their original state.

61. B. Integration testing is correct because when data is transferred from one system to another, it is important to verify that the transference of data occurs correctly, and that data represented in the source system is properly represented in the destination system. This can help the source and destination systems work as an integrated whole.

Unit testing is incorrect because it is the testing of sections of code by the developers who write or update them. Regression testing is incorrect because it is the testing of functionality of software to ensure that it operates as expected. Functional testing is incorrect because it is used to confirm the correct operation of a system.

62. D. The main purpose of encapsulation in object-oriented system development is to hide the internal details of objects. It allows a class to hide its internal data and behavior and expose only certain interfaces, keeping implementation details private and protecting the integrity of the data. This enhancement of method interaction simplifies the complexity of the system for end users while truly linking behavior with data in a controlled manner. Increasing code complexities contradicts the purpose of encapsulation, which is intended to manage complexity by hiding unnecessary details. Enhancing inheritance is unrelated to encapsulation, as encapsulation focuses on data protection and method accessibility rather than class hierarchy. Lastly, encapsulation does not eliminate the need for code reuse; rather, it facilitates code reuse by providing well-defined interfaces and protecting the internal data structures.

63. A. After discovering the absence of a policy guiding sales reconciliation, the most appropriate next step for the IS auditor is to expand the scope of audit testing to obtain sufficient evidence. This approach helps to better understand the extent and impact of the issue and gather the necessary information to support the audit findings, ensuring a comprehensive assessment of the internal control environment. Issuing a report stating that the controls in the Finance Department are inadequate without further evidence could lead to an incomplete or biased report. Requesting a written management representation from the Finance Director might provide some insight, but it would not substitute for proper audit evidence and analysis. Abandoning the audit until a sales policy is in place would leave the unresolved issues and potential risks unexamined, failing to fulfill the auditor's responsibility to provide assurance.

64. D. Confirming that the certificate was issued by a trusted Certificate Authority (CA) is essential because the trustworthiness of a digital certificate relies heavily on the credibility of the issuing CA. This ensures that the certificate can be validated and that the entity presenting the certificate can be trusted. While checking if a Registration Authority (RA) was involved in the issuance process could be informative regarding the chain of trust, it is not as critical as validating the CA itself. Verifying whether the certificate contains the organization's name is relevant for identifying the certificate holder but does not attest to the certificate's validity or trust level. Although confirming the date the certificate was issued helps check if the certificate is within its valid period, it does not directly impact the essential trust the CA provides.

65. C. A data classification policy, along with its data-handling guidelines, is the most specific item that is apparently missing from the organization.

"Document shredders" is incorrect because the absence of shredders, while possible, is not the most likely scenario. "Security policy" is incorrect because the absence of a security policy is not a probable cause. "Acceptable use policy" is incorrect because the absence of an acceptable use policy is not a probable cause.

66. D. The primary aim of initial access provisioning for new employees is to provide the appropriate access privileges. Ensuring that employees have the necessary access rights from the start is crucial for them to perform their job functions efficiently and securely. Reviewing employee access is a separate process that typically occurs periodically to ensure that access levels remain appropriate over time rather than being the primary goal of initial provisioning. Providing employee training is a fundamental aspect of onboarding, but it is distinct from provisioning access and deals more with familiarizing employees with their roles and responsibilities. Assessing employees' technical skills is unrelated to access provisioning, since it is typically done during recruitment or evaluation phases, not during the process of setting up access rights.

67. A. There is no guarantee that an SSAE 18 audit (or any other external audit report) covers all areas of interest. Generally, an auditor will not be required to audit a service provider, particularly when it has an SSAE 18 report. The fact that a service is outsourced does not determine a lack of need to audit it.

The answer stating that the SSAE 18 audit will cover all areas of interest is incorrect because the SSAE 18 audit report may not cover all areas of interest. The answer stating that the auditor may not rely on the SSAE 18 audit is incorrect because the auditor may rely upon the SSAE 18 audit report. The answer stating that the external report service provider need not be audited is incorrect because the auditor does need to audit, or view an audit of, the expense report service provider.

68. D. Phishing simulations are an effective training technique to assist users in recognizing and responding to phishing attacks because they provide realistic scenarios where users can practice identifying and managing phishing attempts in a safe environment. By simulating real phishing threats, users can gain practical experience and immediate feedback, which helps reinforce learning and improve their ability to recognize phishing attempts in actual situations. Role-based training, while valuable, focuses on specific roles within an organization and may not specifically cover phishing for all users. Targeted training, although aimed at specific groups, may not offer the hands-on experience that simulations provide. On-the-job training is more general and might not specifically address phishing threats or provide the interactive practice needed to effectively prepare users to contend with phishing attacks.

69. C. ITIL is the correct choice because it is a globally recognized framework that provides best practices for IT service management, focusing on aligning IT services with business needs. ISO 9000 is unrelated to IT service management, as it deals with quality management systems. SABSA focuses on security architecture and does not address IT service management processes. ISO 27001 pertains to information security management, not the broader scope of IT service management.

70. D. The application had inadequate requirements is the correct conclusion because numerous design changes after implementation typically indicate that the initial requirements were incomplete or poorly defined, leading to unforeseen adjustments. Meeting performance targets would not explain the need for extensive post-implementation design changes. Properly conducted application testing would likely have identified issues earlier, reducing the need for major changes after deployment. Inadequate testing could lead to unaddressed defects, but it does not account for fundamental design changes, which are more closely tied to requirements gathering and analysis.

71. B. Performance and Supervision provides guidance to ensure that all IS audit tasks are performed within the required competence levels because it involves overseeing audit activities and reviewing work to ensure that tasks are completed effectively and within the set standards. It focuses on the roles of supervisors and managers in making sure the audit team adheres to professional standards and fulfills their responsibilities competently. Due Professional Care is more about ensuring that auditors exercise professional skepticism and diligence in their work, but it doesn't directly address competence levels. Organizational Independence refers to the auditor's ability to remain unbiased and free from influence from the organization being audited, which is important for impartiality but not related to competence levels. Proficiency refers to the skills and knowledge required for the job, but it doesn't inherently provide a framework for ensuring tasks are performed at required competence levels, unlike Performance and Supervision which incorporates oversight mechanisms.

72. A. An audit program is the plan for conducting audits over a certain period, and involves planning resources, scope, objectives, and procedures. The other terms don't signify the overall audit plan.

An audit system is not the correct term to describe the strategy and audit plans. An external audit is incorrect because an external audit is an audit of another organization's controls. An internal audit is incorrect because an internal audit is an audit of an organization's own controls.

73. B. A missing critical hardware component directly impacts the ability to restore systems promptly after a disruption, which implies a recovery delay issue. Without this component, the time taken to get systems back online would be longer than planned, thereby delaying the recovery process. Syntax error refers to mistakes in the documentation or code, unrelated to physical components. Resumption effect is the impact of restarting operations on a system, focusing more on processes rather than missing physical components. Walkthrough error involves mistakes found during a read-through or step-by-step review of procedures, primarily related to executing the plan correctly, not missing components.

74. A. The IS auditor would not expect to find "Tags" as a classification level at a financial institution because it is not a standard classification level. Instead, "Tags" generally refers to labels or metadata used for organizing and identifying data but not for classifying its confidentiality or sensitivity. "Public," "Confidential," and "Secret" are established classification levels used to designate the sensitivity of information. "Public" refers to information intended for public distribution without restrictions. "Confidential" indicates data that contains sensitive information intended for restricted access, while "Secret" typically signifies a higher level of sensitivity, requiring stringent access controls. These terms are commonly used across various organizations to ensure appropriate data protection and access control based on sensitivity levels, whereas "Tags" lacks the specificity of security classification.

75. C. Web content filtering is the appropriate solution for preventing users from accessing sites that violate organization policy. For example, web content filters can block access to gambling, weapons, and pornography sites.

Intrusion prevention system is incorrect because the role of an IPS isn't to block user access to websites that violate organization policy. An IPS can, however, be used to block user access to malicious websites. Cloud access security broker is incorrect because a CASB is used to provide visibility and control of end user access to specific cloud service providers. Advanced antimalware is incorrect because its role is to block advanced malware from successfully executing on a system.

76. B. Segregation of Duties (SODs) is the principle being violated in this scenario. SOD requires that critical tasks be divided among different individuals to reduce the risk of error and inappropriate actions, such as fraud. By allowing one person the ability to create supplier accounts, request payments, and make payments, the organization fails to separate these responsibilities, which compromises the integrity of financial processes. Aggregation of Duties is not a recognized control principle like Segregation of Duties and therefore does not apply. Dual control refers to a system wherein two individuals are required to complete a task together as an additional layer of security, but this does not specifically address the separation of tasks. Process workflow generally refers to the sequence and management of processes within an organization, which doesn't directly relate to the issue of overlapping duties being highlighted in the scenario.

77. B. Noting the audit exception is appropriate because this finding indicates a control weakness but does not present an immediate or urgent risk requiring immediate notification to management. Immediate notification is typically reserved for critical or time-sensitive issues, which this is not. Examining business records focuses on past occurrences rather than addressing the systemic issue of inadequate controls. Continuing the audit without documenting the finding overlooks an important weakness in the user account management process.

78. B. Vulnerability management is the correct process to implement because it involves identifying, assessing, prioritizing, and tracking vulnerabilities for remediation in a structured manner. Penetration testing focuses on simulating attacks to identify vulnerabilities but does not address the ongoing tracking and remediation process. Patch management ensures that software updates and patches are applied but does not encompass the broader scope of identifying and tracking vulnerabilities. Change management oversees the proper implementation of changes to systems and processes but does not directly handle vulnerability tracking and remediation.

79. C. In business terms, a configuration management database (CMDB) is a record of all of the configuration changes made to IT systems.

Information about the configurations of IT systems is incorrect because this only partly explains the purpose of a CMDB. Record of approvals for changes made to a system is incorrect as a record of approvals for changes would reside in a change management business record. Record of the most recent change made to IT system components is incorrect because configuration management is not only concerned with the most recent changes made to a system but all changes.

80. C. Aligning IT strategy with business strategies is the most important aim of implementing an IT governance framework for a pharmaceutical firm because it ensures that the IT initiatives support the organization's overall goals and objectives, thus facilitating better decision-making and efficient resource allocation. By aligning IT with the business strategy, the firm can better support its unique needs, such as research and development, regulatory compliance, and market responsiveness. While increasing sales and profitability levels is crucial, it is a consequence rather than a direct goal of IT governance. Improving transparency is essential, but it primarily supports accountability and does not directly align IT with business strategies. Improving managerial performance is also beneficial, but it is typically a byproduct of better alignment and processes, not the primary goal of implementing such a framework. Therefore, aligning IT strategy with business strategies remains the most significant aim of IT governance in this context.

81. C. A statement of impact is a qualitative or quantitative description of the impact if the process or system were incapacitated for a time.

Criticality analysis, an inventory of processes and systems, and risk analysis are all incorrect because they are activities performed during a BIA but for other purposes.

82. C. A device that ensures only authorized traffic enters the network from the Internet while performing application-layer inspection is best described as a next-generation firewall. This type of firewall combines traditional firewall capabilities with advanced features like application-layer inspection, intrusion prevention, and deep packet inspection. A web application firewall focuses specifically on protecting web applications by filtering and monitoring HTTP traffic, which is narrower in scope. An intrusion detection system is a passive device that monitors and alerts on potential threats but does not block traffic. An intrusion prevention system actively blocks malicious traffic but lacks the comprehensive application-layer inspection and broader feature set of a next-generation firewall.

83. C. ISO/IEC 20000 is the international standard for IT service management, a process model adaptable to most any IT organization.

ISO/IEC 27701 is incorrect because it is a privacy standard. ISO 27002 is incorrect because it is a security controls standard. NIST 800-53 is incorrect because it is a security and privacy controls standard.

84. A. The stratified sampling technique permits auditors to select samples with very low or high values, or any other rarity, whereas the other sampling techniques are not likely to provide the needed samples.

Statistical sampling is incorrect because it will probably result in few or no high-value purchase orders being selected. Variable sampling is incorrect because it will probably result in few or no high-value purchase orders being sampled. Discovery sampling is incorrect because it is used when an auditor is looking for at least one exception in a given population.

85. C. A collection of servers that appear as a single entity and provide high availability is known as a cluster. Clustering involves linking multiple servers together to work as a unit, ensuring that if one server in the group fails, the others can take over, thereby enhancing uptime and reliability. Backup refers to the process of copying data to safeguard against loss, which is not directly related to improving server availability as it is more about data recovery. Resilience generally refers to the ability of a system to withstand failures and continue operating, but it does not specifically describe the composition of multiple servers working together. Virtualization involves running multiple virtual instances on a single physical server to maximize resource utilization, rather than focusing on high availability through multiple servers appearing as one entity.

86. B. Many IoT devices cannot be patched once they have been manufactured. This means that vulnerabilities that have been identified after their manufacture cannot be easily fixed, making them vulnerable to attack. For this reason, IoT devices as a rule should occupy separate networks with strict access controls so that compromised IoT devices cannot bring harm to the rest of the organization.

The answer mentioning an insecure multicast protocol is incorrect because it is not a fact that IoT devices usually communicate via multicast. The answer referring to high volumes of syslog messages is incorrect because it is not a fact that IoT devices produce a high volume of syslog messages. The answer stating that many IoT devices cannot be field upgraded is incorrect because, while the statement is true, the larger problem is that they cannot be patched (which may or may not be a part of a field upgrade).

87. C. A privacy policy is the appropriate choice for guiding an organization in handling Personal Identifiable Information (PII) because it specifically addresses the protocols and procedures associated with collecting, storing, managing, and protecting personal data. Privacy policies are designed to cover rules and guidelines on how PII is processed, ensuring legal compliance and maintaining trust with individuals whose information is being managed. Operations policies generally pertain to the internal processes and procedures that support business functions, typically unrelated to privacy concerns. Strategic policies are typically concerned with the long-term direction and goals of the organization, focusing on broad objectives rather than the specifics of PII handling. Personnel policies deal with human resources aspects, covering employee-related concerns rather than data management or privacy issues. Therefore, only a privacy policy directly relates to the management and protection of PII.

88. B. A problem is defined as an incident that is recurring on a system.

"Open a new incident" is incorrect because opening incidents repeatedly does not help the organization get to the root cause of this chronic condition. "Reboot the server" is incorrect because rebooting the server is not necessarily going to resolve this problem. "Report a security incident" is incorrect because this situation is not a security problem but an operations problem.

89. D. A PCAP file contains information generated by a packet-capturing tool. A network sniffer is the best tool for reading a PCAP file.

Web application scanner is incorrect because this does not typically include the ability to read a PCAP file. Password cracker is incorrect because this does not typically include the ability to read a PCAP file. Fuzzer is incorrect because a fuzzer does not typically include the ability to read a PCAP file.

90. B. Unit testing ensures that individual software modules work properly. It focuses on examining the smallest parts of an application, like functions or methods, to verify their correctness in isolation from other parts of the program. Integration testing, in contrast, deals with testing the interaction between combined modules to identify any compatibility issues. System testing is broader, encompassing the entire application, and aims to validate the end-to-end functionality. Penetration testing is unrelated to module verification as it focuses on evaluating the security of the application and discovering vulnerabilities that could be exploited by malicious actors. Therefore, only unit testing is directly concerned with validating the functionality of individual modules.

91. A. A confidence coefficient of 70% is considered low, meaning the samples do not accurately represent the entire population. More samples should be selected.

Stopping sampling will not improve this low confidence coefficient. Switching to judgmental sampling is not likely to improve it either. Starting over is unnecessary as this would represent greater expenditure of time and effort.

92. A. Examining user account lockout settings is essential in assessing how the system handles repeated unsuccessful login attempts, which can indicate potential security breaches or brute force attack attempts. By evaluating these settings, an auditor can determine whether accounts are appropriately locked after a certain number of failed attempts and ensure that unlocking procedures are secure and effectively manage risks. Removing all unlocked accounts is not a viable option, as user accounts need to remain active for legitimate access, and locking all accounts could disrupt business operations. Determining the complexity of passwords is a separate issue related to password policies, not directly related to lockout configurations, as lockout settings deal with failed login attempts rather than password characteristics. Similarly, determining password sharing among users is another aspect of identity management concerned with user behavior and policy compliance, not directly assessed by examining lockout settings.

93. B. A CISO should not ordinarily report to a CIO for conflict of interest reasons. The CISO will not be able to act with independence regarding IT personnel, controls, and processes.

Personality conflict is not necessarily a reason to change reporting lines. Separation of duties would not ordinarily be a reason to separate the CISO and CIO. Few, if any, regulations require the CIO and CISO to be in different reporting lines.

94. D. Competitive analysis takes place during the feasibility study, prior to requirements definition, design, and testing phases.

Testing, design, and requirements definition are all incorrect because competitive analysis should take place prior to these phases.

95. C. Ensuring rapid recovery of primary systems in the event of a cutover failure is the best answer because a functional contingency plan ensures that the organization can quickly restore operations if the cutover does not proceed as planned. Speeding up the cutover process is not the primary purpose of a contingency plan, as its focus is on managing risks, not efficiency. Providing guidance for personnel is a valid concern but is typically addressed through training or process documentation rather than a contingency plan. Enhancing the ability to identify system bottlenecks is unrelated to contingency planning and pertains more to performance testing and optimization.

96. D. A questionnaire or intake form is the instrument used to collect data so that all processes and systems may be identified. Other methods, such as documentation and network diagram review, may be helpful but will probably not capture all relevant data.

Network diagram review is incorrect because a network diagram is unlikely to reveal all business processes. Documentation review is incorrect because this is unlikely to reveal all business processes, particularly in less mature organizations that do not document all of their processes. Criticality analysis is incorrect because this examines business processes already identified by other means.

97. C. The Chief Audit Executive (CAE) retains ownership of internal IS audit engagements because the CAE is responsible for overseeing and managing the internal audit function, including the planning, execution, and reporting of audit activities. This centralization of ownership ensures accountability and strategic oversight aligned with organizational objectives. Management does not retain ownership, as their role is to be the subject of audits and use the audit reports to improve processes and controls. Internal auditors conduct the audits but operate under the direction and ownership of the CAE. External auditors are independent of the internal audit process and focus on external assessments; hence, they do not own internal audit engagements.

98. B. The general counsel, whose job is to understand and interpret applicable laws and regulations, should have the final say in whether the organization notifies law enforcement in the event of a security breach.

The CISO, CPO, or IA should not be the party that approves notification of law enforcement.

99. A. Main memory is out of scope for media management and destruction because it is volatile and typically does not require the same management and destruction processes as non-volatile storage mediums like hard drives, optical media, or hard copies. Main memory loses its contents when power is lost, making it less of a concern for long-term data exposure. In contrast, hard drives and optical media are forms of non-volatile storage that retain information even without power, necessitating careful management and secure destruction to prevent unauthorized data recovery. Similarly, hard copies represent physical documentation that can contain sensitive information, requiring established processes for their secure disposal to protect data confidentiality.

100. C. The CIS Benchmarks are well-known hardening standards for common types of information systems.

The answer mentioning encryption is incorrect because CIS Benchmarks are not encryption standards but rather system-hardening standards. The answer referring to incident case history is incorrect because CIS Benchmarks are not an incident case history but rather system-hardening standards. The answer referring to maturity is incorrect because CIS Benchmarks are not maturity standards but rather system-hardening standards.

101. C. Automatically applying encryption is the correct approach for a network-based Data Loss Prevention (DLP) system to prevent the loss of sensitive information during email transmission. Encryption ensures that sensitive data remains unreadable to unauthorized parties, thus securing email contents as they traverse the network. Monitoring all hosts for attack attempts is more relevant to intrusion detection or prevention systems rather than DLP, which focuses on data protection. Applying labels to information is more associated with data classification and management; while important, it doesn't actively prevent data loss during transmission. Allowing unencrypted transmissions to pass through runs counter to the objective of a DLP aimed at protecting sensitive information, as it would not prevent data interception by malicious actors.

102. D. The design of a database is known as its schema.

Index is incorrect because an index is a structure that facilitates the rapid retrieval of data in a database. View is incorrect because a view is a mechanism that reveals data as a result of a search, as though it was persistent data. B-tree is incorrect because a B-tree is a type of binary search tree that facilitates the rapid retrieval of data in a database.

103. C. Quantitative risk analysis is the appropriate method when analyzing IT risk based on specific dollar figures because it uses numerical data to estimate the financial impact of risks, often involving calculations of probability and potential loss. Qualitative risk analysis focuses on subjective assessments using categories such as high, medium, or low and does not provide specific monetary values. Business impact analysis identifies the effects of disruptions on business processes but is not primarily focused on financial quantification of IT risks. Critical path analysis is a project management tool for identifying the longest sequence of dependent tasks, unrelated to assessing IT risk in dollar terms.

104. D. The standard interval for the retention of video security surveillance data is 90 days.

The answer options referring to 7 days, 28 days, and 30 days all are incorrect because they are shorter than the typical 90-day retention practice.

105. C. Establishing the maximum tolerable downtime (MTD) for each critical process is crucial to ensure the organization's continued survival during a disaster. This is because understanding the MTD allows the organization to prioritize its recovery efforts and allocate resources effectively to ensure that mission-critical processes are restored within a timeline that prevents severe operational or financial impact. Setting the MTD does not directly set the maximum acceptable data loss, as that is more related to recovery point objectives (RPOs) rather than MTD. Similarly, it is not about setting a maximum level of tolerable risk, which is more of an overarching risk management strategy rather than a focus on downtime. While MTD can assist in coordinating recovery efforts, its primary purpose is more about preventing organizational failure during disruptive events than the broader coordination of recovery efforts.

106. A. A full restore is the best method for recovering a server with a corrupted root file system because it restores the entire system, including the operating system, applications, and configurations, to a known good state. A data restore only recovers user files and does not address system-level corruption. A transaction log restore applies changes to a database but does not restore the operating system or file system. Rebuilding from scratch is time consuming and requires reconfiguring everything manually, making it less efficient than restoring from a full backup.

107. C. A primary goal of a digital signature is to assure nonrepudiation by the sender. Digital signatures provide proof of the origin of a message, allowing the recipient to confirm that the message was indeed sent by the purported sender and preventing the sender from denying their involvement later. This is crucial for accountability and trust in digital communications. Ensuring the fast arrival of the message is not a function of digital signatures; that aspect pertains to the efficiency of the communication channel itself. Encrypting a message in transit is related to confidentiality, which is achieved through encryption methods, while digital signatures focus on authenticity and integrity.

Proving message ownership is similar to nonrepudiation, but digital signatures specifically emphasize identity verification and real-time consent by the sender, rather than indicating ownership.

108. D. Showing concern for the audit client and an interest in its success improves the auditor-auditee relationship.

It is generally not an auditor's role to remind the client of an upcoming audit. Neither reminding an audit client of any needed audit remediation nor asking for a reference is the best answer.

109. A. An organization might choose to discontinue an older information system if it has serious incompatibilities with new applications. This creates challenges in integrating with current technology and can hinder overall operational efficiency, making the system less viable in a modern IT environment. In contrast, compliance with new laws and regulations is generally a reason to keep or upgrade a system rather than discontinue it. If a system has recently been updated, it would likely improve its functionality and extend its lifespan, negating the need to discontinue it. A system with sufficient data storage space typically means it can continue to handle data needs effectively, which wouldn't necessitate discontinuation. Incompatibility with new applications is the most stress-inducing factor, leading to potential system failure and increased costs, outweighing the reasons provided by the other options.

110. A. Because the process is performed consistently, an auditor would probably cite only a minor finding due to the lack of business process documentation.

Major finding is incorrect because the process is being performed consistently. No finding is incorrect because the lack of documentation should be considered a finding. Lack of process documentation is rarely grounds for a material weakness finding.

111. A. The concept of organizational independence is crucial for ensuring that an internal IS auditor can conduct audits independently. This ISACA standard specifically addresses where the IS auditor should be placed within the organization to maintain independence and unbiased auditing processes. An internal auditor's organizational independence ensures that they are free from influence and can provide objective assessments of the entity's controls, without interference from those being audited. An audit charter, while important, primarily defines the overarching purpose, authority, and responsibility of the audit function rather than focusing on independence per se. Reasonable expectation pertains more to the expectations placed on audit outcomes and deliverables, ensuring they are in line with stakeholder needs, rather than the structural independence of the auditing function. Objectivity relates to the auditor's mindset and approach to performing audits free from bias but does not specifically handle the auditor's placement within the organization, which directly impacts independence.

112. B. A document that instructs users on the levels of protection of information along with handling guidelines is better known as a data classification policy.

The answer referring to information security policy is incorrect because although such a policy may indeed contain levels of protection and handling guidelines, the best answer is a data classification policy. The answer mentioning data privacy policy is incorrect because, while a data privacy policy may indeed contain levels of protection and handling guidelines, the best answer is a data classification policy. Data disposal procedure is incorrect because this procedure describes the steps to be taken to destroy data.

113. A. An organizational chart is a visual representation of an organization's structure, showing roles, responsibilities, and reporting lines. It is designed to clarify lines of reporting and responsibility, which are fundamental elements of organizational structure. Key risk indicators, while important for monitoring risks, do not pertain to structural relationships or hierarchy. Audit objectives are specific to the goals and focus areas of audits, unrelated to the depiction of organizational roles. Key performance indicators track progress toward strategic or operational goals and are also not part of an organizational chart's purpose.

114. A. Protocol data unit (PDU) is the term used to describe a single unit of information transmitted through the protocol, and the PDU for the UDP protocol is the datagram.

Checksum is incorrect because a checksum is not a PDU but rather a part of a frame (or packet) used to ensure the integrity of the frame (or packet). MTU is incorrect because MTU (maximum transmission unit) is a specification of the largest frame or packet that may be transmitted on a network. Header is incorrect because a header is a part of a frame or packet that contains information about the source and/or destination of the frame or packet.

115. A. Symmetric cryptosystems use a single shared secret key to enforce confidentiality, where the same key is used for both encryption and decryption. Asymmetric cryptosystems use a pair of keys – public and private – making them different from symmetric cryptosystems. Quantum cryptosystems employ quantum properties for secure communication but do not rely on a single shared secret key. Homomorphic cryptosystems enable computations on encrypted data without decrypting it, focusing on data privacy during processing rather than simple confidentiality through a shared key.

116. C. The CMMI, or Capability Maturity Model Integration, is a well-known maturity model used by organizations to understand the maturity of their business processes.

CMMI is not a control model. CMMI is not a risk model. CMMI is not an infrastructure model.

117. A. Validating the length of input data is primarily aimed at preventing buffer overflow attacks. Buffer overflow attacks occur when more data is entered into a field than it can handle, potentially leading to arbitrary code execution or system crashes, making length validation a critical security measure. Spell-checking the data would relate more to text correctness rather than security concerns, thus irrelevant for validation focused on input length. Ensuring accurate totals is related to data integrity but not specifically to input length validation, as it involves cross-verifying summation or similar operations. Producing hash totals is a method used for verifying data integrity but does not address the need to control input size specifically, making it unrelated to input length validation.

118. C. IT personnel perform system testing, functional testing, and quality assurance testing. End users perform user acceptance testing (UAT).

System testing, functional testing, and quality assurance testing are all incorrect because they are all performed by IT personnel and not by end users.

119. A. Top secret data classification requires the highest degree of protection because its unauthorized disclosure could lead to exceptionally grave damage to national security or organizational interests. This is a common classification in military and government contexts, indicating the critical nature of the information. Secret classification, while still significant, suggests that the release of information could cause serious damage, but not to the same extent as top secret. Private data classification typically refers to personal or sensitive information that should be protected from public viewing but does not necessitate the same high-level controls as top secret. Confidential data is generally considered sensitive and proprietary within an organization, with its unauthorized disclosure potentially causing damage; however, it is deemed less critical than top secret in terms of potential impact.

120. C. Host and guest operating systems all need to be patched.

The answer stating that only host OSs listen on the network is incorrect; guest OSs also listen on the network. The answer stating that hypervisors pass immunity to their guests is incorrect because hypervisors do not pass immunity to their guests. The answer stating that only guest OSs are patched is incorrect because host OSs also need to be patched, in order to prevent their compromise by attackers.

121. A. Data controls are the least relevant safeguard because they primarily focus on ensuring the accuracy, completeness, and integrity of data rather than restricting system communication with APIs. Interface controls are relevant as they manage how systems interact with APIs. Access controls are critical because they enforce authentication and authorization for systems connecting to APIs. Firewalls are also important as they help restrict unauthorized network-level access to the APIs.

122. A. The privileged access review is a detective control because it is used to detect potentially unauthorized privileged access assignments.

"Preventive" is incorrect because this procedure does not prevent unwanted outcomes. "Administrative" is incorrect because an administrative control is generally implemented in the form of a policy. "Recovery" is incorrect because this procedure is not being used to recover a system.

123. B. Gathering relevant information is the first step in applying a risk-based auditing approach because it lays the foundation for understanding the context in which the audit will occur, which includes company objectives, processes, and external factors. This understanding is crucial before identifying potential risks, which can only be accurately assessed with comprehensive background information. Understanding existing internal controls comes after identifying and assessing risks to evaluate how these controls mitigate identified risks. Developing a risk-based audit program is a subsequent step that relies on the information and analysis gathered from the previous steps, ensuring the program is effectively tailored to address specific risks. Identifying potential risks should follow the initial gathering phase, as it requires an understanding of both the external and internal environments of the auditing entity.

124. D. Third-party service providers are often required to produce metrics to ensure that quality standards are met.

GDPR does not necessarily require detailed metrics of the third-party service provider. Reporting to a regulator is a vague answer and would not necessarily require third-party metrics. Understanding how much to pay the service provider is incorrect because it would be more important to have this information for the purposes of determining the quality of the provider's services rather than using this information to help determine monthly cost.

125. B. Switches operate at Layer 2 of the OSI Model, known as the Data Link Layer, where they use MAC addresses to forward data to the appropriate destination within a local area network (LAN). This functionality allows switches to efficiently manage traffic within a network by making forwarding decisions based on the devices connected to their ports. Firewalls, on the other hand, typically operate at Layers 3 (Network Layer) and above, inspecting and filtering traffic based on IP addresses and other criteria for security purposes. Proxies also operate at higher layers, typically the Application Layer (Layer 7), where they manage requests and responses between clients and servers, often for the purpose of anonymity or caching. Repeaters work at Layer 1, the Physical Layer, where they regenerate signals to extend the distance a network can cover without any data re-routing capabilities associated with Layer 2 devices.

126. A. The testing phase is used to confirm correct design, implementation, and operation of a system.

Maintenance is incorrect because the maintenance phase is the entire period in which changes are made to a system in production. Design is incorrect because the design phase is used to create the makeup of the system; the system cannot at this time be verified because it has not been built. Implementation is incorrect because systems are verified not only during the testing portion of implementation, but in all testing after implementation.

127. B. The balanced scorecard (BSC) includes multiple perspectives to provide a comprehensive evaluation of an organization's performance toward its objectives. The Financial perspective is a crucial component of the BSC as it measures the financial performance and profitability of the organization, which is fundamental for understanding the economic impact of its strategies. The Customer perspective is also a key component, focusing on customer satisfaction and relationships, which link directly to market performance. Internal processes are captured within the Internal perspective, a core element of BSC that examines internal operational goals and how well business processes align with organizational objectives. External processes, however, are not explicitly considered within the conventional BSC framework. Instead, the BSC focuses on factors that the organization can directly control and improve, emphasizing internal parameters over external.

128. D. The zero trust model assumes that, in this context, end-user devices are not to be trusted, and may even be hostile.

Least privilege is incorrect because this is related to access control. VDI is incorrect because this stands for virtual desktop infrastructure, which is not an architecture but a technology. Implicit trust is incorrect because "implicit trust" is not an information security architecture term.

129. B. MFA (Multi-Factor Authentication) is effective in mitigating the risk of identity theft because it requires users to provide multiple forms of verification (e.g., something they know, have, or are) to access systems, making it much harder for attackers to compromise accounts even if credentials are stolen. CASB (Cloud Access Security Broker) focuses on securing cloud applications and may help with broader security but does not directly prevent identity theft. IPS (Intrusion Prevention System) detects and blocks suspicious activities but is not specifically designed to address credential misuse. IDS (Intrusion Detection System) only identifies potential threats without actively mitigating them, making it less effective for directly addressing identity theft.

130. B. RIP, or Routing Information Protocol, is an obsolete routing protocol that is not secure and not suitable for DMZ environments.

The answer mentioning a dual-homed server is incorrect because RIP is not associated with whether a server is dual-homed. The answer referring to multiple paths to the Internet is incorrect because the presence of RIP does not necessarily indicate multiple paths to the Internet; RIP could be in use because of the architecture of the internal network. The answer mentioning promiscuous mode is incorrect because promiscuous mode is related to network sniffing, not routing protocols.

131. B. Disaster Recovery Planning (DRP) focuses more on the restoring of systems after a disaster, as it specifically addresses the recovery of IT infrastructure, data, and technical operations to ensure business continuity. Less critical business functions are not the primary focus of DRP, as it prioritizes critical systems. Operational functions and human resources aspects of a recovery effort are covered more broadly under Business Continuity Planning (BCP), which ensures overall organizational resilience and continuity beyond just IT systems.

132. D. The minimum essential practice for administering security awareness training is to require training at the time of hire and annually thereafter.

At the time of hire is incorrect because the standard for training is not only at the time of hire but also annually thereafter. Annually is incorrect because the standard for training is not only annually but also at the time of hire. At the time of hire and quarterly is incorrect because the standard for training is not quarterly but instead annually. Quarterly is, however, a good practice.

133. B. Conducting walkthroughs is the most effective way for an IS auditor to gain an understanding of a client's operating procedures as it allows for real-time observation of processes and provides an opportunity to ask questions and obtain clarifications from personnel performing the tasks. This interactive approach gives insight into the actual execution of operations compared to the theoretical or documented procedures. Reviewing instruction manuals and management procedure documentation can offer some level of understanding but may not reflect real practices or informal controls that are not documented. Utilizing control checklists is a useful tool to ensure that specific controls are in place or to assess compliance, but it does not provide a holistic overview of operating procedures or their practical implementation.

134. C. The purpose of assigning severity levels to a security incident is to bring the right level of resources to respond to the incident, and to notify specific personnel according to severity level.

The answer referring to an appropriate level of reporting is incorrect because severity levels are not only about reporting levels but also for determining the level and type of response. The answer that mentions the method of evidence collection is incorrect because severity levels are not related only to levels or types of evidence collection. The answer that refers to evidence protection is incorrect because severity levels are not related only to evidence protection but instead are mainly about response procedures overall.

135. B. Reporting the email to your Information and Communications Technology (ICT) department and deleting it is the best course of action because it minimizes the risk of falling for a phishing attempt while allowing the IT department to investigate and potentially mitigate any threat to the organization. Opening the email link is risky because it could lead to a phishing website designed to steal personal information or install malware. Forwarding the email link to ICT could potentially spread the phishing content or malicious link further, depending on the email software and company policies regarding such content. Storing the link in the email archive is not advisable because it preserves the potential threat, possibly compromising future email security or inadvertently leading to the malicious link being accessed later.

136. A. Obtaining screenshots that capture requested security configurations and then giving those screenshots to the auditor during the walkthrough nearly eliminates the possibility that the interviewee might falsify the information.

It is incorrect to ask the engineer to take screenshots during the walkthrough and send them via email because he could manipulate or substitute screenshots before mailing them to the auditor. It is incorrect to ask the engineer to take screenshots after the walkthrough because he could take screenshots of a different system or manipulate the screenshots. It is incorrect to ask the engineer to write a narrative because a narrative does not represent direct evidence from the system being audited.

137. B. The purpose and scope of the audit are the most critical determinant in the allocation of resources for an audit engagement because they define the audit's objectives, breadth, and depth, ensuring resources are allocated effectively and efficiently to address the most crucial areas. Without a clear understanding of what the audit aims to achieve and how broad it will be, it's difficult to allocate resources such as time, personnel, and tools appropriately. While the availability of skilled personnel is important, it follows the determination of scope and purpose, as the necessary skill set is based on these factors. The extent of the organization's geographic footprint is a logistical consideration that affects the audit plan rather than the initial allocation of resources based on criticality. The availability of automated audit tools, while beneficial for efficiency, is secondary to defining what needs to be achieved through the audit, as tools should be selected based on the audit's specific requirements.

138. A. ISO 9000 is the world-recognized standard for quality management systems. While initially targeting manufacturing, software development and IT organizations are known to employ ISO 9000 as well.

ISO 27001 is incorrect because it is a security management standard. ISO 27002 is incorrect because it is a security controls framework. IT BSC is incorrect because it is the IT balanced scorecard, a reporting methodology.

139. B. The development of a program charter is critical in commencing a program because it serves as a formal document that defines the program's objectives, scope, stakeholders, and high-level requirements. This foundational document provides guidance and benchmarks for decision-making and aligns stakeholders with the program's purpose and direction. Appointing a non-technical program manager might not cater to all programs, especially those needing technical expertise. Although appointing the CEO as a program sponsor can be valuable for support and visibility, it may not always be practical or necessary for every program, depending on its size or strategic importance. Setting a tight program timeline can add unnecessary pressure and may compromise the quality and feasibility of the program deliverables.

140. D. CMMI was developed by Carnegie-Mellon University.

COBIT, the Risk IT Framework, and Val IT were developed by ISACA.

141. B. The primary consideration for establishing audit terms on turnaround time for requests from external auditors is the availability of key personnel, as they are essential for providing information and support during the audit process. The schedule of IT upgrades, while important for system stability, is not directly tied to meeting audit requests. The availability of the CEO is rarely relevant for routine audit requests, as these are typically handled by operational or financial personnel. Terms for payment of audit fees pertain to the financial agreement but do not influence the turnaround time for handling auditor requests.

142. D. Video surveillance where cameras and other apparatus are hidden serves as a detective control. When video surveillance equipment is visible, it acts as a deterrent and detective control.

"Stealth" is incorrect because "stealth" is not a control category. "Deterrent" is incorrect because the video surveillance system cannot be seen by personnel. "Preventive" is incorrect because a video surveillance system does not prevent unwanted events.

143. B. Migration testing's primary purpose during the IT system testing phase is to ensure that data is correctly transferred from an old system to a new one. This testing is crucial because it helps verify data integrity and consistency during the transition process, addressing potential issues such as data loss or corruption that may arise during migration. Validating system functionalities pertains to functional testing rather than migration testing, as it focuses on whether the system performs specific functions as intended. Assessing whether user requirements are met falls under acceptance testing, where the implemented system is verified against the initial requirements specified by the users or stakeholders. Verifying the proper interface of individual modules is part of integration testing, which examines how different components of a system work together, rather than focusing on data migration from a previous system.

144. B. Delay of software escrow is not considered a risk to a project.

Delivered software not adequately meeting business needs, purchased software not meeting efficiency needs, and key design personnel resigning from the organization are all incorrect because they are all considered risks to a software development project.

145. B. Implementing a "gate process" in the systems development life cycle (SDLC) is primarily to review and approve each phase before proceeding. This structured approach ensures that all requirements and assessments are satisfied before advancing to the next phase, which helps maintain project integrity and alignment with organizational goals. Removing the need for project reviews contradicts the purpose of a gate process, which is inherently about periodic evaluation and assessment. Addressing project challenges during each phase is broader than what a gate process specifically targets, as the primary focus of the gate process is approval based on meeting specific criteria rather than resolving issues. Assessing the amount of funds utilized at each phase may be a component of the gate process but is not the main reason for its implementation, as the focus is more on project verification and viability than solely financial tracking.

146. B. "Active-active" refers to a specific server cluster architecture in which all servers are actively performing production tasks.

The answer referring to different VLANs is incorrect because active-active is related to server clustering, not their association with VLANs. The answer mentioning multiple power supplies and NICs is incorrect because active-active is unrelated to multiple power supplies and NICs. The answer referring to database management systems is incorrect because other types of servers besides database servers can be in a cluster in active-active configuration.

147. B. Performing qualitative risk analysis before quantitative risk analysis allows an IS auditor to quickly identify the most critical risks. This step is essential because it provides a clear understanding of areas that require immediate focus and helps prioritize risks based on factors like impact and likelihood without delving into complex calculations. Identifying critical risks promptly sets a foundation for more detailed analysis. This approach does not strive for precision in the financial impacts of threats, which is a goal of quantitative analysis. It does not aim to reduce the extent of risk analysis; rather, it ensures that the subsequent quantitative analysis is more directed and efficient. Measuring risk in numerical terms is the essence of quantitative risk analysis, not qualitative.

148. A. An MDM (mobile device management) system is used to manage and protect mobile devices, including smartphones, tablets, and laptop computers.

Monitoring of data exfiltration is incorrect because an MDM system is not used to monitor data exfiltration but rather to manage mobile endpoints. Prevention of data exfiltration is incorrect because an MDM is not used to prevent data exfiltration but instead is used to manage mobile endpoint systems. User self-service password reset is incorrect because an MDM is not used for self-service password reset but rather to manage mobile endpoint systems.

149. B. Systems configuration standards are critical for an IS auditor to examine because these standards provide the baseline for how systems should be configured to ensure consistency, security, and compliance across the organization's IT infrastructure. Configuration standards help prevent unauthorized changes and secure the environment against vulnerabilities. Systems operations procedures focus on the day-to-day functioning of the system, which, while important, do not specifically address the configuration settings. Disaster recovery procedures are concerned with restoring systems after a disruption, not with their initial setup and configuration. Systems update processes pertain to how software updates are handled, which, while part of system maintenance, do not provide the comprehensive view needed for initial configuration settings. Therefore, configuration standards directly relate to ensuring the correct settings are applied initially, which is why they are the aspect the auditor should examine.

150. B. A zero-day attack always involves exploiting a previously unknown vulnerability because it targets software flaws that developers are unaware of and have not yet patched. Evil twin attacks involve setting up fake wireless networks to trick users into connecting, which does not depend on exploiting unknown vulnerabilities. DDoS attacks overwhelm a system with traffic to disrupt its operations, relying on resource exhaustion rather than undisclosed flaws. Social engineering attacks manipulate individuals into revealing sensitive information or performing actions, focusing on human behavior rather than exploiting software vulnerabilities.

Practice Test 2

1. C. A data flow diagram (DFD) is used to illustrate the flow of information between IT applications in business terms. It visually represents how data moves through a system, including inputs, processes, storage, and outputs. The Zachman model is a framework for enterprise architecture that organizes information about an organization but does not specifically illustrate data flow. The OSI model describes networking layers and how data is transmitted over a network, rather than how information flows between business applications. The Clark-Wilson model is a security model focused on maintaining data integrity through well-formed transactions and separation of duties, not on illustrating data movement.

2. A. DevSecOps is effective in resolving conflicts between software development and operations teams while ensuring the development of secure software, as it integrates security practices into every part of the software development life cycle. This approach fosters collaboration among development, security, and operations teams, emphasizing the importance of security from the outset. The focus is on automating security checks and processes, which helps in early detection and resolution of security issues. Agile, although it promotes collaboration among cross-functional teams and can include security practices, primarily concentrates on delivering iterative and incremental project progress and may not inherently emphasize security. Scrum focuses on the management and organization of team tasks within a framework that supports Agile processes but does not explicitly include security considerations in its practice. DevOps enhances collaboration between development and operations teams for faster and more reliable software delivery but, similarly, does not explicitly integrate security considerations throughout the development life cycle. Therefore, although Agile, Scrum, and DevOps improve general collaboration and efficiency, they do not specifically address security integration as DevSecOps does.

3. B. In the context of network border devices, such as routers and firewalls, ACLs filter network traffic by criteria such as port, protocol, service, and host/destination IP address.

The answer stating that ACLs allow network traffic to pass unfiltered is incorrect because ACLs do not "audit" network traffic. The answer referring to administrative access to the router or firewall is incorrect because ACLs do not determine who has administrator access to a router or firewall (however, ACLs can be used to limit the origins of administrator logons to network devices). The answer stating that only inbound traffic is filtered is incorrect because ACLs can be used to filter both inbound and outbound traffic, or either, or neither.

4. A. Applying for cyber-risk insurance represents risk transference because the financial impact of cyber risks is shifted to the insurance provider. Risk avoidance involves eliminating the risk entirely, such as by discontinuing a risky activity. Risk acceptance means acknowledging the risk and choosing not to act, accepting any potential losses. Risk mitigation involves reducing the likelihood or impact of the risk through controls or measures, which is not the case with transferring financial liability via insurance.

5. A. Defining Requirements is not one of the top-level processes in the PRINCE2 project management framework.

Starting Up a Project (SU), Directing a Project (DP), and Managing Product Delivery (MP) are all part of PRINCE2 top-level processes.

6. A. An audit program is not considered a core artifact of effective IT governance. IT governance focuses on establishing structures, policies, and processes to ensure that IT aligns with business objectives, typically involving resource management, standards, and policies. Resource management ensures optimal use of IT resources, standards provide consistent practices, and policies establish rules and guidelines. An audit program, although important for evaluating compliance and effectiveness, is a tool for assessment rather than a foundational element of governance itself.

7. B. Grid computing is a technique used to distribute a problem or task to several computers at the same time, taking advantage of each computer's processing power to solve the problem or complete the task in less time. Grid computing is a form of distributed computing, but in grid computing the computers are coupled more loosely and the number of computers participating in the solution of a problem can be dynamically expanded or contracted at will.

"Server clusters" is incorrect because computers in server clusters perform individual tasks. "Cloud computing" is incorrect because this represents the use of virtual servers or services that are hosted by external organizations. "Network-attached storage" is incorrect because this is used to store information and is accessed over a network.

8. A. An IS auditor's independence and internal audit objectivity are most likely impaired if they operated a payroll system subject to audit in the past month, as this directly involves them in the operations they are supposed to audit, creating a conflict of interest and a bias due to their prior involvement. Advising on the implementation of an enterprise resource planning (ERP) system does not inherently impair independence or objectivity because providing advice is different from making decisions; auditors can still independently review the system after implementation. Not holding the CISA qualification does not directly impair independence or objectivity, as it is a credential for demonstrating knowledge rather than a requirement for unbiased auditing work. Failing to report CPE credits affects professional credentials and continuous education but does not impact the ability to remain independent or objective in auditing tasks.

9. C. 1204, Performance and Supervision because it addresses the operational aspects of conducting an audit, focusing on how audit work should be performed and overseen rather than outlining ethical behavior. In contrast, Due Professional Care (2005) directly relates to ethical standards by emphasizing the responsibility of auditors to apply skill and diligence in their work. Standard 1207, Irregularities and Illegal Acts pertains to the auditor's duty to recognize and respond to unethical or unlawful behavior, aligning closely with ethical obligations. The ISACA Code of Professional Ethics explicitly defines the ethical principles auditors must follow, such as integrity, objectivity, and confidentiality.

10. A. IT value delivery should not form part of the security requirements because it focuses on ensuring that IT investments deliver business value, which is a strategic and governance concern rather than a security-specific requirement. Encryption is critical for protecting data confidentiality. Authentication ensures that only authorized users can access systems or data. Authorization determines what actions authenticated users are allowed to perform, ensuring that appropriate access controls are in place. These elements are fundamental to a security requirements specification.

11. B. RAD is a response to the slower and more structured application development methodologies (such as waterfall) that were developed in the 1970s. Among its characteristics are small, highly experienced development teams; integrated development and design tools; and frequent design and analysis sessions with end users.

DOSD is incorrect because data-oriented system development is a data-centric design often found in large environments such as airline reservation systems. OO is incorrect because object-oriented system development is a concept that is based on objects, methods, classes, and inheritance. Component-based development is incorrect because this is based on a system architecture consisting of components that operate separately in support of the whole.

12. A. Hiring contractors or consultants during seasonal periods is typically due to varying demand. Seasonal fluctuations can greatly affect workload, necessitating a temporary increase in the workforce that contractors and consultants can fulfill, offering the flexibility to scale up or down as needed. This is distinct from issues like financial discipline, which relates more to internal fiscal management practices rather than staffing decisions aligned with demand fluctuations. A lack of skills relates to a shortage of specific expertise rather than the cyclical nature of work volume; if skills were consistently absent, hiring permanent staff could be a better solution. High labor turnover also would not typically justify employing temporary workers, as this is an ongoing issue, whereas contractors are more suited to addressing temporary peaks in workload rather than persistent staffing problems.

13. B. A risk assessment performed prior to an audit helps auditors better understand which processes, systems, or locations should receive greater scrutiny in an upcoming audit.

The answer that refers to performing a risk assessment during the audit is incorrect because auditors perform a risk assessment prior to the audit. The answer that states that auditors determine the highest risks is incorrect because risks are determined prior to the audit. The answer referring to determination by management is incorrect because management should not direct the course of the audit.

14. A. Data management is the most suitable category of utility software for tools that are used to manipulate, query, import, and export data in an organization. These tools are specifically designed to handle data-related tasks, facilitating organization-wide data handling and integration processes. Data manipulation, although seemingly similar, typically refers to the specific act of altering data to achieve a desired format or structure, not encompassing the full range of data management activities. Systems health tools relate to monitoring and maintaining the performance and integrity of IT systems, not managing or processing data. Software testing involves verifying and validating software functionality and performance, which is unrelated to the direct handling of organizational data for import, export, or manipulation purposes.

15. C. A switch will listen to traffic, learn the MAC address(es) associated with each port (connector), and send packets only to destination ports.

"Gateway" is incorrect because a gateway does not so much forward traffic as it does translate or transform traffic. "Router" is incorrect because a router uses IP addresses to forward traffic from one network to another. "Firewall" is incorrect because firewalls are used to block packets based on the firewall's rules.

16. A. Prioritizing the analysis of critical applications is the most effective strategy for managing a large number of applications because it allows the organization to focus its resources on the most important systems that could have the biggest impact if compromised. These critical applications typically handle sensitive data or key operations that support business continuity. Analyzing each application individually is impractical for a large number of applications due to resource constraints and could lead to delays, leaving some critical vulnerabilities unaddressed for extended periods. Performing a single analysis for all applications may miss specific vulnerabilities unique to certain applications, reducing the overall effectiveness of the analysis. Focusing on intangible assets does not directly address application vulnerability management, as vulnerabilities reside within the applications themselves, not within intangible assets. Prioritizing critical applications ensures that the highest risks are mitigated more promptly.

17. D. Tunnel mode is used by IPsec to create a secure link between two networks, especially across a insecure network (such as the Internet).

Both "encryption mode" and "authentication mode" are incorrect because these are not IPsec modes. "Transport mode" is incorrect because it is typically used within a local network.

18. A. Invoicing for services rendered in the IS audit is addressed under the scope of non-audit work, as this section typically includes details about financial arrangements, including billing practices, fees, and payment terms. The executive summary provides an overview of the engagement and does not cover invoicing. The report distribution list specifies who will receive the audit report and is unrelated to invoicing. "Confidentiality and nondisclosure" addresses the protection of sensitive information but does not pertain to billing or payment matters.

19. D. The Risk IT Framework is the risk management framework developed and maintained by ISACA.

"Zachman" is incorrect because it is an enterprise architecture model. "NIST 800-30" is incorrect because this is a risk management standard created by the National Institute of Standards and Technology (NIST), not ISACA. "COBIT" is incorrect because this is an IT process framework.

20. A. The primary objective of availability management in IT systems is sustaining IT services to support organizational objectives, as this function ensures that IT services are consistently available and reliable to meet the needs of the business, aligning with the overall goals and objectives of the organization. Allocating skilled human resources to IT programs, although important, focuses more on personnel management rather than ensuring system availability. Increasing the monitoring of IT systems performance is part of availability management, but it serves more as a means to an end rather than the primary objective itself. Finally, ensuring that IT assets are properly safeguarded relates more to security and asset management than directly addressing service availability or its primary objective.

21. C. Application software should be managed with the recovery site type in mind. For cold sites, it is not normally installed. Warm sites have application software installed but not running; and at hot sites, application software must be up and running to minimize transition time.

The answer referring to software running at a cold site is incorrect because application software will not be running at a cold site; there may not even be computers for applications to run on. The answer referring to installation at a hot site is incorrect because application software MUST, be running at a hot site. The answer referring to a warm site is incorrect because application software may be installed at a warm site.

22. A. Mergers and acquisitions introduce business integration objectives, which increases audit complexities because integrating disparate systems and processes often presents significant challenges that can complicate the audit environment. As these complexities arise, auditors need to address new risks and ensure that controls are effectively designed and implemented across merged entities. The option suggesting that mergers and acquisitions create a stable environment for IS audit operations is incorrect because such activities typically result in substantial changes rather than stability. The suggestion that they reduce the audit budget is incorrect as, in reality, the need for thorough audits generally increases costs rather than decreasing them. Finally, although mergers and acquisitions do increase the demand for audits, which may suggest a need for more skilled IS auditors, this is a consequence of the complexity introduced and not a direct effect they have on audit programs.

23. A. A preaudit is generally performed on an audit client that has not been audited before, as a means for helping it prepare for an upcoming audit. A preaudit can be considered a "practice" audit or a "dry run."

The answer mentioning examples of evidence is incorrect because a preaudit is not used to provide examples of evidence. The answer referring to coaching the client is incorrect because a preaudit should not be used for unethical activity, such as guiding auditees to deceive auditors. The answer mentioning training for new auditors is incorrect because preaudits are not used for training auditors.

24. A. Informing key stakeholders and authorities of the disaster status and any changes in operations is critical because it ensures effective communication, helps manage expectations, and supports coordinated responses to minimize disruptions. It is not merely a matter of courtesy, as timely notification has practical and strategic importance. Stopping the processing of transactions for the organization is not typically the primary reason for such notifications unless explicitly required by the situation. Although compliance with laws and regulations is important, it is only one aspect of stakeholder communication and does not encompass the broader necessity of keeping stakeholders informed during a disaster.

25. B. One of the easiest ways for an intruder to attack a system is through known default passwords. Before being connected to a network, every system should be changed so that all accounts have organizationally assigned passwords instead of the default passwords.

Complex passwords, unique passwords, and password vaulting are incorrect answers because they are all good password protection measures.

26. A. The likelihood of threat realization is the key factor for determining vulnerability severity because it directly assesses how probable it is that a threat will exploit the vulnerability, combined with its potential impact. The duration of time the vulnerability has existed is not a direct indicator of severity, as older vulnerabilities may still be low-risk or mitigated. The effectiveness of IT controls implemented relates to the current defenses in place but does not prioritize the inherent severity of the vulnerabilities themselves. The cost of mitigating vulnerabilities is a consideration for planning remediation but does not affect the ranking of severity.

27. A. A CRO (chief risk officer) is most often responsible for building and managing an organization's enterprise risk management (ERM) program and processes.

The answer referring to the information security program is incorrect because a CISO would build and manage an information security program. The answer referring to IT governance is incorrect because a CIO would build and manage IT governance. The answer mentioning product development is incorrect because a development leader (sometimes a CTO) would build and manage product development.

28. A. Examining IT problem management records is crucial in determining the effectiveness of problem management activities. This allows auditors to assess whether issues are identified, analyzed, and resolved efficiently, ensuring that the problem management process is functioning as intended and contributing to overall IT service management goals. Rectifying all problems is unrealistic for an audit focus, as the goal is to evaluate processes rather than fix individual issues. Enhancing media control is unrelated to the purpose of reviewing problem management records because media control is more about managing storage and data access. Improving the effectiveness of recovery efforts is more related to disaster recovery and business continuity plans, rather than routine problem management records, which focus on the ongoing handling of incidents and problems.

29. A. Modern LAN environments are protected from outside threats with firewalls. Many larger organizations also employ internal firewalls that create separate zones of trust within the organization, thus separating sensitive information assets from users who do not require access.

The answer referring to communication between two departments is incorrect because although preventing communication between two departments is a potential objective for internal firewalls, this explanation is too narrow. The answer citing external threats is incorrect because although operating in a defense-in-depth posture to slow down Internet threats is a potential reason for layers of firewalls, internal firewalls typically do not serve to assist border firewalls in stopping external threats. The answer referring to the prevention of propagation of malware throughout a network is incorrect because although blocking malware from moving laterally through a network is a common objective for internal firewalls, this is not the best available answer, as there are often additional reasons for internal firewalls.

30. A. Implementing an employee policy manual in an organization primarily serves to specify the terms and conditions of employment. This is correct because such manuals typically outline company rules, employee rights, roles, responsibilities, and organizational procedures, providing a comprehensive guide to the employment relationship and expectations. The other options are not the primary purposes of a policy manual. Although a manual may include some guidance related to training, it is not specifically designed to train employees; separate documents and programs are typically used for thorough employee training and development. Advertising internal vacancies is generally managed through different communication channels like emails, notice boards, or HR portals, not the employee policy manual. Training employees in controls is typically addressed through specific compliance or control training programs and not a general policy manual.

31. A. Control self-assessments help process owners see how effective their controls are (or are not) through a structured assessment program. This can help process owners take more ownership in their controls and be more receptive to improvements. The other activities are not as effective at accomplishing this objective.

"Internal audit" and "external audit" are incorrect because although internal and external audits will identify improvement opportunities, these are not as effective as a control self-assessment, where control owners have more involvement in control evaluation and improvement. "Balanced scorecard" is incorrect because the balanced scorecard is used for strategy measurement and management.

32. A. Data minimization in the early stages of the information life cycle focuses on collecting only the amount of data necessary to meet specific business requirements. This approach helps reduce storage costs, limits exposure to data breaches, and ensures compliance with data protection regulations by not retaining unnecessary personal or sensitive information. Collecting data for multiple purposes could lead to over-collection, increasing the risk of mismanagement and compliance issues. Maximizing the extent of data sources is contrary to the concept of data minimization, which aims to restrict data collection to what is strictly needed. Speeding up the data collection process is not a principle of data minimization; instead, it emphasizes purpose-driven, prudent data handling rather than focusing on efficiency in collection.

33. B. It is relatively easy for an intruder to establish a rogue access point with the same name as a legitimate access point (evil twin). The intruder can use this rogue access point as a gateway to forward legitimate traffic in both directions while watching for and intercepting any sensitive information that may pass by. Or the intruder may use the rogue access point to steal logon credentials from users trying to connect to the real access point.

"MAC address spoofing" is incorrect because although this is a method for gaining access to a network that uses MAC address filtering, by itself it does nothing to help an intruder steal authentication credentials. "Wireless sniffing" is incorrect because it does not redirect traffic. Additionally, sniffing by itself it does little these days to help an intruder steal login credentials; this is because the vast majority of authentication is performed via encrypted channels such as TLS and other encrypted protocols. "MAC address filtering" is incorrect because this is not an attack on a network but instead a defensive measure.

34. A. The hybrid model for end-user computing involves the organization providing some computing resources while allowing employees to use their personal devices to access specific resources. This approach balances control and flexibility, enabling employees to use personal devices for work while maintaining security over key systems. Providing all computing resources is a fully managed approach, not a hybrid one. Restricting the use of personal devices represents a strict corporate-controlled model rather than a hybrid approach. Requiring employees to provide all devices and software describes a bring-your-own-device (BYOD) model without corporate provisioning, which differs from a hybrid setup that includes both personal and corporate resources.

35. C. A maturity model helps an organization better understand the integrity and reliability of a business process.

"Control framework" is incorrect because this would be used to organize specific desired outcomes. "Risk assessment" is incorrect because this is used to identify risk, not measure the integrity of a process. "Clark-Wilson model" is incorrect because this is a data integrity model.

36. A. IT audit and assurance guidelines are the optional component of the ITAF because they serve as recommendations to support auditors in implementing the IT audit standards effectively but are not mandatory to follow. IT audit standards and the Code of Ethics are not optional because they establish mandatory requirements for the audit profession and outline the professional conduct expected of ISACA members and certification holders, respectively. These standards ensure the quality and rigor of IT audits, and adherence to the Code of Ethics maintains the integrity and professionalism of practitioners, making them essential components of the framework. Thus, guidelines provide flexibility and support, whereas standards and the Code of Ethics are foundational and compulsory.

37. A. A business case defines the business problem, feasibility study results, budget, metrics, and risks associated with a new business initiative.

"Financial stability" is incorrect because this is not a document used by IT. "Budget request" is incorrect because it does not usually take this form. "Migration plan" is incorrect because this is a description of the steps to move from one system to another.

38. A. Architecture improvements are typically implemented during the Development stage of the business continuity planning (BCP) process life cycle. This stage involves the creation and updating of plans and procedures to enhance the organization's capability to maintain operations or quickly resume them following an interruption. Development focuses on creating detailed plans and implementing improvements to existing infrastructure and processes. The Analysis stage is primarily concerned with understanding potential risks, impacts, and requirements without altering the architecture. Training is about educating employees on their roles within the BCP, not developing or improving systems. Testing evaluates the effectiveness of the BCP and validates the plans without incorporating changes at that point, focusing instead on identifying gaps and areas that need improvement, which would then lead back to further development work.

39. C. Firewall change records should contain a business reason for the change so that the auditor will have an idea of why each firewall rule exists. It would be useful (but not necessary) if the firewall change records contained references to a record number in the organization's change management system.

The answer stating that the change approval is absent is incorrect because the change approval information usually resides in the change management system. The answer stating that the records are complete is incorrect because they are not complete: there is no reference to a business reason for the change. The answer stating that the backout plan is lacking is incorrect because the presence or absence of a backout plan is not relevant.

40. B. An NGFW (next-generation firewall) is the best option for protecting systems facilitating online transactions because it combines the capabilities of stateful inspection with advanced features like intrusion prevention, deep packet inspection, and application-layer filtering. These capabilities provide robust protection against sophisticated threats in transactional environments. Stateful firewalls track the state of connections and are effective for general use but lack the advanced features of NGFWs. Stateless firewalls and packet-filtering firewalls only analyze individual packets without context, making them less effective against modern, complex attacks targeting online transactions.

41. C. Secure Multipurpose Internet Mail Extensions (S/MIME) is an email security protocol that provides sender and recipient authentication and encryption of message content and attachments.

"POP" is incorrect because Post Office Protocol does not encrypt its transmissions. "S-HTTP" is incorrect because this is not an email security protocol but is instead the deprecated secure HTTPS protocol. "HTTPS" is incorrect because this is not an email security protocol but is instead the popular TLS-encrypted HTTP protocol.

42. B. Volcanic eruptions are classified as a natural disaster because they are natural events that can cause significant disruption and damage to both human life and the environment. Unlike human-induced actions, natural disasters arise from geological processes that are beyond human control. Theft, hacking attempts, and insider threats, however, are all examples of human-related incidents rather than natural disasters. Theft involves the illegal taking of property, hacking attempts refer to unauthorized efforts to access computer systems, and insider threats refer to individuals within an organization who might misuse their access for personal gain or other reasons. Each of these involves deliberate or negligent human action instead of natural, nonhuman phenomena.

43. C. The other choices all describe activities that could be important to the organization during the BCP and DRP processes; however, they are not statements of impact as defined by ISACA. A statement of impact describes the impact on the organization if the process or system were incapacitated for a predefined period.

The answer referring to an outline of downtime is incorrect because this answer closely describes maximum tolerable downtime (MTD). The answer referring to the cost of recovery is incorrect because recovery expense is only part of a complete statement of impact. The answer mentioning financial losses due to a natural disaster is incorrect because financial losses in the event of a natural disaster are only part of a complete statement of impact.

44. B. Interface testing is used to confirm that an application is communicating effectively with other applications. It focuses specifically on the interactions between systems, ensuring that data is exchanged accurately and efficiently. In contrast, regression testing is conducted to verify that new code changes do not adversely affect the existing functionality of an application, rather than monitoring communication between applications. Unit testing involves examining individual components or functions of the software, primarily focusing on their independent operation rather than their interaction with other systems. Functional testing assesses whether the software performs its intended functions but does not specifically address application-to-application communication. Thus, interface testing is the most appropriate choice for verifying communication effectiveness between applications.

45. D. Resource management is the practice of managing budgets, personnel, and equipment in an organization.

"Capacity planning" is incorrect because this is the practice of ensuring that there is sufficient processing capacity to meet current and future needs. "Internal audit" is incorrect because this is used to independently confirm the effectiveness of processes and controls. "Benchmarking" is incorrect because this is used to compare one organization's processes to another organization's processes (or an individual organization's processes over time).

46. B. Management representations are not critical to the operation of the IS audit function because they are statements provided by management to auditors and serve as evidence during audits rather than foundational documents for the audit function itself. The audit charter defines the authority, purpose, and responsibility of the audit function, making it essential. Audit objectives outline the goals of the audit, ensuring alignment with organizational needs. Audit scope specifies the boundaries and focus areas of the audit, ensuring clarity and direction. These documents are critical for defining and guiding the audit function.

47. D. A back door is a section of code that permits someone to bypass access controls and access data or functions. Back doors are commonly placed in programs during development but are removed before programming is complete. Sometimes, however, back doors are deliberately planted so that the developer (or someone else) can access data and functions.

"Trojan horse" is incorrect because this is a program that is promoted as having one function but also (or instead) has a malicious function. "Bot" is incorrect because a bot is not a section of code but rather an autonomous program designed with one or more purposes. A logic bomb is code inserted into a system that triggers a malicious action when specific conditions are met, but it doesn't inherently provide unauthorized access like a back door does.

48. B. RAID-0 is the correct option because it implements disk striping, where data is distributed across multiple disks without redundancy, which enhances performance by allowing simultaneous read/write operations. However, it offers no fault tolerance, so a single disk failure results in data loss. RAID-1 provides mirroring, where data is duplicated across two or more disks, which improves fault tolerance rather than performance. RAID-2 is an outdated method that uses Hamming codes for error correction and interleaves data at the bit level across multiple disks, which is not efficient for modern systems. RAID-10 combines mirroring and striping of data, which offers both increased performance and fault tolerance but does not solely focus on performance improvement due to its redundant configuration.

49. A. Process owners themselves are the right persons to perform control self-assessments. The primary objective of a control self-assessment program is ownership of the results of self-assessments; what better way to achieve this than to have process owners performing them?

The answers mentioning auditors and the Chief Audit Executive are incorrect because self-assessments are performed by control owners, not auditors.

50. B. Management review of key measurements is crucial in quality management because it allows management to assess performance expectations. This ensures that the processes meet the set performance and quality standards, thereby facilitating continuous improvement and alignment with organizational goals. Identifying data leakages would be more related to information security audits than quality management processes. Focusing solely on developing new quality processes may lead to neglect of existing ones that may also require enhancement or adjustments. Preventing poor-quality product development is an outcome of effective quality management, for which management reviews performance metrics as a crucial input; however, it is not the primary reason for conducting such reviews.

51. C. Although it's appropriate to examine the hosting provider's audit report for audit findings and file the report for future reference, the company really needs an audit report for the cloud service provider itself, not just its hosting provider. However, cloud service providers sometimes do not have audits of their own development and operations. Sending the data center hosting provider's audit report is useful, but that report probably does not include the service provider's systems and processes.

The answer referring to thanking the service provider is incorrect because the data center audit report is not the report that was requested. The answer referring to examining the audit report is incorrect because the company is expecting an audit report for its service provider, not its service provider's hosting provider. The answer that mentions filing the report is incorrect because although the service provider's hosting provider audit report may be interesting, the company is expecting the service provider's audit report and did not receive it.

52. B. Implementing multifactor authentication (MFA) is the best solution because it adds an additional layer of security beyond just a password, making it more difficult for fraudsters to gain unauthorized access to customer accounts even if they have stolen credentials. Regularly rotating passwords can help to a degree, but it is not foolproof against sophisticated phishing or hacking methods that can capture the new password immediately. Enforcing the use of ATMs does not address the threat as it does not mitigate risks associated with mobile platforms, which is where the identity theft is occurring. Conducting staff training and development sessions is beneficial for raising awareness and improving practices, but it does not directly safeguard against immediate threats of identity theft through technical controls as effectively as MFA.

53. C. A documentation review does not interfere with business operations.

    The answers referring to either cutover or parallel tests are incorrect because these tests involve organization personnel, and there is some risk of disruption of business operations as well. "Walkthrough" is incorrect because this involves several people, taking them away from business operations.

54. B. A Gantt chart is the correct choice because it is specifically designed to display project tasks along a timeline, showing the start and end dates for each task while also visualizing dependencies between tasks. This makes it an ideal tool for managing and planning project schedules in a clear and sequential format. PERT focuses on the analysis and representation of a project's tasks and their timelines using a network diagram to calculate the time needed to complete tasks. Although PERT is useful for depicting project execution activities and identifying the most critical path, it lacks the straightforward visual clarity of a Gantt chart regarding time sequencing. A project timeline, in the general context, merely refers to a list of dates without necessarily showing task dependencies, which is a limitation when aiming to visually manage a complex project's dynamics. CPA identifies the sequence of essential tasks to determine project duration, using network diagrams similar to PERT.

55. B. The call tree is a pyramid-style notification system used to quickly notify as many key personnel as possible and get assistance in dealing with the disaster.

    "Direct notification" is incorrect because this is not a common term for the notifications described here. "Conference call" is incorrect because it is not the method being used in this example. "Wide area alert" is incorrect because it is not a common term for the notifications described here.

56. B. COBIT 2019 is the recommended model for determining the maturity of governance processes because it includes a detailed maturity assessment framework specifically

designed for IT governance and management. CMMI focuses on process improvement for software development and engineering rather than governance. Agile methodology is a project management approach for software development and is not designed to assess governance maturity. Val IT is focused on the value delivery of IT investments rather than governance maturity assessments.

57. B. 99.9% uptime means that out of 8,760 hours in a year, an organization can experience no more than 0.1%, or 8.76 hours, of unscheduled downtime.

88 hours, 52 minutes, and 52 seconds are all incorrect because these values do not represent 99.9% uptime.

58. B. Capacity issues on IT systems often result in SLA violations due to overutilized IT systems. Overutilization can lead to slower system performance, increased response times, and, ultimately, failure to meet the agreed-on service levels defined in SLAs. Reduced system response times might occur if capacity issues were managed or optimized, which isn't the case when discussing problems with capacity. Optimizing system performance would imply that capacity issues are being effectively managed, rather than creating problems. Reducing the need for incident monitoring would suggest fewer issues or incidents, which is contrary to the challenges posed by capacity constraints, which often lead to more frequent monitoring and incident management to ensure SLA compliance.

59. D. Hashing is the process of applying a cryptographic algorithm on a block of information that results in a compact, fixed-length "digest." The purpose of hashing is to provide a unique "fingerprint" for a message or file – even if it is large. A message digest can be used to verify the integrity of a large file, thus ensuring that the file has not been altered.

"Session encryption" is incorrect because this is not a cryptographic function that is used to confirm the integrity of a message. Session encryption instead is used to ensure the confidentiality of a message. Both "symmetric encryption" and "asymmetric encryption" are incorrect because these actions are used to encrypt a message to ensure its confidentiality, not its integrity.

60. B. Management is responsible for starting the first phase of the SDLC because they identify business needs, set priorities, and approve the initiation of projects. Functional users provide input regarding requirements but do not initiate the process. Developers execute the technical aspects of the life cycle once it begins but are not responsible for initiating it. IS auditors review and evaluate the processes but do not play a role in starting the SDLC.

61. A. Active Directory provides key escrow capabilities to facilitate administrative access to encrypted hard drives in the event end users forget their passwords or leave the organization.

"Password hints" is incorrect because these do not provide a service desk with a method of accessing a BitLocker encrypted hard drive when the end user has left the organization. "Back doors" is incorrect because using a back door, generally referred to as a malicious or accidental pathway for bypassing controls, is not an appropriate method for administrators to access an encrypted hard drive. "Password recovery" is incorrect because this is not an available mechanism when passwords are protected appropriately with one-way hashes.

62. B. When auditing the user access provisioning process, the IS auditor should examine whether access requests are consistent. This means verifying that the process for requesting and granting access is uniform across the organization, adhering to established policies and procedures. Consistent access requests ensure that users are provisioned with permissions appropriate to their roles and responsibilities, mitigating the risk of unauthorized access. Examining whether access requests are always denied or approved does not address the core issue of consistency and does not ensure compliance with access control policies. Ensuring that access requests are encrypted primarily concerns data confidentiality during transmission and does not relate directly to the provisioning process's integrity. Finally, verifying whether all users have requested access is irrelevant to evaluating the adequacy and consistency of the provisioning process itself, as not all users may need or have reasons to request access regularly.

63. A. The best choice for members of an IT steering committee in an organization are senior executives and department heads.

"Board members" is incorrect because these are not the best choice for an IT steering committee. "End users" is incorrect because although their input is valuable, end users are not suited for a steering committee. "Customers" is incorrect because they should instead be part of a customer advisory board, if the organization values their input.

64. B. Including a statement of impact as part of impact analysis is essential to clearly present business impact in relatable terms. This ensures that stakeholders can understand the potential consequences of various risks in the context of their specific business environment, facilitating better decision-making and prioritization. Simply showing the results of risk analysis is insufficient because it does not contextualize those results in terms of their actual relevance or severity for the business. Stating threats that have no impact would not be a rationale as this would undermine the focus of risk management processes by cluttering them with irrelevant information. Finally, ensuring that risk analysis addresses all impacts is a broad objective of risk management, but the statement of impact specifically aids in communicating the implications of those risks, rather than ensuring comprehensive risk coverage.

65. A. Procedures for continuing operations have more to do with business processes than they do with IT operations. All other operations (disaster recovery, data restoration, and so on) support the ultimate goal of continuing the business processes that enable the organization to survive.

"IT operations" is incorrect because business continuity operations are not primarily focused on IT operations but on business processes. "Disaster recovery" is incorrect because business continuity operations are focused on business processes, not on disaster recovery. That said, in some situations, business continuity operations may need to be *aware* of disaster recovery operations so that business processes can obtain IT system support for critical processes. "Data restoration" is incorrect because data restoration is part of IT disaster recovery, not business continuity.

66. B. Don should use his private key to digitally sign the message. A digital signature is created using the sender's private key to ensure authenticity and nonrepudiation, as only Don has access to his private key. Don's public key is used by Zara to verify the signature, not to sign the message. Zara's private key is unrelated to the signing process, as it is used by Zara for her own encrypted communication. Zara's public key would be used by Don to encrypt messages for Zara but not for signing.

67. D. CSA is not a viable substitute for internal audit, although it is sometimes perceived that way.

The answers referring to detecting risks, the stake of process orders, and the speed of improvements are incorrect. These *are* all advantages of a control self-assessment.

68. B. Value and range checking is the appropriate type of input validation to ensure that each field on an online registration form accepts only valid dates within a specific range. This method assesses whether the input data falls within the defined lower and upper boundaries, making it suitable for verifying date ranges. Typing checking simply verifies that the input is of the correct data type (e.g., integer, date) but does not enforce specific range limits. Validity checking generally ensures that input values adhere to predetermined standards or formats, but it may not necessarily enforce range restrictions. Check-digit validation is a technique often used in identifiers like credit card numbers to verify authenticity and does not apply to date range validation.

69. B. Type checking examines input data to see if the characters are of the proper type. For instance, a person's name field would contain lowercase and uppercase letters, as well as an apostrophe and a hyphen.

"Range and value checking" is incorrect because this is used to confirm the correct values of input data of the expected type. "Spell checking" is incorrect because this is used to confirm the correct spelling of words. "Batch totals" is incorrect because these are used to confirm numeric values of batches of transactions.

70. B. Activating the incident response plan is the immediate action an IS auditor should recommend because this plan provides a structured procedure for addressing and managing the aftermath of a security breach, ensuring that the organization responds efficiently and effectively. This plan typically includes steps for containment, eradication, and recovery, as well as communication strategies, both internal and external. Disconnecting all network connections and devices may be necessary in some situations, but as an initial step, it could disrupt essential ongoing operations and prevent the collection of forensic evidence. Notifying law enforcement agents is important but should follow the activation of the response plan to ensure that any communication is done through proper channels and with accurate information. Evacuating people from the premises is generally unnecessary for a data breach, as these incidents typically do not endanger physical safety.

71. A. It is advisable to wait for some time to report on business benefits, mainly to provide time for transaction data, response times, and other measurements to accumulate and be reported on.

The answer referring to the shakedown period is incorrect because the metrics captured during the shakedown period may not accurately reflect system activities. The answer referring to post-implementation issues is incorrect because waiting for these issues to be resolved may still not provide sufficient time for enough stats to be collected. The answer referring to external resources is incorrect because the use of external resources should not be a factor.

72. B. Criminal syndicates are the most likely threat actors behind a ransomware attack because these groups primarily seek financial gain, which aligns with the typical motive for deploying ransomware to extort money from victims. Nation-states are generally involved in cyber espionage or politically motivated attacks rather than seeking direct financial compensation. Hacktivists, although motivated by ideological purposes, typically aim to make a statement or promote an agenda, not necessarily to gain financial profit. Script kiddies are usually less skilled attackers using premade tools without a deep understanding of how they work, making them unlikely to execute a sophisticated and potentially financially lucrative attack like ransomware.

73. D. Hardware monitoring is the best available solution for monitoring the performance of servers in a server farm.

"Egress filtering" is incorrect because this is an activity performed by firewalls that do not reveal server performance. "Network monitoring" is incorrect because this does not reveal server performance. "Event logging" is incorrect because event logging does not reveal server performance.

74. B. Risk assessment is the initial input into determining the audit scope because it helps to identify the areas with the greatest potential for material impact or the highest likelihood of issues, thereby guiding the allocation of audit resources effectively. This step ensures that the audit focuses on significant risks, aligning the audit objectives with areas of potential vulnerability or noncompliance. Management input, although important, typically informs the process after key risks have been identified to ensure alignment with organizational priorities. Prior audit reports may offer historical insights into problem areas but are retrospective and do not necessarily identify current risks. The strategic plan guides organizational goals and long-term objectives but does not specifically identify risks that should drive the audit focus.

75. B. It is important to determine the scope of an audit before the audit is executed. This defines the time schedule, physical geography or location of the audit, technologies and business processes to be audited, and which parts of the organization will be affected by the audit. The other terms describe different components or characteristics of an audit.

"Charter" is incorrect because a charter describes an audit program and its objectives, scope, and roles and responsibilities. "Audit program" is incorrect because an audit program is an organization's strategy and resources for performing audits. "Audit plan" is incorrect because an audit plan is the information that defines the scope, resources, and procedures for an individual audit.

76. B. After specifying the business objectives in the BCP process, the next logical step is to conduct a BIA. This step involves identifying critical business functions and assessing the impact that a disruption could have on them, which is essential for developing effective continuity plans. Risk analysis, although crucial, typically follows the BIA as it involves evaluating risks that could affect those identified critical areas. Testing and maintenance are further down the process; testing ensures that the plan works as expected, and maintenance ensures that the plan remains relevant and up to date. Therefore, BIA precedes risk analysis, testing, and maintenance in the progression of developing a comprehensive business continuity plan.

77. D. It is essential that all primary components be patched to reduce the likelihood that vulnerabilities will be exploited in an attack. This includes the base OS, the hypervisor, as well as all guest operating systems.

The answer referring to patching the base OS only is incorrect because this does not protect guest OSs from all attacks. The answer mentioning patching only the hypervisor is incorrect because this does not protect guest OSs from all attacks. The answer referring to patching both the base OS and the hypervisor is incorrect because this does not protect guest OSs from all attacks.

78. C. In the scenario described, the IS auditor is undertaking a forensic audit. Forensic audits are specifically designed to gather and maintain evidence that can be used in legal proceedings, which matches the IS auditor's goal of collecting evidence for legal purposes. A financial audit, on the other hand, focuses on the accuracy and integrity of financial records and statements, not on collecting evidence for legal cases. Operational audits aim to evaluate the effectiveness and efficiency of operations within an organization, rather than preparing for litigation. There is no specific "legal audit" in the context of IS auditing; thus, it doesn't align accurately with the objective of collecting evidence for legal proceedings. Therefore, forensic audit is the only option explicitly tied to the legal evidence-gathering process.

79. A. A procedure document describes steps to be taken to accomplish a task.

"Standard" is incorrect because a standard defines specific protocols, techniques, or brands to be used. "Process" is incorrect because a process is a set of procedures, not a single procedure. "Policy" is incorrect because a policy is a statement of expected behavior.

80. C. A repeater would be the recommended device to solve the issue of signal attenuation because it serves the primary function of receiving a network signal and retransmitting it at a higher power level, thereby extending the signal distance within the network. This helps in overcoming the degradation or weakening of a signal as it travels over longer distances. A switch, although useful for connecting multiple devices within a network and segmenting traffic, does not address signal attenuation directly. A firewall is designed to provide security by controlling incoming and outgoing network traffic based on predetermined security rules, without the capability to amplify signals. A router directs data packets between networks, determining the best pathway for data transfer, but does not enhance or amplify signals. Therefore, only a repeater has the specific functionality needed to combat signal attenuation.

81. C. An SLA, or service-level agreement, is a statement that defines minimum service levels to be provided by an entity to other entities.

The answer referring to improper function is incorrect because this is not a measure of service level but of service quality. The answer mentioning agreed sales levels is incorrect because sales are not related to SaaS operations. The answer referring to overcharging is incorrect because this is not a service-level problem but a billing problem.

82. C. HTTP is the insecure protocol in this list as it transmits data in plain text, making it vulnerable to interception by malicious actors. Its lack of encryption means sensitive information, like passwords and personal data, can be easily accessed if intercepted. TLS, on the other hand, is a secure protocol used for encrypting communications over a network, providing confidentiality and integrity, which ensures that data is not tampered with or exposed to unauthorized parties. SFTP (Secure File Transfer Protocol) also uses encryption to secure data transfer, safeguarding information during file uploads and downloads. Similarly, SSH (Secure Shell) provides secure access to remote systems through encrypted communication channels, ensuring privacy and data integrity in remote administration tasks.

83. B. Judgmental sampling enables the auditor to select some stores with older technology and some stores with newer technology. The other answer options are not sampling techniques that are best suited for this audit.

"Statistical sampling" is incorrect because this is not the best sampling choice, as it might not reflect the distribution of older and newer technologies. "Attribute sampling" is incorrect because it is not the best sampling technique to be used. "Discovery sampling" is incorrect because this is the method to be used when an auditor is looking for at least one exception in a given population.

84. C. TLS provides message confidentiality by using both symmetric and asymmetric encryption. At the start of a TLS session, asymmetric encryption is used for key establishment or key agreement, followed by the usage of symmetric encryption for the actual data transmission, ensuring efficient and secure message confidentiality. Symmetric encryption alone would not provide a secure way to initially establish encryption keys, which is why asymmetric encryption is also necessary. On the other hand, asymmetric encryption alone would not be efficient for encrypting large volumes of data due to its computational intensity. Claiming that TLS uses neither form of encryption contradicts its fundamental purpose, which is to secure data through encryption.

85. D. Discovery sampling enables the auditor to examine records until an exception is found, whereas the other sampling techniques are not likely to provide the needed samples.

"Stratified sampling" is incorrect because this method is used to ensure that samples from various value ranges (such as purchase order amount) are selected. "Statistical sampling" is incorrect because this method is used for randomly selecting samples from an entire population. "Variable sampling" is incorrect because it is used to calculate the total value represented by the samples.

86. C. Attestation is a formal statement in which the IS auditor confirms the results of an audit as it involves providing assurance regarding the subject matter audited, ensuring stakeholders that the findings are accurate and reliable. "Interim report" is incorrect because it is typically a progress report provided during the audit process and does not serve as a confirmation of final audit results. "Audit program" refers to the plan and procedures that outline how an audit is conducted rather than the confirmation of findings. "Audit test results" are the outcomes of specific tests or procedures conducted during an audit, but they do not constitute a final statement of confirmation of audit results.

87. B. Competency quiz results reveal the most about user comprehension of security awareness training content.

"Attendance records" is incorrect because attendance alone may not improve efficacy at all, particularly if the content is outdated or irrelevant. The answer referring to duration of training is incorrect because the length of time spent in training with outdated or irrelevant content does nothing but waste users' time and does not contribute to better security practices. The answer referring to the Gartner MQ rating is incorrect because a rating of a security awareness program by an advisory firm may not necessarily mean that the program is well socialized or relevant to any particular organization.

88. C. Performance optimization primarily aims to obtain maximum benefit from the use of IT services with minimum resources. This focus ensures that organizations leverage their IT investments to deliver maximum value while conserving resources, aligning perfectly with the core goal of performance optimization. Cost effectively developing new systems is more related to project or system development objectives than the ongoing process of optimizing existing systems. Enhancing the complexity of IT processes would be counterproductive to optimization, as it typically seeks to simplify and streamline. Enhancing employee productivity, although beneficial, is a secondary outcome of optimized IT processes rather than a primary focus. The main goal of performance optimization revolves around maximizing efficiency and effectiveness in IT resource utilization.

89. B. A "subject" is the person, system, or thing accessing a resource (often, but not always, data), and "object" is the resource being accessed.

The answer defining "object" as the file containing the data is incorrect because "object" refers to the resource being accessed. The answer defining "subject" as the security context is incorrect because "subject" refers to the person or thing accessing the data. The answer defining "subject" as a person accessing the data and "object" as the person who created the file is incorrect because the person who created the file does not factor into the subject/object model.

90. C. Watermarking in DLP systems helps prevent data loss by identifying and blocking the exfiltration of unencrypted information. Watermarks are embedded identifiers that allow DLP systems to recognize and control sensitive data when it is moved or shared. DLP systems cannot decrypt encrypted information, so watermarking does not assist in managing encrypted data. It also does not detect data corruption, which involves verifying data integrity rather than tracking its movement. Watermarking is not used as a honeypot, which is a decoy system designed to attract and study attackers.

91. A. A smaller agent footprint is not a result of a centralized console.

"Centralized monitoring and reporting" is incorrect because this practice facilitates organization-wide visibility into the health and configuration of protected endpoints. "Consistent agent configuration" is incorrect because this practice permits consistent organization-wide actions. "Bulk scan and update capabilities" is incorrect because these practices facilitate consistent organization-wide actions.

92. C. An organization should have an IT disaster declaration procedure primarily to clarify conditions for declaring a disaster. This ensures that all stakeholders understand the specific criteria and thresholds that trigger the disaster recovery plan, facilitating a swift and coordinated response during critical incidents. Without clear criteria, there could be confusion and delays in mobilizing resources when a disaster occurs. Providing guidelines for evacuation is not the primary purpose of an IT disaster declaration procedure, as evacuation pertains more to physical safety and may be managed by another protocol. Training employees in the disaster recovery process is important but typically happens separately as part of broader disaster recovery planning and drills. Eliminating the need for disaster recovery plan testing would be detrimental, as testing is essential to validate and improve the recovery strategies put in place.

93. A. A chain of custody is a business record that is used to track the safeguarding and transfer of evidence as part of the overall record to demonstrate the protection and integrity of evidence.

"Evidence log" is incorrect because this is typically a business record showing what items reside in an evidence repository, but not any details about the handling of evidence. "Hash file" is incorrect because this should not be updated, because the hard drive itself should not be altered. "Time sheet" is incorrect because this does nothing to ensure the integrity of a hard drive in evidence.

94. C. Unit testing is typically performed during the coding phase of the software development life cycle. This is because unit testing involves testing individual components or pieces of code to ensure that they function correctly before being integrated with other components. The coding phase is where these components are being actively developed and written, making it the most suitable time for unit testing to occur. In contrast, user acceptance testing focuses on validating the overall functionality of the application against user requirements and takes place after unit testing. The migration phase involves moving software into a production environment, which is well after unit testing has taken place. The design phase is more abstract and focuses on planning the architecture and design of the software, rather than on the actual writing and testing of code, which happens later during the coding phase.

95. A. By refusing to deliberate over a risk matter, an organization has – by default – accepted the risk.

"Risk avoidance" is incorrect because this involves cessation of the activity that introduced the risk. "Residual risk" is incorrect because this term does not refer to a type of risk treatment but is instead leftover risk after risk treatment has been completed. "Risk transfer" is incorrect because this is the act of acquiring insurance for a risk – or outsourcing the activity, where the outsourcer agrees to share the risk.

96. C. Media analysis is the appropriate technique for recovering deleted files from a physical disk because it involves examining the storage media directly to retrieve lost files. This method focuses on the data storage aspects and file existence within the medium, making it ideal for file recovery. Hardware analysis does not specifically address file recovery as it focuses on the physical components of the computer, which is more related to hardware diagnostics. Live analysis generally involves analyzing running systems and processes, not focusing on previously stored and deleted data in nonvolatile storage, which makes it unsuitable for this specific task. Network analysis pertains to examining network traffic and communications, which is unrelated to the recovery of deleted files from a physical disk.

97. C. The answer referring to written process documents, interviews of process owners, and business records is correct because gathering all three types of evidence will give the auditor a more complete picture of the state of the business process.

The answer referring to process documents and business records is incorrect because these items alone are insufficient; interviews should also be performed. The answer mentioning written process documents and interviews of process owners is incorrect because business records should also be examined. The answer referring to business records and interviews of process owners is incorrect because process documents should also be examined.

98. C. IS skills development is least directly related to IT governance because it focuses on enhancing individual capabilities rather than addressing organizational policies, processes, and controls. IS strategic planning is a core component of IT governance, ensuring alignment of IT with business goals. IS risk management is integral to governance, addressing threats to IT systems and data. IS laws and regulations are directly tied to governance as they establish compliance requirements and guide governance frameworks.

99. B. OS patch levels are not included in hardware monitoring.

The answers referring to resource availability, system health, and CPU utilization are all incorrect because hardware monitoring assists with all three functions, as well as other aspects of hardware capacity and utilization.

100. C. Using a standard report template from similar engagements ensures consistency in audit reporting, which is critical for maintaining uniformity and clarity across various audit reports. This consistency allows for easier comparison between reports, facilitates understanding among stakeholders, and upholds the auditor's professional standards. The other options do not directly address the primary benefit of a standard reporting format. Reusing a template is not primarily about avoiding the need to rewrite a report, but about maintaining a consistent structure and language. Reducing the length of the report is not a fundamental reason to use a template, as clarity and completeness are typically more important. Although including client responses is part of the reporting process, it is not a reason for utilizing a standard template, which focuses on the report's format and consistency rather than its content.

101. C. Noting a lack of staff qualifications is a legitimate finding in an audit.

Training the systems engineer is incorrect because it would be inappropriate for an auditor to train anyone in the client organization. Recommending training for the systems engineer is incorrect because this is not the most important responsibility of an auditor in this situation. The auditor must include a finding in the audit report and should also go on to recommend the solution of training the engineer. Immediately notifying audit client management is incorrect because this is not an emergency situation warranting immediate notification.

102. C. Data serves as the central focus in DOSD, so it is the correct choice. This approach emphasizes the significance of data in shaping and guiding system development processes, ensuring that the system can effectively manage data resources throughout its life cycle. People, although crucial to development processes, are not the core focus in DOSD methodologies. Information is the outcome of effectively managing data, but it isn't the primary focus of developing the system. Evidence, although essential for supporting conclusions and findings, is not the main component around which DOSD activities are structured. Therefore, data remains the pivotal element in DOSD, distinguishing it from other methodologies focused on different aspects.

103. C. The data protection officer, who is responsible for privacy, is concerned about data collection and aggregation.

The answers citing the chief risk and chief information security officers are incorrect because the CRO and CISO, although concerned about the unauthorized collection and aggregation of data, are not the roles that are *most* concerned about this practice. "Chief marketing officer" is incorrect because the CMO is the least concerned with the unauthorized collection and aggregation of data.

104. C. To verify the authenticity of a digital certificate, it is essential to check the CA signature because the CA is the trusted entity that issues and digitally signs the certificate, confirming its validity and authenticity. The RA signature is not relevant in this context because the RA primarily handles the process of accepting requests for digital certificates and verifying the entity's identity but does not issue or sign the certificate itself. The last date the certificate was audited is unrelated to the authenticity of the certificate; auditing pertains more to security management practices rather than verifying certificate integrity. The certificate's encryption algorithm, although critical for ensuring secure communications, does not directly confirm the authenticity of the certificate itself; it merely indicates the method used to encrypt the data.

105. C. Identification is the act of asserting one's identity without providing proof. Once proof is provided, this is authentication.

"Authorization" is incorrect because this refers to the granting of permission to objects, not the act of asserting your identity. "Authentication" is incorrect because this refers to the assertion of your identity after some kind of proof, such as a password, is provided. "Logging" is incorrect because this is the recording of events, not the assertion of your identity.

106. C. An application should reject the entire batch when transaction counts and control totals do not match expected values. This approach prevents incorrect or invalid data from being processed, maintaining data integrity and accuracy. Accepting the entire batch and creating an error report or warning would mean that potentially erroneous data could still be processed, which is undesirable for maintaining accurate records. Reprocessing the entire batch is not an immediate solution as it does not address the root cause of the mismatch; the data still needs to be examined for errors before reprocessing. Rejection ensures the issue is identified and corrected before any further processing takes place.

107. B. Load balancers are used to evenly distribute work across a collection of servers. This ensures better resilience through the redundancy of servers performing work.

The answer referring to process threads is incorrect because load balancers are not used to ensure a balanced load across process threads. The answer mentioning measurement of network utilization is incorrect because load balancers are not used to measure network utilization. The answer referring to testing of network utilization is incorrect because load balancers are not used to test network utilization.

108. C. Utilizing a "PBC list" (Prepared/Provided by Client list) for tracking evidence collection is essential because it is a tool specifically designed to organize and manage requests for client-provided documents and information, ensuring clarity, accountability, and a structured approach. Although email can be used for communication about evidence, it is not a dedicated evidence tracking tool and can lead to disorganization and missed requests. "Inspection" refers to physically examining assets or documents but does not provide a method of tracking what evidence has been collected or is still needed. "Document review" pertains to analyzing the evidence for auditing purposes but lacks the systematic process to track and manage ongoing requests and collections throughout the audit. Thus, a PBC list aligns directly with the purpose of tracking and managing evidence collection efficiently.

109. C. Reconciling the two databases is the best first step; this will help identify the reason the scanning and inventory systems differ.

The answer referring to removal of the devices from the vulnerability scan database is incorrect because this exacerbates the problem by permitting these previously unknown devices to continue to reside on the network, and without knowing what vulnerabilities may exist in them. The answer referring to stopping scanning the devices is incorrect because the new devices should continue to be scanned, like all other devices on the network. The answer mentioning waiting for the asset inventory system to be trued up is incorrect because any time delay related to the installation of inventory agents could represent a window of time where serious exploitable vulnerabilities may exist, endangering the environment.

110. C. "Script kiddies" best describes the threat actor in this scenario because they rely on automated tools to exploit vulnerabilities without deep technical knowledge, often targeting systems indiscriminately. APT actors are highly skilled and typically conduct targeted, sophisticated attacks over extended periods, which is not the case here. Hacktivists are motivated by ideological or political goals and typically target specific organizations or causes. Insiders are individuals within the organization who misuse their access, which does not align with the description of external, indiscriminate attacks using automated tools.

111. A. Cloud-based web content filtering will protect laptop computers regardless of their location – on network or off network.

The answer referring to on-premises protection is incorrect because this is not an advantage of cloud-based web content filtering. "GDPR compliance" is incorrect because cloud versus on-premises web content filtering has little, if any, bearing in GDPR compliance. The answer referring to circumvention of filtering by end users is incorrect because the ability of users to circumvent web content filtering does not correlate with whether web-based content filtering is cloud-based or on-premises.

112. C. Requirements development is represented by X in the systems development life cycle (SDLC) diagram because it is typically the initial phase of the SDLC where the organization determines the needs for the project. A project plan would not be represented by X as it is typically developed after the feasibility study when the project is deemed feasible. The project charter is developed before requirements development, serving as a formal authorization of the project once feasibility is established. Risk assessment is an ongoing process throughout the SDLC rather than a distinct phase at the very beginning; thus it is inappropriate to label it as X in the context of the SDLC phases.

113. D. GDPR, or General Data Protection Regulation, is an example of an international privacy regulation.

"Maturity model" is incorrect because GDPR is not a maturity model. "OSI model" is incorrect because GDPR is not an OSI model. "US State privacy regulation" is incorrect because GDPR is not a US State regulation but instead a European regulation.

114. D. ISO/IEC 27001:2022 should be recommended for implementing an ISMS because it specifically provides requirements for establishing, implementing, maintaining, and continually improving an ISMS within the organizational context. This framework is internationally recognized and focuses on managing and safeguarding information security risks effectively. COBIT 2019, although useful, is primarily aimed at IT governance and management rather than specifically focused on information security management. NIST CSF is designed as a voluntary framework to guide organizations in improving their cybersecurity posture but does not specifically provide a structured approach for implementing an ISMS like ISO/IEC 27001. TOGAF is an enterprise architecture framework and not specifically tailored to the implementation of management systems, including those for information security, making it less suitable for this purpose compared to ISO/IEC 27001.

115. A. A session cookie is used to uniquely identify each user visiting a website. When encrypted, a session cookie is difficult to hijack.

The answer mentioning responses sent to a user is incorrect because an encrypted session cookie does not itself force the encryption of responses sent to a user. The answer mentioning queries sent by a user is incorrect because an encryption session cookie does not by itself force the encryption of queries sent by a user. Credit card security standard compliance may require the use of secure cookies, but there is no mention of the use of credit cards in this question and many systems do not involve credit card processing.

116. D. Judgmental sampling (also known as nonstatistical sampling) involves the use of professional judgments by the IS auditor to select a sample for testing, making it suitable for situations where the auditor has specific expertise or where random selection is not feasible or appropriate. Unlike judgmental sampling, discovery sampling relies on a predetermined method to identify at least one occurrence of a critical error, mainly used when the presence of an error would have significant consequences. Stratified sampling is a statistical method used to divide a population into separate groups, or strata, to ensure that each subgroup is adequately represented, and does not involve professional judgment for selecting individual samples within those groups. Systematic sampling involves selecting samples based on a

fixed interval from a random starting point, which is more structured and doesn't rely on the auditor's judgment for individual selections.

117. A. An operational audit is the most appropriate engagement to assess whether the CSP is adhering to the stipulated SLAs. This type of audit focuses on evaluating an organization's operations to ensure that they are efficient and effective and will specifically examine if the service delivery processes and procedures align with the agreed standards in the SLAs. A compliance audit, although relevant to adhering to regulations and standards, may not delve deeply into the service levels provided by the CSP. A quality audit focuses on maintaining product or service quality standards, which is narrower in scope than operational efficiency and effectiveness related to SLAs. An integrated audit, although comprehensive and covering multiple aspects such as IT, operational, and financial facets, is broader in scope and may not specifically emphasize the SLA adherence as an operational audit would.

118. D. PCI DSS is the highly effective non-law standard that is widely adopted by financial institutions globally. It is specifically designed to secure credit/debit card and financial transactions and has become a crucial part of compliance for financial organizations. ISO/IEC 27001:2022 is a global standard for information security management systems, but it is not exclusively tailored for financial institutions. NIST provides a comprehensive framework for cybersecurity but is primarily used within the United States, limiting its global adoption compared to PCI DSS. The CSF, or Cybersecurity Framework, developed by NIST, is a robust framework for managing cybersecurity-related risks but lacks the specific and widespread industry application focus seen in PCI DSS for financial institutions worldwide.

119. A. Test plan development is key to the requirements definition and design phases because it ensures that testing objectives and strategies align with the defined requirements, establishing a clear foundation for evaluating whether the system meets those needs. It is not central to the maintenance phase, which focuses on updates and fixes after deployment. The deployment phase involves delivering the system to users, not planning tests. Although testing occurs in the testing phase, the development of the test plan must precede it to guide the testing activities effectively.

120. D. Incident preparation is the first stage in the incident response process as it involves developing policies, procedures, and plans necessary to effectively manage and respond to incidents before they occur. This stage sets the foundation, ensuring that the organization is ready to deal with potential security events. Incident detection, on the other hand, occurs after preparation and involves identifying potential security events that might affect the organization. Incident analysis is the process where detected incidents are further assessed to understand their impact and severity, typically following detection. Incident response involves the actions taken to manage and mitigate the effects of a security incident and is executed after detection and analysis have provided sufficient information about the incident at hand.

121. B. A non-exportable digital certificate on company-owned workstations can be used to automatically enforce the "company computers only" policy regarding the use of a VPN.

The answer stating that personally owned devices are permitted to connect to the VPN is incorrect because the practice of using non-exportable certificates on company-owned workstations does not relate to whether personally owned devices can connect to a VPN. It is the role of the VPN switch, through mechanisms such as embedded digital certificates, to make that determination. The answers which refer to either encrypting or hashing all traffic over the VPN are incorrect because non-exportable digital certificates do not influence the encryption or hashing of VPN traffic.

122. D. Ensuring IT alignment with the business strategy is the most critical objective of implementing an IT governance framework in an organization because its primary purpose is to support and extend the organization's strategies and objectives. This alignment ensures that IT resources are used effectively and efficiently to drive business success, creating value for the enterprise. Although enforcing accountability is an important aspect of governance, it is more of a mechanism to achieve alignment rather than the primary objective itself. Reducing operating costs and enhancing productivity are potential outcomes of successful IT governance, but they are more tactical objectives. If IT is not aligned with business goals, cost reduction and productivity improvements may not contribute positively to realizing overall business strategies.

123. D. Event management and capacity management are monitoring processes performed on a production system after it has been implemented.

The answer referring to maintenance and change management is incorrect because these activities are not related to monitoring. The answer referring to service and configuration management is incorrect because these activities are not related to monitoring. "Problem management" is incorrect because this is not related to monitoring.

124. D. A vulnerability assessment primarily involves the identification and detection of vulnerabilities within a system or network without actually exploiting those vulnerabilities. It aims to provide a list of potential security weaknesses that could be targeted by an attacker, allowing organizations to address these vulnerabilities proactively. This contrasts with a penetration test, which goes beyond detection to actively exploiting vulnerabilities to determine the real-world impact and potential risks posed by those vulnerabilities. The suggestion that vulnerability assessment is similar to a penetration test is misleading because the two processes differ fundamentally in their approach and goals, with penetration testing involving active exploitation. The notion that vulnerability assessment is only applicable to physical assets is incorrect because it targets a wide range of assets, including network and software components. Finally, although vulnerability assessments may benefit from experienced professionals, there is no strict requirement for a scanner to possess a security certification to perform an assessment; however, certifications can enhance credibility.

125. C. A recovery control is a control that is used to return a system to a previous state.

"Compensating" is incorrect because a compensating control is used when another primary control cannot be used. "Restorative" is incorrect because this is not a control category. "Automatic" is incorrect because automatic is not a type of control and a bare-metal restore of a server is not typically an automatic activity but instead one that is human initiated.

126. D. Implementing a design freeze is crucial after design reviews as it signifies that the design is finalized, preventing further modifications that could destabilize the project. This step ensures stability as it locks the design specifications, allowing the team to progress to the next development phase with a clear and unchangeable guideline. Developing system test plans, although important for verifying and validating the system, is more relevant in the requirements definition and design phases stages where testing is paramount to system quality rather than maintaining design stability. Storyboarding sessions with staff are useful for clarifying and illustrating design concepts but occur earlier to gather requirements or refine designs, rather than after freezing them. Performing requirements analysis is generally done before design development and reviews and is meant to ensure that the correct needs and specifications are captured; this should not be confused with maintaining design stability post-review.

127. B. The balanced scorecard (BSC) is a management tool used to measure the performance and effectiveness of an organization.

"Zachman scorecard" is incorrect because there is no such thing as a Zachman scorecard. Benchmarks compare performance to external standards or peers but don't inherently offer insight into internal process effectiveness or alignment with strategic goals. "Control self-assessments" is incorrect because CSAs may be subjective and biased; the CIO should obtain unbiased information.

128. D. Deterrent controls are specifically designed to warn and discourage potential unauthorized access before it occurs, making them suitable when the aim is to prevent individuals from attempting to breach systems. Preventive controls, although also aimed at stopping unauthorized access, do so by blocking unauthorized actions rather than merely warning or discouraging them. Detective controls, on the other hand, identify and alert the system to unauthorized access attempts after they have happened, allowing for a response to the breach. Logical controls involve software-based measures like authentication and encryption, which are more closely aligned with preventing access rather than warning against it. Therefore, a deterrent control is most aligned with the auditor's recommendation in this context.

129. A. A software distribution system is the best method to be used to distribute and install patches to a large server environment.

"Gold images" and "hardened images" are incorrect because images are not advised, as they are only used to build, not maintain, servers. "Auto-update" is incorrect because automatic updates are not advised, as some patches may impair operation.

130. D. Multitenancy is the term used to describe a major advantage of cloud computing where multiple users share resources without knowing or interacting with each other. This allows for efficient resource utilization and cost-effectiveness, which is a fundamental aspect of cloud services. "Measured service" refers to the cloud computing feature that allows for monitoring and controlling resource usage, which is essential for billing but not directly related to the simultaneous sharing of resources. On-demand access involves users obtaining resources as needed, which facilitates flexibility and rapid provisioning but doesn't inherently describe shared resource use among multiple users. Scalability pertains to the ability of a cloud service to handle increasing or decreasing workloads, allowing organizations to adapt resource use to demand levels, but it doesn't directly address the idea of resources being shared among multiple users without awareness.

131. C. An IT steering committee, with members consisting of executives and leaders from end-user departments, is the best option for getting the IT organization into better alignment with the business.

"Control self-assessments" is incorrect because CSAs are used to determine control effectiveness. "Benchmarking" is incorrect because this technique is used to compare one organization to another. "Balanced scorecard" is incorrect because this is a management reporting methodology.

132. D. Each functional requirement must be verifiable because the primary aim of functional testing is to ensure that the software meets specified requirements and performs its intended functions. Verification involves checking that requirements are properly implemented and operating as intended, which is crucial for validating that the application works correctly. A functional requirement being recent is not inherently critical as older requirements could remain relevant and unchanged, thus not impacting the validity of the testing. Although having developers test each requirement may be beneficial, it is not a critical component because testing can be performed by other parties such as a QA team to ensure objectivity. Resilience of requirements relates to the application's ability to recover from issues, which is important for nonfunctional testing rather than functional testing, where the focus is on verifying specification adherence. Therefore, verifiability is essential for comprehensive and effective functional testing.

133. D. Burp Suite is a tool used to test web applications, specifically to identify vulnerabilities in web applications. It is not used for stress testing, which evaluates performance under heavy load. It does not facilitate user acceptance testing, which involves validating that the system meets user needs and requirements. Functional testing focuses on verifying that the application functions as intended, but Burp Suite's primary purpose is to assess and enhance application security.

134. D. The main purpose of disaster recovery procedures is to bootstrap services supporting critical business functions after a disruption. These procedures are essential to ensure that an organization can quickly recover and continue its operations during and after a disaster. Creating new procedures is not the main purpose of disaster recovery; it's about having existing, tested, and updated procedures ready to implement. Eliminating the need for a disaster recovery plan is unrealistic, as such a plan is crucial for organizational resilience. Although training staff is important, it supports the execution of the procedures rather than being the primary purpose of having the procedures in place.

135. C. The prevalent reason for using two NICs is for system resilience purposes; in the event of the failure of one NIC or its corresponding switch or switch port, the server can continue communicating through the other NIC.

The answer referring to multiple VLANs is incorrect because a single NIC can be associated with multiple VLANs. The answer citing the unreliability of NICs is incorrect because NICs are not inherently unreliable. The answer referring to connection of servers to a supernet is incorrect because network addressing and masking are unrelated to the number of NICs in use.

136. D. Engaging in audit planning is essential for IS auditors to determine the amount of audit resources required. Proper planning ensures that auditors allocate sufficient time, personnel, and tools to effectively and efficiently carry out the audit. This not only helps in managing limited resources but also enhances audit quality by addressing key risk areas and ensuring sufficient coverage. Compliance with legal requirements may guide the scope of the audit but isn't the primary reason for engaging in planning – it's more about regulatory adherence during execution. Reducing the workload is not the primary focus of audit planning; rather, planning ensures that workloads are managed wisely without compromising the audit's integrity. Avoiding external audits is not a valid reason for planning, as audits – whether internal or external – focus on accountability and assurance rather than avoidance.

137. A. Passive monitoring of database schema changes is the correct answer because dynamic DLP has nothing to do with the monitoring of database schema changes.

Automatic enforcement of data classification policy, prevention of exfiltration of data, and identification of instances of sensitive data on file shares are all incorrect because they are all purposes of a dynamic DLP system.

138. D. Remediating the issues is an acceptable way for client management to respond to IS audit findings because it demonstrates a proactive approach to addressing and correcting the identified deficiencies, which aligns with the ultimate goal of improving information system controls and processes. Denying the findings is not constructive as it does not address the issues or contribute to risk mitigation and improvement. Approving the report is not a response to the findings themselves but merely an acknowledgment of the report's existence, which does not provide a plan of action to address the issues. Rewriting the audit report undermines the integrity of the audit process and fails to provide any tangible plan for addressing or correcting the identified issues, instead jeopardizing the independence of the audit findings.

139. B. The best source of an event population for a change control process is log data of some kind from the systems in scope for the change control process. Obtaining records from change management would only include approved changes.

The answer referring to approved changes is incorrect because the list of approved changes represents only approved changes, not unapproved changes, or changes that were not requested at all. The answer referring to events stored in the SIEM is incorrect because the SIEM may not have records of all changes made in the system. The answer referring to the number of administrator logins is incorrect because administrators can log in to a system and not make changes, and administrators can make changes to systems without logging in to them.

140. D. In component-based development environments, applications are typically structured as several components working together because this approach promotes reusability, scalability, and ease of maintenance, allowing different components to be independently developed and then integrated into a larger system. Unlike monolithic systems, which are large, single-tiered architectures where updates or changes are more complex and riskier, component-based environments are more modular and flexible. Standalone applications do not take advantage of the collaborative interaction between components to build a comprehensive system. Unrelated modules lack cohesion and coordination, which fails to leverage the potential for components to effectively interact and support the application's functionality as a whole.

141. C. A SIEM, or security information and event management system, is used to collect log data from systems and to devise and produce alerts when security events are suspected.

    The answer referring to server farm management is incorrect because a SIEM is not used to manage server farm sessions but instead is a log collection, correlation, and alerting system. The answer referring to log data is incorrect because a SIEM is not used *only* to aggregate log data but also to correlate and alert on events. The answer referring to privacy encryption keys is incorrect because a SIEM is not used as a means for protecting privacy encryption keys but instead is used to store, correlate, and alert on security event logs.

142. D. Risk Assessment in Planning is the ISACA standard that outlines a requirement for adopting a risk-based approach when determining the controls and activities to audit. This standard ensures that auditors focus on areas with the highest risk, thereby optimizing audit resources and increasing the effectiveness of the audit process. Audit Planning, although a crucial element of preparing for an audit, is more general and doesn't specifically mandate a risk-based approach. Risk Assessment is more about identifying and evaluating risks rather than applying those assessments specifically within audit planning. The Audit Charter provides authority to the audit function but doesn't dictate the methods, such as risk-based planning, that an audit should employ.

143. C. The IT steering committee formally commissions the feasibility study, approves the project, assigns IT resources to the project, and approves the project schedule.

    "CTO" is incorrect because the CTO does not typically approve a feasibility study. "Project manager" is incorrect because a project manager does not typically approve a feasibility study. "CISO" is incorrect because the CISO does not typically approve a feasibility study.

144. D. Conducting a simulation test for business continuity and disaster recovery plans primarily serves the purpose of simulating a disaster scenario and evaluating the response to it. This approach is critical as it allows organizations to test the effectiveness of their disaster recovery plans in a controlled environment, ensuring that the response mechanisms are efficient and can be improved if necessary. Responding to a current disaster is not the main purpose of a simulation test; instead, it's meant to prepare for potential future scenarios. Simulating a disaster scenario without evaluating the response undermines the purpose of a simulation test as it does not provide any insights or improvements to existing plans. Assessing the effects of the disaster focuses more on the aftermath rather than testing preparedness and response strategies, which is what a simulation test aims to address.

145. C. A standard is a document that specifies technologies, architectures, protocols, and vendors to be used in an IT organization.

    "Process" is incorrect because a process is a series of related procedures. "Architecture" is incorrect because an architecture describes the relationship between system components. "Policy" is incorrect because a policy is a statement of expected behavior.

146. D. Numerous back-out procedures indicate to an IS auditor that emergency changes were frequently made to an application, because these procedures are often employed when unforeseen issues arise after an emergency change. This suggests that those changes were not thoroughly tested or that emergent issues required a quick rollback, revealing a pattern of reactive rather than proactive changes. Although an absence of a change management policy

could contribute to a chaotic change environment, it doesn't directly indicate the frequency or presence of emergency changes. A well-documented change management process suggests effective control and organization in managing changes, which is the opposite of what numerous emergency changes imply. Finally, inadequate test cases imply poor testing but do not themselves indicate the occurrence or frequency of emergency changes; they might lead to errors, but the immediate evidence of emergency changes would be the numerous back-out procedures.

147. C. The lack of alignment of an organization's security controls to an international standard is not necessarily a deficiency. The organization may have a sound risk management program that has driven the development of security controls that are adequate for the organization. A manufacturing organization is not necessarily under an obligation to adopt a specific control framework standard.

"Material weakness," "major deficiency," and "minor deficiency" are all incorrect. The use of any particular controls framework is not grounds for creating any level of issue, whether a minor deficiency, major deficiency, or material weakness. Only a failure of control design or control effectiveness would result in such a finding.

148. D. In the COBIT 2019 Goals Cascade, X represents stakeholder drivers and needs. This is because the Goals Cascade begins by identifying the needs and expectations of stakeholders, which then guide the development of enterprise goals. These stakeholder drivers and needs are fundamental in shaping the governance and management objectives within the COBIT framework. Board of directors directives reflect the specific governance decisions within an organization but are not the starting point in the cascade. The Chief Executive Officer's strategic plans are a result of aligning organizational strategies with stakeholder needs rather than the initial input. Environmental scanning is an analysis technique used to understand external influences and is part of strategic planning but not the primary focus of the Goals Cascade. Therefore, stakeholder drivers and needs logically initiate the cascade, as they are the foundational elements on which the framework builds its objectives and processes.

149. D. Using two sets of backup media – one near the primary system and one at an offsite storage facility – permits the organization to rapidly restore data in normal operations circumstances (with the nearby backup media) as well as for disaster recovery purposes (using the backup media at the offsite storage facility).

"Business continuity purposes" is incorrect because business continuity alone is not a sufficient reason for having two sets of backup media. "Disaster recovery purposes" is incorrect because disaster recovery (DR) alone is not a sufficient reason for having two sets of backup media; for DR, having one remote set of backup media is sufficient. "Because backup media cannot be trusted" is incorrect because backup media is not inherently untrustworthy.

150. D. An API allows applications to interact directly with a web service, bypassing the normal user interface, by providing a set of functions and protocols for communication. A GUI is designed for users, not applications, to interact with systems visually. A user interface is a broader term for any interface designed for user interaction, not for application-to-application communication. A system interface refers to internal interactions within systems and is not specifically designed for web service interaction.

Index

S